Beginning with
the Word

culturalexegesis

William A. Dyrness
and Robert K. Johnston, series editors

The Cultural Exegesis series is designed to complement the Engaging Culture series by providing methodological and foundational studies that address the way to engage culture theologically. Each volume works within a specific cultural discipline, illustrating and embodying the theory behind cultural engagement. By providing the appropriate tools, these books equip the reader to engage and interpret the surrounding culture responsibly.

Beginning with the Word

the Word

MODERN LITERATURE
AND THE QUESTION OF BELIEF

Roger Lundin

Baker Academic

a division of Baker Publishing Group
Grand Rapids, Michigan

Published by Baker Academic
a division of Baker Publishing Group
P.O. Box 6287, Grand Rapids, MI 49516-6287
www.bakeracademic.com

Printed in the United States of America

Library of Congress Cataloging-in-Publication Data
Lundin, Roger.
    Beginning with the word : modern literature and the question of belief / Roger Lundin.
        pages cm. — (Cultural exegesis)
    Includes bibliographical references and index.
    ISBN 978-0-8010-2726-0 (pbk.)
    1. Religion and literature. 2. Literature and morals. I. Title.
PN49.L77 2013
801—dc23   2013029543

14   15   16   17   18   19   20   7   6   5   4   3   2   1

To Sue,

for all things,
once again,
and forever

Contents

Acknowledgments

This book grows out of a long experience of reading, teaching, and writing about literature and theology, and my debts are many and varied to the guides who have helped along the way. As an undergraduate, I learned the joys of theology from Morris Inch and the late Bob Webber; in seminary, the late Stuart Barton Babbage showed me how bring that theology together with my love of literature; and in the graduate study of English, the late Milton Stern provided an incomparable model of dynamic teaching and reflection.

Early in my career, my student Mark Walhout introduced me to the work of Paul Ricoeur and Hans-Georg Gadamer, and I have spent the past three decades trying to bring those theorists together with Karl Barth and Dietrich Bonhoeffer on the one hand, and the likes of Emily Dickinson, Frederick Douglass, and William Faulkner on the other.

I wish to pay special thanks to four former colleagues: to Alan Jacobs, for rollicking conversations marked by flights of metaphor and arresting discoveries; to Ashley Woodiwiss, for loyalty and laughter in a friendship that has ranged widely over the political, cultural, and theological landscape; to Mark Husbands, for his perceptive understanding and his joyful articulation of the importance of Karl Barth's theology; and to Mark Noll, for his friendship and unstinting encouragement, his sustained and stimulating engagement with my work, and his exemplary commitment to the life of the mind under the lordship of Christ.

Two pastors in particular—let me call them pastoral teams—trained me in the ways of faithful obedience to Christ and the gospel: JoAnn Harvey and the late Bob Harvey (Wheaton) and John and Hazel Timmer (Grand Rapids). And for more than three decades, Paul Heidebrecht has been a source of wisdom, hilarity, and insight as a fellow parishioner, former pastor, and lifelong friend.

Beyond my local provinces, I owe a great deal to friends and colleagues from around the world. Three of them, all from the British Isles, head the list: Jeremy Begbie, David Livingstone, and Tony Thiselton. I also have in mind Katherine Clay Bassard, Andrew Delbanco, Denis Donoghue, Jim Dougherty, Tracy Fessenden, John Gatta, Stanley Hauerwas, Harold Heie, David Jeffrey, George Marsden, the late Barbara Packer, Manfred Siebald, Jim Turner, Clare Walhout, John Webster, Ralph Wood, and Nick Wolterstorff.

At Wheaton College, during the years that I have worked on this book, Provost Stan Jones, Dean Jill Baumgaertner, and my department chair, Sharon Coolidge, have consistently provided tangible support and a steady stream of encouragement. I am grateful to the donors who have funded the chair I currently hold as the Arthur F. Holmes Professor of Faith and Learning, just as I am thankful to God for all I learned from Art Holmes over the course of more than four decades as his student, colleague, and friend.

And finally, I want to thank two student assistants at Wheaton who provided remarkable help, one at the beginning of this project and one at its close. At the start, Annie Erhardt Reed faithfully took and transcribed notes from my lectures in two different courses, and those notes provided the seeds from which this book eventually flowered. At the close, Benjamin Holland was equally diligent in the proofreading and fact-checking he did on the page proofs. Like Annie, he was a quick learner, a painstakingly careful worker, and a person of consistent good cheer.

At Baker Academic, I thank Bob Hosack for his perseverance and Lisa Ann Cockrel for her proficiency. For years, Bob waited patiently for this manuscript, and in a matter of months, Lisa shepherded it through a complex production process.

I want to close by giving my deepest word of thanks to Sue Lundin. For the whole of our adult lives, Sue and I have shared in the building of a household, the raising of our family, and the fellowship and service of the church. We've delighted together in mutual friendships, shared a love of the arts, embraced robust rounds of activity—from tennis to mountain climbing to cycling without end—and found endless encouragement and challenges in the life of the mind. Sue is my most perceptive critic and receptive reader, and although my debt to her is endless, nothing in life gives me greater joy than trying to repay it.

Introduction

When our three children were very young, I happily spent countless evenings playing zany games we had invented. Many involved physical comedy and stunts of some kind—I had been raised, after all, on a solid diet of Buster Keaton, Laurel and Hardy, and the Three Stooges. My children and I came up with Burger Bumpers, for example, in which we strapped pillows to ourselves and gently careened into one another in the wide open spaces of our living room; Sea Drop involved my lifting two of them bundled together in a blanket and carrying them around the house, until I dropped them onto a mattress or cushioned chair; and then there was Daddy Mountain, in which I stood and assumed a craggy pose as each one in succession grappled his or her way up my 6-foot-6½-inch frame, only to be dislodged from the mountain by rumbling tremors.

These were great games, but they could be exhausting, so I looked forward each night to the way we brought our play to a close, just before the kids went to bed. At this point we turned from the slapstick of the Stooges to verbal games inspired by the likes of Ogden Nash and Dr. Seuss. My favorite was one in which I would begin a story of some kind by making up two lines of quasi-poetry, with the last word in the second line left blank. Any one of the children was free to slap down a rhyme to complete the line, and we would go on from there, as I scrambled to weave a story with the thread of those unforeseen rhymes.

What a delight I took in those games! Our verbal escapades brought back memories of my own childhood fascination with the shapes of letters and the sounds of words, even as they tapped into a vein of pleasure and perplexity that I was mining in my new job as a college English professor. "The sound is the gold in the ore," Robert Frost once wrote in an effort to describe poetry's uniqueness. The "mystery is how a poem can have wildness and at the same time a subject that shall be fulfilled." The heart of this mystery, he concludes, is "the figure a poem makes. It begins in delight and ends in wisdom" (776–77).

This book is an effort on my part to think, along with you, about words—about what we do with them, how we think of them, what we make of them, and what they make of us. It is an effort at thinking rooted in the spirit and practice of playfulness that marked my childhood musings, that inspired my play as a father with my children, and that continues to energize my teaching and research. Throughout *Beginning with the Word* I seek to keep alive a sense of delight by anchoring our search for wisdom in personal experience and the infinite play of possibilities that literature opens before us. To that end, the argument that unfolds in these chapters will be replete with images, characters, and episodes from poetry and fiction along with a few key incidents from my own past.

The Task of Thinking and the Joy of Theology

For all its emphasis on the delights of language, this book remains unapologetically a search for wisdom and an exercise in thinking. Several years after Emily Dickinson died in 1886, her sister Lavinia tried to explain the seclusion that had marked the last two decades of the poet's life. "As for Emily," Lavinia observed, "she was not withdrawn or exclusive really. She was always watching for the rewarding person to come, but she was a very busy person herself. She had to think—she was the only one of us who had that to do."[1]

In describing her sister's calling, Vinnie Dickinson got it right, for thinking is a vital kind of work, a genuine form of human action. To think creatively, to struggle with an opaque text or confounding idea, to seek connections between periods of history or disciplines of thought, and to search for the precise word or the right rhythm for a single sentence—these are human actions every bit as worthy as the wielding of a hammer, the manipulation of a surgical scalpel, or the making of a courtroom argument.

To be a Christian means to be something of an idealist about such work, since the Gospel says of Jesus Christ, "In the beginning was the Word, and the Word was with God, and the Word was God. . . . All things came into being through him, and without him not one thing came into being" (John 1:1–3). Or as the Letter to the Colossians says of Christ, "he is himself is before all things, and in him all things hold together" (1:17).

Confidence of this kind—confidence in the connection between the majesty of Christ and the power of language and thought—is not always easy to come across, for suspicions about the value of thought are deeply embedded within American culture in general and the evangelical church in particular. Such suspicions are as old as fundamentalism and as fresh as the therapeutic moralism that permeates the culture of today. As I was writing this introduction, for example, the evangelical Protestant magazine *Christianity Today* posted an online interview with a popular author and gave it the title, "You Can't Think Your Way to God." The interviewer, a former editor of the magazine, introduced his subject by saying flatly that "when we try to think our way" out of "the inconsistencies between what we think and what we do," we find ourselves stymied. "Our behavior keeps coming back to bite us. That's because behavior is not driven by ideas. It is a bodily thing that reflects the way we order—or disorder—our loves and desires."[2]

This sweeping claim points to a need for us to think creatively and rigorously about what I term the *tacit creed* of contemporary intellectual life. This creed, which is a version of philosophical naturalism, provides the key elements for a master narrative that claims to explain all natural phenomena and human experience. David Brooks paid tribute to the ruthless efficiency and comprehensive sweep of that narrative in a column published several years ago in the *New York Times*. "Once the Bible shaped all conversation, then Marx, then Freud, but today Darwin is everywhere," Brooks argued. "Confident and exhilarated, evolutionary theorists believe they have a universal framework to explain human behavior." In this narrative, humans are like any other living organism; they are simply "machines for passing along genetic code." We are, the naturalist creed asserts, "jerry-built creatures" crammed with "sophisticated faculties . . . piled on top of primitive earlier ones." And the purpose of it all is as simple as it is sobering. None of us has a particular destiny, for all of us live and die merely to propagate the general species.[3]

Given the power of naturalism's account of human nature and destiny, it would seem to matter what the Scriptures say about these things and what Christians from St. Paul to Flannery O'Connor have believed about them. Yet here again, we encounter skepticism about the relevance of belief for an understanding of faith, and this is as true outside the church as it is within its walls.

As a case in point, just days after "You Can't Think Your Way to God" appeared, the *New York Times* published an opinion piece titled "Belief Is the Least Part of Faith." It was written by T. M. Luhrmann, a distinguished anthropologist who has closely studied evangelical Christianity and "the puzzle of belief." Her study has led Luhrmann to conclude that "the deep questions" about faith—"Why do people believe in God?" or "What is our evidence" for the existence of God?—are the ones that "university-educated liberals ask." She says such "abstract and intellectual" issues do not interest evangelicals, for they are concerned with "fundamentally practical questions" that have to do with feeling God's love and being aware of God's presence. Indeed, Luhrmann says, not all evangelicals have even "made up their minds whether God exists or how God exists." Many, perhaps most, of them "put to one side" the question of belief, and in doing so, they confirm something social scientists discovered more than a century ago:

> The role of belief in religion is greatly overstated, as anthropologists have long known. In 1912, Émile Durkheim, one of the founders of modern social science, argued that religion arose as a way for social groups to experience themselves as groups. . . . Religious ideas arose to make sense of this experience of being part of something greater. Durkheim thought that belief was more like a flag than a philosophical position: You don't go to church because you believe in God; rather, you believe in God because you go to church.

Luhrmann suggests that we should "think about faith as the questions people focus on, rather than the propositions observers think they must hold." If we look at faith this way, she promises, we will see that "the evangelical view of the world is full of joy. God is good. The world is good. Things will be good, even if they don't seem good now." Because they take the life of the mind seriously and seek rational and empirical grounds for their own beliefs, "it is understandably hard for secular observers to sidestep the problem of belief." Yet Luhrmann says the secularists must set this problem aside if they are to understand that, for evangelicals, belief is nothing more and nothing less than "the reach for joy."[4]

Luhrmann's is a lucid formulation of the tacit creed of contemporary naturalism. According to it, the world is a closed system governed by impersonal laws. To be human is to live within the system while remaining slightly askew from it due to the accident of consciousness and the mystery of language. As both Durkheim and Luhrmann assert, we employ that language to devise beliefs that can "make sense of [our] experience of being part of something greater." To them, the key to sensible living and intellectual respectability appears to involve remembering that whatever therapeutic power such beliefs may have, they have nothing to do with values that endure or truths that transcend the moment of their usefulness.

As I have thought over the years about how a Christian might engage the naturalist creed both charitably and cogently, I have been guided by the invigorating example of Karl Barth. Near the close of *Evangelical Theology*, a book written at the end of his storied career, the theologian explains what it means to think about the modern world through the category of Christian hope. "They build on a firm foundation if they work in profound happiness as well as in profound terror," Barth writes of those who think of the world in theological terms. We live and die in communion with Christ, through whose resurrection "the glory of the children of God" has already been revealed. Through this person and this power, we are enabled to endure and bear all that is before us "with alacrity, hilarity, and spiritual joy."[5]

In explaining his unapologetic approach to Christian belief, Barth observes that for several centuries, "theology has taken too many pains to justify its own existence." The result has been to make theology "hesitant and halfhearted," yet in return for all its self-abasing tentativeness, it has "received no more respect for its achievements than a very modest tip of the hat." Barth urges Christian thinkers to set themselves on firmer ground by letting theology act "according to the law of its own being" and "to follow this law without lengthy explanations and excuses."[6]

To that end, I have sought to have *Beginning with the Word* develop in the same manner as my two most recent books on literature, theology, and modern culture.[7] My guiding principle is a simple one. It is to engage modern culture with confidence and a degree of brio. The goal of this book in particular is to reflect upon questions of literature, language, and belief by engaging a wide array of modern theorists and imaginative writers—from Ferdinand de Saussure to Frederick Douglass, Jean-François Lyotard to Emily Dickinson, and Hans-Georg Gadamer to Flannery O'Connor—and to do so by treating these dialogical partners with the respect they deserve.

At the same time, without hesitation or defensiveness, I deliberately wish to introduce strong theological voices into the conversation about language and belief. I do so in an effort to break the silence that so often seems to surround literary theory and cultural studies when it comes to the question of theology.[8] The reason for this silence cannot be that the partners are so woefully mismatched that a genuine dialogue between the theorists and the theologians would be unthinkable. It is not as though Ferdinand de Saussure, Richard Rorty, and Frank Kermode are tilling some lofty plateaus of the intellect, while Karl Barth, Hans Urs von Balthasar, and John Paul II toil away out of sight on barren landscape in the valleys far below.

I suspect the lack of a theory and theology dialogue is largely due to the simple fact that those who embrace the naturalist creed find it difficult to fathom the sincerity or authenticity of those who recite the Apostles' Creed. Pastor and author Timothy Keller made this point in a pitch-perfect way recently in a discussion with mainstream journalists. He told them that whatever else conservative Protestantism entails at the beginning of the twenty-first century, it contains an element of "supernatural Christianity." When asked, "Did the resurrection really happen?" the conservative "says 'Yes.' And other people say, 'Well, that depends on how you look at it.'"

At that point in the conversation Keller mentioned a distinguished secular professor of the humanities with whom he had served on a panel at a symposium. The professor was trying to determine just where Keller stood on religious matters. Then it came to him: "Oh, I get it," he told the pastor. "You don't take the Apostles' and Nicene Creed metaphorically, do you?" To which Keller replied, "Bingo. That's it."[9]

There are, to say the least, great differences between critics who take religious claims metaphorically and believers who place their trust in them—or even stake their lives on them. As I will argue in *Beginning with the Word*, a great number of literary and cultural critics join with T. M. Luhrmann in defining religious belief as a matter of personal formation and social aspiration rather than as an endeavor to know and obey the truth. To give but one example of what I mean, I quote from the introduction to a superb work of contemporary literary criticism:

> The question for the writers I take up in these central chapters is not what they believe about God or any other supernatural being or world order—a question that isn't answerable for most of them—or how their religious beliefs and practices are reflected in their writing, but what they believe about literature.[10]

Try telling that to David Kern, a boy in his early teens who undergoes a mid-twentieth-century crisis of faith in John Updike's "Pigeon Feathers." Deeply troubled by a naturalistic account of the life of Jesus that he has read in H. G. Wells's *The Outline of History*, David finds his faith in God and his confidence in life shaken deeply. To Wells, Jesus was little more than a "hobo" from a "minor colony of the Roman Empire," and twenty centuries of credulous Christian history had been set in motion by the "freakish" fact that Jesus had somehow survived his crucifixion and thus inspired his followers to found a religion. "Had Christ ever come to him, David Kern, and said, 'Here. Feel the wound in My side?' No." Indeed, the facts of nature and the incidents of history seem instead to have "proved the enemy's point: hope bases vast premises on foolish accidents, and reads a word where in fact only a scribble exists" (14–15).

David undergoes several more trials, including a terrifying vision of death and a dishearteningly awkward encounter with his unbelieving pastor. The latter confrontation unfolds during a Sunday afternoon catechetical class at the Lutheran church. They are discussing the third and final section of the Apostles' Creed, and David has a question for Pastor Dobson about the resurrection of the body. He wants to know, "Are we conscious between the time when we die and the Day of Judgment?" In response, Dobson blinks, and "the faces of the other students went blank, as if an indiscretion had been committed." When Dobson says, "no," David shoots back, "Well, where is our soul, then, in this gap?"

As the sense grows of a "naughtiness occurring," with one girl giggling and others on edge, "all he [David] wanted was to hear Dobson repeat the words he said every Sunday morning. This he would not do. As if these words were unworthy of the conversational voice." Instead the pastor puts his heaven-denying, death-embracing point as bluntly as he can to David: "You might think of Heaven this way: as the way in which the goodness Abraham Lincoln did lives after him." When David counters with yet another question—"But is Lincoln conscious of it living on?"—Dobson closes off the conversation with "a coward's firmness": "I would have to say no. But I don't think it matters" (22–23).

Yet such questions—about the meaning of the creeds, the nature of the truths they claim to encompass, and the likelihood of the resurrection whose victory over death they trumpet—matter to young David Kern, as they have to women and men for almost two millennia. But they matter, not simply because they provide "a way for social groups to experience themselves as groups" and "make sense of this experience of being part of something greater."

No, such questions make a difference today, as they have for the centuries, because they speak directly to our nature and destiny as creatures who sense, feel, *and* think. In the justly famous opening paragraph of *Confessions*, St. Augustine addresses God and says that "man, a little piece of your creation, desires to praise you," for "you have made us for yourself, and our heart is restless until it rests in you."[11] Following the lead of Augustine, the contemporary Catholic philosopher Alasdair MacIntyre describes self-knowledge as a process of coming to understand "the true objects of our desires." Augustine, he says, believes "that I cannot be in error about the fact that I love, but that I may always be in error about what it is that I love."[12] Like St. Augustine, in other words, young David Kern is desperate to learn whether there are any "true objects" for his desires and whether there is any place, person, or everlasting state in which his fearful and longing heart may find its rest.

Christ and the Modern Creed

The questions posed by the David Kern of fiction and the St. Augustine of history have to do with language and its relationship to truth. All David wants, after all, is for Pastor Dobson to repeat in private—"I believe . . . in the resurrection of the body and the life everlasting"—what he proclaims in public each Sunday. But this the pastor "would not do. As if these words were unworthy of the conversational voice" (23).

It is a guiding conviction of *Beginning with the Word* that the gospel is the story of a God who seeks, embraces, and gives himself over to the conversational voice. The prologue to the Gospel of John (1:1–14) and the Pauline hymn to Christ (Phil. 2:5–11) serve as the touchstones of this book's argument. John declares that "in the beginning was the Word," that "all things came into being through him," and that in due season "the Word became flesh and lived among us, . . . full of grace and truth" (John 1:1, 3, 14). And to the apostle Paul, the remarkable fact about Jesus Christ is that "though he was in the form of God," he did not regard his "equality with God as something to be exploited, but emptied himself, taking the form of a slave, being born in human likeness" (Phil. 2:6–7).

To comprehend what such affirmations might mean to us today, the book's first four chapters focus on language and the nature of the word. Language is a many-faceted gem, and these chapters look at it from distinctly different, yet ultimately adjacent, angles. Scripture provides guidance and a framework. My own experiences of loss enter into the discussion, as do experiences and images put forth in plays by Shakespeare, novels by William Faulkner, and passages from several modern poets. In turn, these literary and experiential accounts set the background for a discussion of naturalism, modern theories of language, and Christian thought.

In the early chapters, I offer a critique of naturalism and what I call the *structuralist paradigm* of contemporary language theory. My analysis here is deeply indebted to Hans-Georg Gadamer's *Truth and Method*, a work that shows the profound imprint of the history of Christian thought even though its author made no claim to profess the Christian faith. What Gadamer's work demonstrates, however, is the difference that Christian belief—in particular, the doctrine of the Incarnation—can make in the way we think about the nature, scope, and power of words. That difference is made explicit in the theology of Karl Barth, whose voice first enters fully into the discussion in chapters 3 and 4.

In the second half of *Beginning with the Word*, our attention shifts from the building blocks of words to the structures made by stories. In these chapters a number of writers and their works from the past two centuries make their way into the discussion. We hear from the contemporary Dutch novelist Harry Mulisch and the incomparable Fyodor Dostoevsky; Emily Dickinson weaves her way in and out of several chapters, while Don DeLillo's *White Noise* and a story by Isak Dinesen (Karen Blixen) illuminate the argument; and discussions of Frederick Douglass's autobiography and the stories of Flannery O'Connor play essential parts in the closing arguments of the book.

In the two final chapters, literature's *play of possibilities* comes to the fore. It does so in the case of Douglass, through his extraordinary account of his struggle to learn how to read. Throughout the slaveholding states, laws forbade teaching black men, women, and children to read. To be a slave, Douglass said, was to be "within the circle" and to have no idea of the possibility of liberty or justice, and as he discovered, it was through reading and through the alternate worlds it opened to him, that young Frederick came, in his words, to understand "the pathway from slavery to freedom" (*Narrative*, 37–38).

The closing chapter extends the reach of this *play of possibilities* by setting it within a dynamic of nineteenth-century cultural questions and twentieth-century theological responses. In the nineteenth century the citizens of the industrialized world began to take the full measure of the callous indifference of modernity's engines of power, be they natural or social. In the poetry of Dickinson and the fiction of Herman Melville, in the writings of Friedrich Nietzsche and the novels of Dostoevsky, we encounter sharp, sometimes devastating questions about the justice, silence, and very existence of God.

One place these questions received a robust response in the twentieth century was in the church's vigorous renewal of the doctrine of Christology. In his *Church Dogmatics* Barth both summarizes and advances that renewal in a remarkable section titled "The Way of the Son of God into the Far Country." In his treatment of the Incarnation, Barth speaks of the "unnecessary and extravagant" choice made by God to become flesh and travel to our far country, so that we might be saved from the folly and ravages of our "own devices" (*CD*, IV.1.158).

The journey through nineteenth-century literature and twentieth-century theology brings us back at the end of the book to the point at which it began. A personal experience (involving death and birth), a work of art (Roland Hayes's song-cycle of African American spirituals), and a passage of Scripture (Phil. 2:5–8, once more) come together to bear witness to the grace and truth of the Word made flesh.

That last sentence contains a phrase—"to bear witness"—that beguiles me and sums up as well as anything could the approach I seek to take to the literature and theory of modern culture and to the Christian faith I practice *and* believe. Near the end of chapter 4, I quote a passage from Richard Wilbur's "Lying," one of the great modern poems on language and belief. In it the poet stresses the need for us to remain humble as we think about language and our self-constituting powers. We may believe that the truth is something we invent in order to make sense of our experience and cushion the blows a seemingly indifferent universe deals out to us, yet Wilbur begs to differ. "In the strict sense, of course," he writes, "we invent nothing, merely bearing witness / To what each morning brings again to light" (83).

The French Protestant philosopher Paul Ricoeur wrote several decades ago that we in the modern world "must choose between philosophy of absolute knowledge and the hermeneutics of testimony."[13] In *Beginning with the Word*, I side with Ricoeur in choosing the latter. From the serendipitous discoveries we make in the wordplay of childhood, to the wonders we come upon in the world around us and in the depths within us, to the miracle of the Word "through whom all things came into being," there is more than we could imagine to bear witness to and so much, so abundantly much, for which to give thanks.

In a book-length study of Martin Heidegger, critic George Steiner notes that the philosopher was fond of the seventeenth-century German Pietist saying, *Denken ist Danken*, "to think is to thank." Steiner goes on to say that conceiving of *thinking as thanking* "may well be indispensable if we are to carry on as articulate and moral beings."[14] I wholeheartedly agree. So, let us begin to think together. And may we never cease to give thanks.

1

Beginning with the Word

In the beginning was the Word, and the Word was with God, and the Word was God. He was in the beginning with God. All things came into being through him, and without him not one thing came into being. What has come into being in him was life, and the life was the light of all people. The light shines in the darkness, and the darkness did not overcome it. . . . And the Word became flesh and lived among us, and we have seen his glory, the glory as of a father's only son, full of grace and truth.

—John 1:1–5, 14

> 'Tis but thy name that is my enemy.
> Thou art thyself, though not a Montague.
> What's Montague? It is nor hand, nor foot,
> Nor arm, nor face, nor any other part
> Belonging to a man. O, be some other name!
> What's in a name? That which we call a rose
> By any other name would smell as sweet.
> So Romeo would, were he not Romeo called,
> Retain that dear perfection which he owes
> Without that title. Romeo, doff thy name;
> And for thy name, which is no part of thee,
> Take all myself.
>
> —William Shakespeare, *Romeo and Juliet*

A Word dropped careless on a Page
May consecrate an Eye
When folded in perpetual seam
The Wrinkled Author lie

Infection in the sentence breeds
We may inhale Despair
At distances of Centuries
From the Malaria—
                    —Emily Dickinson, #1268

We begin with words. Without them, there would be no literature. We would have no poems or plays, no lyrics or stories, no memories or dreams, not even any names. With words, we pledge our love to one another, we rail against wrongs in our homes and injustices across the seas, we chart the course of the past, we map the contours of the future, and we remember what—and whom—we have lost.

But what are these things we know as *words*? What strength do they possess? What is the source of their power to "breed Infection" and make us "inhale Despair" centuries after they have been written or printed? What weaknesses might words reveal? What do they have to do with the gritty realities of our lives or the glittering visions we imagine for the future?

That words have power of some sort, virtually everyone would agree, including St. John, William Shakespeare, and Emily Dickinson. But beyond that point, out in the vast universe of language usage, the disputes begin and the battles are fought over the nature and meaning of words.

According to the Gospel of John, the Triune God provides the secret to the source and power of words. "In the beginning was the Word," John announces, "and the Word was with God, and the Word was God. He was in the beginning with God. All things came into being through him, and without him not one thing came into being." For John, the Word is personal and powerful beyond imagining. From the nucleus of the smallest cell to the edge of the farthest galaxy, at the heights of joy and in the depths of sorrow, the Word abides. Before "heaven and earth were created, there was the Word of God, already existing in closest association with God and partaking of the essence of God."[1]

To describe the Incarnation and "its connection to all the past and all the future," John used the Greek word *Logos*. This term can only be "faintly and partially imaged by 'the Word,'" argues the eminent Victorian biblical scholar Brooke Foss Westcott, for "as far as the term *Logos* expresses a revelation, it is not an isolated utterance, but a connected story, a whole and not a part, perfect in itself, and including the notions of design and completion."

Beginning with the Word

In addition to pointing to a given revelation, the concept of the *Logos* also speaks of a redemptive purpose that has been revealed in human history and that was present "in the depths of the Divine Being before creation." Yet until the Gospel of John was written, "no one had dared to form such a sentence as that which . . . declares the central fact of Redemption, in connection with time and eternity, with action and with being: '*The Word was made flesh, and dwelt among us.*'"[2]

From the beginning of the Christian era, the theologians of the church found in the *Logos* crucial resources for describing how God relates to creation and what the beautiful order of this world may reveal to us about him. "God is good," St. Athanasius wrote in the fourth century, and "because he does not begrudge being to anything, he made all things from non-being through his own Word, our Lord Jesus Christ." From among all the things he created, God chose to be "especially merciful toward the human race." Since by the logic of our origin, we lack the power to live forever, God "granted [us] a further gift" to distinguish us from the rest of creation. In an act of charity, he created us "according to his own Image, and shared" with us "the power of his own Word, so that having a kind of reflection of the Word," we might "be enabled to remain in blessedness and live the true life of the saints in paradise."[3]

The Word secures the blessedness of the saints, and through its power God also binds, strengthens, and supports the structures of creation and imparts to human life the purposeful dignity it requires if it is to prosper and flourish. Through the power of the Word, we are made, sustained, and reconciled to God, and through the agency of words, we hear of God's faithfulness in the past, God's power in the present, and God's promises for the future. "He is the image of the invisible God, the firstborn of all creation," Colossians says of Christ, "for in him all things in heaven and on earth were created, things visible and invisible, whether thrones or dominions or rulers or powers—all things have been created through him and for him. He himself is before all things, and in him all things hold together" (1:15–17). Astonishingly, according to John's Gospel, the One through whom all things came into being was not content to leave the world he had made to its own devices. So, "the Word became flesh and lived among us, and we have seen his glory, the glory as of a father's only son, full of grace and truth" (John 1:14).[4]

All this is to say that the Scriptures, creeds, and early church councils bore witness to the intimate bond between the power and personality of God, as they are embodied and revealed in the *Logos*, the Word made flesh. Catholic theologian Hans Urs von Balthasar notes that from the beginning, Christianity challenged paganism to recognize all that the "personal God-Logos" had accomplished through his incarnate life, sacrificial death, and miraculous resurrection. All "the ancient world's unifying principles" have been redeemed by the God who "has drawn close to the world" through the history of Israel and the Incarnation of the Word. "The world was created in this Logos, the true 'place of the ideas,' and can therefore be understood only in the light of this Logos."[5] In the words of an eminent twentieth-century historian, "history in terms of the embodied *logos* means history in terms of personality."[6]

Yet unlike God's Word, our own words cannot create something out of nothing and do not have the power to live forever. Indeed, as Shakespeare's Juliet realizes, it is hard for us to pin down just what it is that our words can do. Consider the case of the two lovers. With the force of nature and the pulse of passion running through them, who or what can stand against them? No one. Nothing. Nothing, that is, but their names. She is a Capulet, he a Montague, and for generations a deadly feud has poisoned the relationship between their families.

Knowing that her family's history of hatreds imperils her future as well as that of Romeo, Juliet asks a simple question. What does the name Montague have to do with the man she loves? After all, this name "is nor hand, nor foot, / Nor arm, nor face, nor any other part / Belonging to a man." To Juliet a name may point to something—or someone—of incomparable value, but the name itself is of little worth. "What's in a name? That which we call a rose / By any other name would smell as sweet" (II.ii., 40–44).

Or would it? A part of what it means to smell a rose has to do with everything we carry within us as we draw near to it. Equipped with language and animated by memories, we stoop to a rose with myriad associations already in mind. As we see and smell it, our experience slips into a continuum of contrasts and discriminations, and this enables us to know and name the thing for what it is. We recognize that it is a flower, a living thing, and not an inert object like a stone; in its usual state, it is sweet and not pungent, soft rather than abrasive, and it is red, white, or yellow rather than dark violet or black. We can situate the rose within a field of understanding because we have words to name our experiences, and when we find ourselves at a loss for words, we may turn to metaphor to open new worlds before us.

Still, Juliet's question remains: "What's in a name?" Before we can venture an answer, we need to stand back and take a wider view of the historical, theoretical, and theological dimensions of the question. For although that answer bears on literature, it has broad implications as well, and one of our ongoing concerns in this book will be to explore the myriad ways in which language, literature, and Christian thought mingle and mix in the life of the spirit and the culture of today.

Beginning with the Word

What's in a Name?

As she ponders the meaning of names, Juliet Capulet in many ways sounds like a dutiful graduate student wending her way through the labyrinthine paths of contemporary theories of language and interpretation. To her, a name is an arbitrary sign. It may point to a real person or an actual state of affairs, but it should never be accepted as a sufficient substitute for the real thing. Knowing that names carry with them a history of power and prejudice, Juliet is suspicious of the associations that cling to them, and she regrets how readily names can become markers in conflicts that have nothing to do with those who bear them. In turn, she believes it to be within her rights to rebel against those who might seek to define and limit her through the power of naming.

That is to say, Juliet is a lot like us; for when she asks, "What's in a name?" Shakespeare is raising through her character in the late sixteenth century a concern about language that was to grow ever more pressing in the centuries to come. In simple terms, it is the question as to *whether words somehow belong to reality and embody truths about God and the world or whether they are primarily signs employed by the powerful to order the world according to their purposes.* We come upon debates about this matter in ancient Greek philosophy, we find them renewed in a provocative form with the rise of nominalism in late medieval thought, and in the past century, those arguments—driven by a new variant of nominalism—have resurfaced in powerful ways within the theory of language and the culture at large.

In speaking of nominalism, I am referring to a philosophical theory whose roots reach back to thirteenth- and fourteenth-century arguments about the laws of nature, the workings of the mind, and the power of God. At the heart of these arguments was a dramatic contrast between the laws of nature seen as something imposed upon the universe and those laws being seen as immanent within the structure of reality itself. The latter view was anchored in Stoic thought and the theory of the *Logos*. It held, in the words of Alfred North Whitehead, "that the order of nature expresses the characters of the real things which jointly compose the existences to be found in nature." When we understand those things in their essences, we also are enabled to see them in their mutual relations to one another.[7] This understanding of natural law, which took the world to be "impregnated with reason," dominated the Aristotelian science that was promoted by the early medieval church and its centers of learning.[8]

What came to be known as nominalism first surfaced in the late thirteenth century and became fully developed in the thought of William of Ockham. As historian Francis Oakley explains, Ockham grounded natural law solely on the arbitrary, unobliged will of God; as a result, that law ceased to be a "dictate of reason" built into the creation and became instead "a divine command" addressed to it. By grounding natural law and ethics in the divine will, Ockham and other nominalists believed they were vindicating and preserving the "freedom and omnipotence of God." Yet the price to be paid was steep, for their defense of the divine will came "at the expense of the ultimate intelligibility of the world." Order could no longer be discerned as being *immanent* within the structures and relationships of creation; instead, it was assumed to have been *imposed* upon creation as a result of "the peremptory mandate of an autonomous divine will."[9]

The nominalists considered "all real being" to be individual and particular (as Juliet does when she dwells on the "dear perfection" of Romeo). They took universals to be fictions because "words did not point to real universal entities but were merely signs useful for human understanding. Creation was radically particular and thus not teleological."[10] This meant that the *ends* of human life—the goals, virtues, and visions to which men and women aspire—are not embedded within the creation and its interlocking relationships. Instead, they have been imparted to the world by a transcendent God whose will remains mystifyingly obscure.

To see the link between this medieval philosophical movement and contemporary theories of language, we can turn to a provocative essay by philosopher Richard Rorty. Titled "Nineteenth-Century Idealism and Twentieth-Century Textualism," this work opens with a bold declaration: "In the last [nineteenth] century there were philosophers who argued that nothing exists but ideas. In our [twentieth] century there are people who write as if there were nothing but texts."[11] According to Rorty, the *idealists* believed that all of life and human experience were embedded within a realm of transcendental ideals; the *textualists* assume that same experience to be entangled in an infinite web of words, beyond which there is nothing at all.

To explain how we moved from the one—idealism—to the other—textualism—Rorty zeros in on the antagonism that marks the stance both movements assume toward natural science and its claims to intellectual certainty and supremacy. Both idealism and textualism "insist that there is a point of view other than, and somehow higher than, that of science." And each believes that it—idealism in the nineteenth century, textualism in the late twentieth—is the worthy and rightful cultural successor to science. To Rorty, textualism is nominalism shorn of its transcedent God, who has been supplanted by the dynamic human will.

A second similarity between idealism and textualism "is that both insist that we can never compare human thought or language with bare, unmediated reality," and they use this point "to put natural science in its place." The idealists of the nineteenth century tried to limit science by following the lead of Immanuel Kant, who claimed that scientific concepts were "merely instruments" used by the mind to organize sense-impressions. To the textualists, Kant's insight turned into the claim that scientific language is only one of many language games we might play; they take it to be something "handy" for "predicting and controlling nature." Science is hardly "Nature's Own Vocabulary," and for the idealist and textualist alike, art represents our deepest experiences more fully than science could ever do.[12]

To Rorty, the difference between idealism and textualism is that the former seeks to replace one form of science (natural) with another (philosophy). Textualism, on the other hand, proposes to do away with the concept of science altogether by treating both philosophy and the natural sciences "as, at best, literary genres." In their place, textualism plants literature at the center of the cultural stage, with science, philosophy, and theology banished to the wings.[13]

Having declared the triumph of textualism in the late twentieth century, Rorty devotes the remainder of his essay to defining and defending his terms. He does so by offering a close reading of idealist philosophy from Bishop Berkeley in the mid-eighteenth century to Hegel in the early nineteenth. Rorty reads that history as the story of a gradual decline of the belief that idealism could deliver through language a true picture of "ultimate reality." With the collapse of "metaphysical idealism," what survived was "literary romanticism," which he defines as "the thesis that the one thing needful [is] to discover not which propositions are true but rather what vocabulary we should use." The main legacy of idealism proved to be the ability of literary culture to stand on its own, apart from and superior to science, and "to claim to embody what is most important for human beings."[14]

Rorty says the final step in securing "the autonomy and supremacy of the literary culture" was taken by Friedrich Nietzsche and William James at the close of the nineteenth century. They accomplished that task by replacing romanticism with pragmatism. "Instead of saying that the discovery of vocabularies could bring hidden secrets to light, they said that new ways of speaking could help get us what we want," he explains. "Instead of hinting that literature might succeed philosophy as discoverer of ultimate reality, they gave up the notion of truth as a correspondence to reality."[15]

Regarding "the suggestion that truth, as well as the world, is out there," Rorty said in a later work that it "is a legacy of an age in which the world was seen as the creation of a being who had a language of his own."[16] He is referring, of course, to the Christian era, when the search for truth involved confident efforts to uncover the worded order God had woven into the fabric of reality and to receive the truths by which God's purposes had been revealed in sacrament, Scripture, and redemptive events.

The *Logos* tradition's vision of language and reality holds no interest for Rorty because he is concerned exclusively with those modern intellectual forces—natural science, philosophy, and literature—that he takes to be the rightful successors to a discredited and vanquished theism. Science sought supremacy on the basis of its power to harness nature, while idealist philosophy committed itself to the proposition that "within natural human experience one can find the clue to an understanding of the ultimate nature of reality, and this clue is revealed through those traits which distinguish man as a spiritual being."[17]

As Rorty describes them, science and philosophy are driven by an ideal of mirroring and a standard of calibration. Scientists and philosophers assume that truth entails bringing our linguistic representations of reality into line with that reality as precisely as we can. By joining words to things, we enable the world to reveal its truths to us.

But Rorty considers this a fantasy, for "the world does not speak. Only we do." The world may cause us to hold certain beliefs, "once we have programmed ourselves with a language," but it is powerless to "propose a language for us to speak. Only other human beings can do that." They—"other human beings"—and we collectively propose those languages through the construction of large "language games" that establish the standards of criteria and choice by which we determine the truth within the confines of the game we happen to be playing.[18]

When she began to muse on the nature of names, Juliet did so because she wanted to rescue Romeo from the forces of prejudice and cycles of revenge that threatened to overwhelm him and destroy their hopes of marriage. As radical as her claims about naming may sound, Juliet harbored no hopes of transforming the world and made no arguments touting the virtues of self-definition in a godforsaken world. But many who came after her would do just that, and it is with these individuals and theories that we will largely be concerned in this and the following chapter.

The Word and the Structures

What Rorty calls *textualism* is a late development in a central twentieth-century revolution in language theory known as *structuralism*. This dynamic intellectual movement came into being as a result of "the birth and explosive growth of the twentieth-century science of linguistics." From its base in linguistics, structuralism migrated over the course of the past century to cultural anthropology and sociology before establishing itself—and its offshoots, including deconstruction and poststructuralism—securely within literary and interpretive theory. Language became a central concern of twentieth-century thought, explains philosopher Charles Taylor, and what is "striking is the partial hegemony, if one can put it this way, that linguistics has won over other disciplines. From Saussure and the formalists there has developed the whole formidable array of structuralisms . . . which seek to explain a whole range of other things," from kinship systems to the operations of the unconscious and the origins of mythology.[19]

In *Beginning with the Word*, I will use the term *structuralism* both narrowly to designate specific developments in linguistics and more broadly to represent that system of philosophical naturalism which has become the tacit creed of literary theory and cultural studies. As the embodiment of key naturalistic assumptions, the structuralist paradigm—with its comprehensive understanding of language, reality, and truth—has mounted a sustained challenge to the premises that inform Christian thought about everything from creation and redemption to revelation and resurrection.

In speaking of naturalism as I do here, I have in mind that set of beliefs that Alvin Plantinga has cogently described in a recent book on science and religion. He takes naturalism to involve the belief that "no such person as God, or anything like God" exists. Naturalism clearly is not a religion, but in a number of ways it plays a religious role for many in the modern world. Like a religion, it poses such questions as: Does God exist, and is God personal? How should we live? What place do we occupy in the universe? What is our relationship to other creatures? In Plantinga's words, naturalism offers unmistakable answers to these questions: "There is no God, and it makes no sense to hope for life after death. As to our place in the grand scheme of things, we human beings are just another animal with a peculiar way of making a living." Yet while naturalism may not be a full-blown religion, Plantinga says we might think of it as a *quasi*-religion that "offers a master narrative" that claims to explain all natural phenomena and human experience, from the primordial explosion of the Big Bang to the fading embers of the last dying star.[20]

In structuralism, the tenets of this "quasi-religion" are wedded to what Jonathan Culler calls the "two fundamental insights" that inform its own master narrative about language and meaning. The first is that we never encounter social realities or cultural phenomena as discrete, factual objects or neutral events. Instead, these phenomena present themselves to us as objects and events replete with *meaning*. They are not *facts* awaiting the inductive study that will yield their meaning; instead, they are *signs* that point to things of *significance*, and their meaning is embedded in the vast, complex networks of relation that constitute the system of language.

The second structuralist insight seems simple yet has profound implications. It is that natural objects and social phenomena "do not have essences, but are defined by a network of relations, both internal and external." That is to say that the meaning of such phenomena is dependent on "an underlying system of distinctions and conventions which makes this meaning possible." By way of explanation, Culler asks us to think of what an observer from a culture in which marriage and soccer do not exist might make of a wedding ceremony or a World Cup match. The observer could probably describe the actions in considerable detail but would have no idea what they meant or what their purpose was. For example, wherever we come upon two posts set apart from one another, we may indeed kick a ball between them. Yet our action will acquire the meaning associated with a soccer "goal" only if it is embedded within a network of rules and conventions that we know as a particular sport. In turn, those conventions are only available in and through the use of language. All human practices and values are the product of a collective human effort to order the world within the boundaries established by language.[21]

Like Rorty's textualism, structuralism relies on a series of tacit metaphors to depict the role and reach of language. Language is the *foundation* on which all human meaning is constructed; it is the *web* in which all human experience is implicated and ensnared; and it is the *fount* of all human meaning. The verbal universe is a self-sustaining world without origin or end. There is nothing before language, no one behind it, and nowhere beyond it. In the words of Robert Scholes: "At the heart of the idea of structuralism is the idea of system: a complete, self-regulating entity that adapts to new conditions by transforming its features while retaining its systematic structure."[22]

What this structuralist theory articulates, with its depiction of a self-sustaining system with nothing or no one beyond it, Ernest Hemingway embodies in a famous story from the 1930s, "A Clean, Well-Lighted Place." This is the tale of an old man who comes each night to a Spanish café to drink himself into oblivion. From the two waiters who discuss the man's condition we learn that he has recently made a failed attempt to take his own life. On the night in question, after the lonely man has left the café, the two waiters have a brief exchange, with the younger of the two saying: "I have confidence. I am all confidence."

"You have youth, confidence, and a job," the older waiter said. "You have everything."
"You have everything I have."
"No. I have never had confidence and I am not young."

Beginning with the Word

After the younger waiter has left for home, where his wife awaits him, his older counterpart lingers at the café, and as he flips the switch that had kept the place "clean and well-lighted," he ponders the darkness:

What did he fear? It was not fear or dread. It was a nothing that he knew too well. It was all a nothing and a man was nothing too. It was only that and light was all it needed and a certain cleanness and order. Some lived in it and never felt it but he knew it all was nada y pues nada y nada y pues nada. Our nada who are in nada, nada be thy name thy kingdom nada thy will be nada in nada as it is nada. Give us this nada our daily nada and nada us our nada as we nada our nadas and nada us not into nada but deliver us from nada; pues nada. Hail nothing full of nothing, nothing is with thee. (382–83)

The world as rendered in Hemingway's story is "a complete, self-regulating entity" of the kind that Scholes celebrates and the structuralist paradigm enshrines. It is a given that from within such a system it is pointless to pray to a Father in heaven, to hallow his name, to pray for the kingdom that is to come, or to thank the deity for our daily bread. It is fruitless to do such things because the system is closed and runs smoothly, even ruthlessly, on its own. Anyone who lives within it ought to have the sense not to waste his or her time by foolishly praying for a god or gods to intervene from anywhere beyond the mechanism, for we live and move and have our being strictly within the confines of what Frederic Jameson calls "the prison-house of language."[23]

At the same time, the structuralists tell us, the imprisoning system needs to be mapped so that we can learn its contours and exploit its resources to our advantage. Everything needs to be accounted for and explained through the study of its relationship to everything else within the system.

According to Scholes, this is a task the structuralist model is well equipped to accomplish since it was born out of an effort to counter the fragmentation of knowledge that characterized the academic treatment in the late nineteenth century and the first half of the twentieth. As disciplines and fields proliferated, the isolated disciplines became "so formidable in their specialization as to seem beyond all synthesis."[24]

Several crucial developments lay behind this fragmentation. As Rorty has already indicated—with his rejoinder that "the world does not speak. Only we do"—one development involved the questioning of the long-standing correspondence theory, which took truth to be a matter of making thought and its instruments—language, mind, ideas—conform to the objects of its attention. What I think and what I say, in other words, should correspond to a reality that stands before me in the present as a fact or is handed down to me from the past as an event. Yet the harder it has become to define what such correspondence or conformity to reality might look like, the more difficult it has become to ground theories of knowledge and morality in the study of the mind's relationship to the world outside it. Ralph Waldo Emerson gave voice to skepticism about the correspondence theory as far back as the early 1840s, when he wrote in "Experience":

> We have learned that we do not see directly, but mediately, and that we have no means of correcting these colored and distorting lenses which we are, or of computing the amount of their errors. Perhaps these subject-lenses have a creative power; perhaps there are no objects. Once we lived in what we saw; now, the rapaciousness of this new power, which threatens to absorb all things, engages us. Nature, art, persons, letters, religions,—objects, successively tumble in, and God is but one of its ideas. Nature and literature are subjective phenomena; every evil and every good thing is a shadow which we cast. (487)

With good reason, then, Rorty concludes that in the early nineteenth century, "the idea that truth was *made* rather than *found* began to take hold of the imagination of Europe."[25] That idea took hold of our modern theories of language, truth, and reality and changed them almost beyond recognition. Looking back on these developments in 1936, William Butler Yeats famously described the transformation of the image of the mind as a mirror held up to nature to that of the mind as a lamp casting light on an otherwise darkened world. "The soul," he wrote, "must become its own betrayer, its own deliverer, the one activity, the mirror turn lamp."[26]

This transformation of the mirror into a lamp was in good measure a legacy of romantic poetry and idealist philosophy. In any number of poems by Samuel Taylor Coleridge, William Blake, or William Wordsworth, we come upon explorations of a dynamic state of tension between the givenness of things and the inventiveness of the mind. This tension is concisely and elegantly depicted in "Tintern Abbey," where Wordsworth describes himself as

> A lover of the meadows and the woods,
> And mountains; and of all that we behold
> From this green earth; of all the mighty world
> Of eye and ear, both what they half-create,
> And what perceive.[27]

This romantic compromise—with the truth divvied up equally between nature and mind—was to last only for a generation. By the end of the nineteenth century, philosophical naturalism and Darwinian theory had stripped from nature its moral and theological significance and left the lamp of the mind as its sole illuminating source.

During the same period that specialization was fragmenting the academic disciplines, the concept of an overarching, theistic framework for knowledge was being undermined by what Hans Frei has termed the "eclipse of biblical narrative."[28] From the beginnings of Christian history to the early stages of the modern era—from the first and second centuries to the seventeenth and eighteenth—"the Biblical narrative . . . [made] its claim to absolute authority," Erich Auerbach observes. "Far from seeking, like Homer, merely to make us forget our own reality for a few hours, it seeks to overcome our reality: we are to fit our own life into its world, feel ourselves to be elements in its structure of universal history."[29] But in the early modern period, the adequacy and trustworthiness of that narrative began to come under suspicion. To a small but increasing number of observers, the Bible, instead of being a unified framework within which all human experience and history could be encompassed, appeared to be a ragged compendium of tales, episodes, and genres whose connections to truth and reality were dubious at best.

A new form of skepticism in the late nineteenth century served as a third source of the fragmentation of knowledge. This line of argument called into question the ability of human consciousness to know even itself, let alone the world outside it, fully or adequately. In a study of Sigmund Freud, Paul Ricoeur famously named this movement "the hermeneutics of suspicion." To Ricoeur, Karl Marx, Friedrich Nietzsche, and Freud were the great "masters" of suspicion who shared a common determination "to look upon the whole of consciousness primarily as 'false' consciousness." With this skeptical turn, they took up the problem of Cartesian doubt and carried "it to the very heart of the Cartesian stronghold" of self-conscious awareness. And in doing so, they shook religious knowledge to its foundations as well.[30]

In the face of these and other sources of fragmentation, the comprehensive naturalistic framework promoted by structuralism appeared to offer a systematic approach to reintegrating knowledge. In the words of Scholes, "structuralism . . . [seeks] nothing less than the unification of all the sciences into a new system of belief." It sets out to meet the need for a "coherent system" that will "unite the modern sciences and make the world habitable for man again." Scholes admits this is a fundamentally "religious need," but he says structuralism can fill it by providing a "believable belief," something he says Christianity can no longer offer. Structuralism shares with Marxism a view of the world as being "both real in itself and intelligible to man." The secret of that intelligibility is to be found in the relationships among words rather than in any supposed correspondence between them and the world outside of language: "For, in its broadest sense, structuralism is a way of looking for reality not in individual things but in the relationships among them."[31] In structuralism the tie between language and reality is never seen to be "a natural bond" because the connection "between [the] sign as a totality . . . and the real thing is arbitrary."[32]

Wherever we look in cultural studies today, we will find a far greater number of theorists who would side with Juliet rather than St. John on the question of the word. Juliet's view grants to language a greater mobility of meaning and flexibility of use than any doctrine of the *Logos* could ever sanction. If language is embedded within an order inscribed by God upon creation and within the human mind, and if it can serve as God's agent of revelatory self-disclosure, then a powerful logic will shape our use of it. Christians may differ on the question of whether we primarily find that order in nature or learn of it through revelation, but they are in essential agreement in believing that language discloses more than the workings of vast systems and the vagaries of arbitrary wills. But if, on the other hand, we believe that power and custom, the agents of the arbitrary and the contingent, alone determine the relationship of words to things, then our possibilities in using language seem unlimited. Hamlet saw this to be the case at the dawn of the seventeenth century: "For there is nothing either good or bad but thinking makes it so" (II.ii.247–48). And Rorty reiterated the point in the closing years of the twentieth century: "Anything [can] be made to look good or bad, important or unimportant, useful or useless, by being redescribed."[33]

Signs and Wonders

Something seemed familiar about all these large themes—the *Logos*, structuralism, nominalism, and philosophical naturalism—when I first learned of them in college, seminary, and graduate school. They struck me not as abstract theories set apart from life but as unique and helpful ways of speaking about something I had come to know in personal, even intimate terms earlier in life.

One way to explain this would be for me to tell you that if I could set before you a series of pictures of me between the ages of nine and twelve, you would quickly spot a quirky habit on full display in the snapshots my mother took during those years. In those pictures, whether I am standing stiffly next to my brother, hamming it up before the camera on a summer day, or sitting on a sofa next to a television, I am likely to be doing one of two things. I am either tossing an object into the air so that it can be caught in midflight or I

Beginning with the Word

am holding up a section of a newspaper, so that the events it reports will be captured next to the face I present to the camera.

At the time, I had no idea why I felt compelled to do such things whenever my mother reached for the camera. Only years later, when I checked the dates on the photos, did it occur to me that my eccentric behavior began only months after my maternal grandmother had died. I was nine years old at the time, and aside from my own mother, "Mormor"—which means "mother's mother" in Swedish—had been the strongest influence on my early life, and her death shocked and saddened me.

I came to realize that with those clumsy and comical poses, I was doing my best to defy death by stopping time in its flight and by freezing the flow of events within the frame of a photograph. It wasn't much, but it was the best I could do; and to a rattled nine-year-old, it seemed better to resist death's menacing power than to submit to it without offering so much as an argument, a protest, even a gesture.

Some years later, when I first read Dylan Thomas's elegiac hymn to childhood, "Fern Hill," I heard in its haunting images and lilting cadences bittersweet echoes of my own serene obliviousness in the years before Mormor died:

> Nothing I cared, in the lamb white days, that time would take me
> Up to the swallow thronged loft by the shadow of my hand,
> In the moon that is always rising,
> Nor that riding to sleep
> I should hear him fly with the high fields
> And wake to the farm forever fled from the childless land.
> Oh as I was young and easy in the mercy of his means,
> Time held me green and dying
> Though I sang in my chains like the sea. (226)

In like manner, when I read Thomas's famous poetic plea to his father—"Do Not Go Gentle Into That Good Night"—I recognized the spirit of my own childhood's resistance to death and "the dying of the light":

> Do not go gentle into that good night,
> Old age should burn and rave at close of day;
> Rage, rage against the dying of the light. (239)

I trace my love of literature to experiences of the kind I had when I came upon these poems by Dylan Thomas. With his evocation of the unknowing bliss of childhood and his furious but futile protest against death, he gave a voice to my grief. I sensed that here and elsewhere the novels and poems

I was reading in English classes had to do with my own deepest fears and longings. I understood Jack London's "To Build a Fire" because I too sensed life's senselessness; like Macbeth, I took life to be a "tale told by an idiot, full of sound and fury, signifying nothing"; and the rigid, icy landscapes in Edith Wharton's *Ethan Frome* captured my feelings of fatality and frustration. As I read these plays and stories, I drew on a deep but inchoate fund of my own experience to understand them and their power.

So it was that in my adolescence, I began to sense both my genuine need for literature and my fledgling love of it. Like most children, I had come to depend on the stories my parents told me about my infancy and our family's life before I came along. Through their stories, I acquired my first sense of where I had come from, who I was, and what I might become. As I grew older, works of literature began to build on the foundation and within the framework my parents had established. Poems and novels rearranged the rooms, flooding some with light and deepening others with shadows, and in my experiences of reading, I began to sense that there might be a pattern to my life and a meaning hidden somewhere within it.

These hints of meaning came to me during a period of quiet desperation. When I was fifteen, my only brother, eighteen-year-old Gordon, died suddenly, several days after routine surgery. Gordy was at the heart of our family's life, and the shock of his death set a devastating grief to work on my mother, my father, and me.

In my case, that grief often manifested itself as an aching dread that stalked me during my waking hours and haunted me while I slept. Every few months, I would have a new version of a troubling dream that was always set in the three-day period between my brother's death and his burial. In the dream, I was always told that if I could touch the body of Gordy before he was buried, he would come back to life. Yet no matter what I did, I bungled the assignment every time. In one dream, I talked with mourners at the funeral until it was too late; while I chatted away for hours, others buried my brother, and I lost my chance to bring him back to life. Invariably, my failure involved a fault having to do with my confusion, incompetence, or worse. I'd forget about the task in the press of other events or get lost on my way to the funeral. When the dream ended, I'd wake up, gaze across the room at Gordy's empty bed, and realize yet again that he would never come back to life.

The silent emptiness of that room stood in stark contrast to the voluble fullness of my memories of Gordy. As he and I were growing up together, whenever I called out his name, he would reply by running upstairs to play with me or by telling me to get lost. As long as Gordy was alive, the sounding of his name could command his presence and draw him into the heart of my experience. But when he died, nothing—neither his name, nor any picture of him, nor any recording of his voice—could call Gordy back from the silent land of the dead. From that point on, whenever any one of us in the family spoke his name, Gordy never came running, and the sound of his name only rattled around the cavernous spaces he once had filled. The *presence* of Gordy's name was only a marker pointing to his *absence* in our lives.

Although I could never have said so at the time, I was learning through these experiences something foundational about the nature of language and its relationship to reality. To be specific, through the loss of Gordy I was beginning to realize that to have the word was not necessarily to have the thing. (This happens to be a central tenet of structuralism and its view of words as signs—but more on that shortly.) I was being schooled in the truth that language deals as much with absence as with presence and that of their own accord, words can work no magic that will bring the dead to life nor cast any light that will flood the darkness they have left behind.

As I continued to read in the midst of grief, I found the fiction of the late nineteenth and early twentieth centuries to provide remarkable and occasionally devastating insights into my own predicament. There I met characters—Thomas Hardy's Tess Durbeyfield and Jude Fawley, and Theodore Dreiser's Clyde Griffiths and Carrie Meeber, along with Edith Wharton's Ethan Frome—who seemed to be perplexed by the same anxieties that vexed me and to be propelled by longings of the kind that were drawing me slowly if unwittingly to God.

"We had the experience but missed the meaning," writes T. S. Eliot in "Dry Salvages," the third of his *Four Quartets*. "And approach to the meaning restores the experience / In a different form" (133). That was the case for me, when I turned toward literature in my late teens. As a child in an unchurched family living in a working-class neighborhood, I had developed a view of life that was in rough accord with naturalism as Plantinga describes it. I doubted the existence of God, but even worse, I feared that if God did exist, he certainly had to be a heartless character. I desperately hoped to believe in life after death, but I suspected it to be a fantasy. And as for my place in the grand scheme of things, I took myself to be an animal afflicted with a consciousness whose sole purpose was to make me aware of death and of my powerlessness before it. I wanted to believe in *truth*, to experience *forgiveness*, and to trust in *eternal life*, but I feared these were simply words that embodied my desires but had nothing to do with anything real or possible beyond my mind. Dreiser seemed to have it right. "People in general attach too much importance to words," suggests the narrator of *Sister Carrie*. "They are under the illusion that talking effects great results. As a matter of fact, words are as a rule the shallowest portion of all the argument. They but dimly represent the great surging feelings and desires which lie behind" (118).

For me, as for a number of the writers I was reading, the most unsettling aspect of naturalism had to do with the fear that such "surging feelings and desires" led nowhere and to no one, and especially not to God. Few writers have registered the pain of that sense of aimless emptiness with greater force than Henry Adams, the grandson of John Quincy Adams and great-grandson of John Adams. In an autobiographical study written early in the twentieth century, Adams tells of his experience of watching his 38-year-old sister die of lockjaw in 1870. As he contrasted the beauty of the Tuscan countryside outside his sister's sickroom with the torment unfolding within it, Adams felt he saw—and *understood*—both nature and death for the first time:

> The first serious consciousness of nature's gesture,—her attitude towards life,— took form then as a fantasm, a nightmare, an insanity of force. For the first time, the stage-scenery of the senses collapsed; the human mind felt itself stripped naked, vibrating in a void of shapeless energies, with resistless mass, colliding, crushing, wasting and destroying what these same energies had created and labored from eternity to perfect. Society became fantastic, a vision of pantomime with a mechanical motion; and its so-called thought merged in the mere sense of life, and pleasure in the sense. The usual anodynes of social medicine became evident artifice. Stoicism was perhaps the best; religion was the most human; but the idea that any personal deity could find pleasure or profit in torturing a poor woman, by accident, with a fiendish cruelty known to man only in perverted and insane temperaments, could not be held for a moment. For pure blasphemy, it made pure atheism a comfort. God might be, as the Church said, a Substance, but he could not be a person. (983)

The universe as Henry Adams envisions it is ruled by brute structural force and not by a personal God. In this world, language appears to serve human needs well for a time, until death shatters the illusion, leaving self and society alike exposed and defenseless.

Throughout this book, I will be taking this naturalistic vision to be one of the core premises of modern understanding that the Christian faith must engage if it is to speak boldly and fearlessly of the Word that became flesh, dwelt among us, and flooded our world with a light that no darkness can ever overcome.

"What's in a name?" Juliet Capulet asks. "In one case, everything," according to a converted Jew from Asia Minor who wrote to a band of fellow converts residing in a European town some three decades after the death of Jesus of Nazareth:

Beginning with the Word

Let the same mind be in you that was in Christ Jesus,
who, though he was in the form of God,
    did not regard equality with God
    as something to be exploited,
but emptied himself,
    taking the form of a slave,
    being born in human likeness.
And being found in human form,
    he humbled himself
    and became obedient to the point of death—
    even death on a cross.

Therefore God also highly exalted him
    and gave him the name
    that is above every name,
so that at the name of Jesus
    every knee should bend,
    in heaven and on earth and under the earth,
and every tongue should confess
    that Jesus Christ is Lord,
    to the glory of God the Father. (Phil. 2:5–11)

2

The Sign in Our Time

Sound and Fury, Suffering and Significance

The Veins of other Flowers
The Scarlet Flowers are
Till Nature leisure has for Terms
As "Branch", and "Jugular".

We pass, and she abides.
We conjugate Her Skill
While She creates and federates
Without a syllable—
—Emily Dickinson, #798

Answer me when I call, O God of my right!
    You gave me room when I was in distress.
    Be gracious to me, and hear my prayer.
How long, you people, shall my honor suffer shame?
    How long will you love vain words, and seek after lies?
—Psalm 4:1–2

Of the many books I read in the first few years after my brother died, one novel in particular spoke to my experience of loss and opened for me new ways of thinking about literature, language, and life. It was William Faulkner's *The*

Sound and the Fury, and in this chapter I will enlist its aid as a guide for our consideration of language, the structuralist paradigm, and the Christian faith.

Through its depiction of character and its use and analysis of language, Faulkner's novel lays before us many of the key challenges and implications presented by modern theories of language in general and by structuralism in particular. Using Faulkner as a base for our explorations, we will be able to move out to see current theories in their historical, literary, and theological contexts.

A Tale Full of Sound and Fury

Faulkner appropriates the title for his novel, of course, from the speech in which Macbeth describes life as "a tale / Told by an idiot, full of sound and fury, / Signifying nothing" (vv. 26–28). To depict what such a tale might sound like, Faulkner created a 33-year-old man named Benjy Compson to be the narrator for the first of the novel's four sections. Benjy has an infantile mind that is trapped within a man's body, and an unspecified crippling condition has rendered him unable to speak, read, or understand the most rudimentary things. He can hear words, see objects, and have experiences, but he cannot make sense of them, nor can he acquire any wisdom by reflecting on those experiences.

Unable to relate one thing to another in any coherent fashion, Benjy is swept down the stream of time by a torrent of rushing phenomena. For him, the past, the present, and the future all flow together in a turbulent confusion. Years later, Faulkner looked back on the novel and said that the concept of Benjy's character had come to him when "the idea struck me to see how much more I could have got out of the idea of the blind, self-centeredness of innocence, typified by children, if one of those children had been truly innocent, that is, an idiot." Benjy could not cope with the world because, "stricken" by God, he was "mindless at birth, [and] there was nothing he could ever do about it."[1]

In Benjy's section, what story there is consists of impressions and associations strung together without any apparent order. Faulkner claimed that as he wrote it, this section of the novel "was incomprehensible, even I could not have told what was going on then, so I had to write another chapter."[2] In the first scene of the novel, for example, Benjy is walking along a fence with Luster, the young black man charged with his care. A short distance away, a man strikes an object and cries out, "Here, caddie." Without warning, Benjy begins to bellow inconsolably, and an obviously annoyed Luster rebukes him: "Listen at you now. Aint you something, thirty three years old, going on that way. . . . Hush up that moaning" (3).

Beginning with the Word

As we read, we have no idea why Benjy howls simply because a man has asked a boy to carry a golf bag. Only later do we come to understand that when the golfer cries, "Caddie!" Benjy hears "Caddy!" That is the name of his sister, the only family member who had ever fully loved the bellowing boy who would grow to be this anguished man. When Benjy was fifteen, the pregnant Caddy had been married off in a hastily arranged ceremony, after which she was banished from the family, never to be welcomed again into her home. To cover family expenses, the Compsons sold the pasture that became the golf course at whose edge Benjy would eventually stand and howl on that day.[3]

Caddy vanishes, and the other members of the Compson family move on, as all of them plunge ahead down the lonely trails of their aimless minds. The parents, siblings, and servants have learned to make of Caddy's absence what they can, but Benjy can never get past the trauma of having lost his sister, and he never comes to comprehend that she is gone for good. As a child, Benjy had shambled down to the front gate each afternoon to await Caddy's return from school. Almost two decades after her banishment, he continues to do so daily. *"You cant do no good looking through the gate,"* a family servant tells Benjy one day. *"Miss Caddy done gone long ways away. Done got married and left you. You cant do no good, holding to the gate and crying. She cant hear you."* To the witless Benjy, such an explanation has no force, and the servant has to concede, *"Aint nothing going to quiet him. He think if he down to the gate, Miss Caddy come back"* (51).

What Benjy never learns is the heartbreaking wisdom that invariably comes to us through our acquisition of experience. In *Truth and Method*, his classic study of language and interpretation, philosopher Hans-Georg Gadamer says such wisdom "belongs to the historical nature of man." We may wish to shield ourselves and those we love from the painful experiences that lead to wisdom, but experience of this kind is not something that any human can be spared. "Experience in this sense inevitably involves many disappointments of one's expectations and only thus is experience acquired." There is in human life a "fundamental negativity" that always involves failed expectations and "emerges in the relation between experience and insight." What we have "to learn through suffering is not this or that particular thing, but insight into the limitations of humanity, into the absoluteness of the barrier that separates man from the divine. It is ultimately a religious insight—the kind of insight that gave birth to Greek tragedy."[4]

"The fear of the Lord is the beginning of knowledge," the book of Proverbs asserts; "fools despise wisdom and instruction" (1:7). Yet because he cannot accept the loss of Caddy, Benjy can neither fear God nor acquire wisdom of any kind.[5] To be wise, we must recognize that our desires are not always satisfied and that our words do not always mean what they say. This is a theme of classical tragedy and Augustinian Christianity alike. Because of human stubbornness and pride, the chorus in Aeschylus's *Agamemnon* says we must "suffer, suffer into truth":

> Zeus has led us on to know,
> the Helmsman lays it down as law
> that we must suffer, suffer into truth.
> We cannot sleep, and drop by drop at the heart
> the pain of pain remembered comes again,
> and we resist, but ripeness comes as well.
> From the gods enthroned on the awesome rowing-bench
> there comes a violent love. (109)

Or as Shakespeare's King Lear agonizingly learns, a stubborn refusal to face the truth may lead to unimaginable suffering. Lear's servant, Kent, says as much, when he pleads with his master to reverse his foolish decision to banish Cordelia, his only faithful daughter, and to reward her sisters, the treacherous Goneril and Regan:

> Thy youngest daughter does not love thee least,
> Nor are those empty-hearted whose low sounds
> Reverb no hollowness.
> LEAR
>   Kent, on thy life, no more!
> KENT
> My life I never held but as a pawn
> To wage against thine enemies; ne'er fear to lose it,
> Thy safety being motive.
> LEAR
>   Out of my sight!
> KENT
> See better, Lear, and let me still remain
> The true blank of thine eye. (I.i.152–59)

If we must suffer before we can "see better" and acquire the wisdom we need to interpret aright the words we use and the lives we lead, then Benjy Compson can never become wise.

At this point, I need to offer a key distinction having to do with the difference between the mental impairment Benjy Compson endures and the moral infirmity the Bible and tragedy refer to when they speak of wisdom and the limits of human understanding. The scriptural perspective dovetails with that of Greek

Beginning with the Word

tragedy, insofar as both link our interpretive limitations to our moral lives. For the Greek tragedians, the tragic hero is a victim of his or her *hamartia*—a fatal flaw often centered in an overweening sense of pride—while for the Christian tradition, it is the human propensity to sin that fuels our penchant for misunderstanding. In either case, for both tragedy and Christianity, there is a distinct connection between our ethical liabilities and our epistemological limitations.

We in the modern world have simply swapped out the ethical categories and replaced them with psychological, chemical, and biological ones. So it is, that to the likes of Gadamer and Faulkner, our interpretive limitations have to do with the fact of our finitude rather than the reality of our sin. The limits we face in all things are those that have been clapped upon us by our status as embodied creatures who live in a constant state of "being-toward-death" (Heidegger's phrase).[6] Our finitude, not our sin, constitutes our enduring dilemma.

Near the end of his life, Gadamer came to refer to the human condition as that of *ignoramus*, by which he meant the admission that we cannot know anything positive or substantial about God or the transcendent realm beyond our finite world. This reduces all religious belief and experience to the common denominator of our experience of transcendence. Yet to Gadamer, transcendence does not involve belief in God but focuses instead on our experience of "something incomprehensible" and unknowable. "Transcendence derives from the admission of our finitude: *ignoramus*—we do not know." In the words of Jens Zimmermann, who conducted the last interview Gadamer ever gave on religion, "transcendence is the absolute limit," and it carries "the power of religious conviction."[7]

The point Gadamer drives at here is largely a given of contemporary thought. Contrary to the claims pressed by the Psalms, by Paul in his Letter to the Romans, or by St. Augustine in his *Confessions*, we in modernity have concluded that there is a fatal flaw in creation rather than in ourselves.[8] Our mortality is the true source of our grief, we believe, and what the ancients called sin has little or nothing to do with our sorrow. That is an underlying message of Dylan Thomas's "Fern Hill," and it is the theme of countless novels, poems, and plays from the past two centuries. Two representative passages from William Butler Yeats illustrate the shift from sin to finitude in a compelling way. In "Sailing to Byzantium," the poet begs a group of sages and spirits to

> Consume my heart away; sick with desire
> And fastened to a dying animal
> It knows not what it is; and gather me
> Into the artifice of eternity. (102–3)

The picture of human life in these lines is painfully poignant. To be human is to know that one is "sick with desire" but also to realize that one's infinite longing is "fastened" to a decidedly finite "dying animal." It is not surprising that a heart filled with such longing "knows not what it is" and yearns to escape into "the artifice of eternity." Or as another Yeats poem from the same period asks, given our mortal plight and all the aimless suffering we must endure,

> But is there any comfort to be found?
> Man is in love and loves what vanishes,
> What more is there to say? (116)

The modern shift from sin to finitude marks a clear break from the doctrinal teachings of historic Christianity.[9] A classic early statement of that position can be found in *The City of God* by St. Augustine. After quoting St. Paul on the "decay of the outer body" (2 Cor. 5:1–4), Augustine says, "So we are weighed down by the corruptible body; and yet we know that the cause of our being weighed down is not the true nature and substance of our body but its corruption." As a consequence, "the corruptible body weighs down the soul," and it depresses the mind, as it reflects "on many questions." He then quotes Virgil in *The Aeneid*, noting that the Roman poet was himself borrowing from Plato's teachings in the *Phaedrus*, when he wrote of the "seeds" of the soul trapped within the body:

> Of those seeds heaven is the source, and fiery
> The energy within them, did not bodies
> Hamper and thwart them, and these earthly limbs
> And dying members dull them.

In Augustine's words, Virgil takes the body to be "the source of . . . desire and fear, joy and grief, which may be called the origins of all sins and moral failings." Augustine counters with what he calls a "very different belief." Although the corruptions of the body weigh down the soul, they are not sin's cause but its punishment. "It was not the corruptible flesh that made the soul sinful; it was the sinful soul that made the flesh corruptible."[10]

The Word and the Thing

Faulkner may portray him as an idiot who can neither read nor speak, but Benjy Compson nevertheless operates with a tacit theory of language. Cleanth Brooks touches on this facet of Benjy's experience when he describes him as living "in a world of primitive poetry. Everything is concrete. Abstractions are beyond him and so is conceptual language."[11] We might describe Benjy's rough understanding of language as a version of the magical theory of words, a view that animated the verbal practices of mythological culture and had its origins in Greek thought from the centuries leading up to Plato.

Like Benjy Compson, the ancient Greeks placed their trust in the powers of language, and like him, they took it for granted that words and things were intimately bound together. For the age of mythology, the era in which *The Iliad* and *The Odyssey* were composed, "the intimate unity of word and thing was so obvious that the true name was considered to be part of the bearer of the name, if not indeed to substitute for him," writes Gadamer. The Greek term for "word" (*onoma*) also means "name" in general and "proper name" in particular. In pre-Socratic thought, words clung to things as tightly as names do to persons, just as in ancient Hebrew culture, where the name of God was seen to participate in his very being.[12]

That is to say that for Greeks and Hebrews alike, names were not labels arbitrarily assigned to persons but mysterious embodiments of the individuals who bore them. This mythological sense of the name is all but impossible for us to imagine, for we have come to consider our own names to be as fluid and flexible as everything else that goes into the making of our identities.

Few things demonstrate our modern sense of names more clearly than a well-known episode from Nathaniel Hawthorne's *The Scarlet Letter*. In this scene, Hester Prynne preaches the gospel of modern renaming to the weary Reverend Arthur Dimmesdale when they meet by chance in the forest outside Boston one day. Like Juliet discoursing on the meaning of "Romeo," Hester considers the pastor's name to be arbitrary, contingent, and inconsequential. "Begin all anew!" she pleads with him. "Hast thou exhausted possibility in the failure of this one trial? Not so! . . . Exchange this false life of thine for a true one." Hester implores Arthur to "Preach! Write! Act!" and to flee with her deep into the wilderness or over the seas to a foreign land. "Give up this name of Arthur Dimmesdale, and make thyself another, and a high one, such as thou canst wear without fear or shame" (288–89).

To feel something of what the ancient view of naming entailed, we might try a thought experiment rooted in our ordinary experience. The situation unfolds like this: You are out in public, on the street or in a crowd, and someone calls out your name. You turn and track the voice to see who has summoned you, only to discover that the person who spoke your name was looking for a different Sarah or another Carlos. Perhaps it was naïve to assume you were being summoned, but your instinctive response was a natural one. You answered reflexively to the sounding of your name because in that name your life is summed up, and more than any other thing, your name serves as the *word* by which the whole of you can be called to account. "The rightness of the name is confirmed by the fact that someone answers to it," Gadamer concludes. "Thus it seems to belong to his being."[13] As Job pleads to God, "Then call, and I will answer; or let me speak, and you reply to me" (Job 13:22).

As powerful as it was, the mythological view of language came under attack during the Greek Enlightenment in the fifth and fourth centuries before Christ. "Greek philosophy more or less began with the insight that a word is *only* a name—i.e., that it does not represent true being," Gadamer argues. The struggle between a reverent trust in words and a problematic skepticism about them emerged for the Greeks as the problem of "the relationship between the word and thing." In the age of Plato and Aristotle, "the word changed from presenting the thing to substituting for it," and the fact that names could be assigned and changed at will called into question both their trustworthiness and their truthfulness.[14]

In the *Cratylus*, Plato examines two markedly different ways of defining the relationship between word and thing, and in the end he finds neither to be satisfactory. Both views begin with the object that language seeks to describe, discuss, or address. According to one theory, the word is *assigned* to the object, while the other view claims the word is *found* for it. The former view, the *conventionalist* theory, asserts that common usage establishes the meaning of words over time, while the latter, the *similarity* theory, posits "a natural agreement between word and object." To Plato, and to Gadamer as well, the "mode of being of language that we call 'customary usage'" shows the limits of both theories.[15]

The limit to *conventionalism* has to do with the impossibility of changing the meaning of words arbitrarily, for "language always presupposes a common world" in which the meaning of words remains independent of any individual's specific judgment. Gadamer offers the example of children and lovers who have their own special "languages" by which they communicate in a world that belongs to them alone. Yet even this is not "because they have arbitrarily agreed upon it, but because a verbal custom has grown up between them." At the other extreme, we see the limits of *similarity* theory when we recognize that we cannot possibly "look at the things referred to" by language and then "criticize the words for not correctly representing them. Language is not a mere tool we use, something we construct in order to communicate and differentiate."[16] Which is to say that we don't stand in our front yard, look up at our dwelling place, and decide on the spot that the word *house* does not accurately represent the structure before us. So it is that "the conventionalist

Beginning with the Word

theory does most justice to our sense of the variability and arbitrariness of words for a given thing, but does least justice to our sense that certain words are right and others not. The advantage and disadvantage of the similarity theory are just the reverse."[17]

According to Gadamer, Plato considered both of these positions untenable and "radically" sought to displace the question to another plane. "Plato wants to demonstrate," he explains, "that no truth can be attained in language—in language's claim to correctness—and that without words, being must be known purely from itself." Whatever the function or value of words may be, for Plato "the pure thought of ideas, dianoia, is silent, for it is a dialogue of the soul with itself." In that dialogue, words are interlopers that have worked their way into a wordless conversation in which they have no essential role to play.[18]

One consequence has been that "in all discussion of language" since Plato, "the concept of the image (eikon) has been replaced by that of the sign (se-meion or semainon)." An image or icon embodies the thing it represents, while the sign points to the thing, which stands apart from it. This displacement of image by sign proved to be an "epoch-making decision," for it implied that the true being of things must "be investigated 'without names.'" By asserting that there could be "no access to truth in the proper being of words as such," Plato managed to establish the independence of thought from language so radically "that the word is reduced to a wholly secondary relation to the thing." It then "follows that an ideal system of signs, whose sole purpose is to coordinate all signs in an unambiguous system, makes the power of words—the range of variation of the contingent in the historical languages as they have actually developed—appear as a mere flaw in their utility."[19]

Unlike the image (*eikon*), the sign does not make present something real but marks its absence even as it points to it. Many of the foundational decisions and central conflicts in church history have their origins in this Greek shift, and we in the modern world continue to reside within the intellectual boundaries established during centuries of dispute within the church over whether words are primarily *icons* or *signs*. We can mark the consequences of these disputes in everything from the liturgies we recite, to the buildings we inhabit, to the poems and stories we read and write. Within the church—and particularly within debates about the sacraments—the distinctions between icon and sign remain lively sources for Christian practice and provocative objects for theo-logical dispute. In the mainstream culture of modern naturalism, however, we live under the rule of the sign, and one of the more remarkable things about that fact is how readily we have come to accept its reign and how reluctant we are to question its ironclad authority.[20]

Signs of the Times

What is it about the modern world and our experience in it that has led to this triumph of sign theory? According to critic George Steiner, one answer to that question has to do with a "retreat from the word" that has been under way for the past four centuries of modern history.[21] He notes that Western civilization "owes its essentially verbal character" to the "Hellenistic conception of the Logos" in particular and to its "Greco-Judaic inheritance" in general. We take this verbal inheritance for granted and live somewhat unconsciously within "the act of discourse" as the heirs of a cultural tradition that assumes the "primacy of the word." Both the classic and the Christian views of the world "bear solemn witness to the belief that all truth and realness—with the exception of a small, queer margin at the very top—can be housed inside the walls of language." In turn, in a Christian understanding, the walls that house that language have been designed, built, and sustained by the Word through whom "all things came into being" (John 1:3).[22]

To say that "all things"—including language and reality—were made "through him" who is the Word is to assume that all of creation participates in a drama that encompasses the whole of reality. In the early twenty-first century, it is admittedly difficult to grasp, or articulate, the idea that the human mind and the Milky Way participate with one another in a grand cosmic drama of creation and redemption. Catholic literary scholar Walter Ong suggests that one way to grasp this idea would be to work our way back through the modern history of language, until we reach that point where such a concept made plausible sense.

To that end, Ong asks us to consider the sense that four Latin words carried in the sixteenth century and the meaning they now have for us. The words Ong highlights—*ornamentum* (ornament), *laus* (praise), *honor* (honor), and *lumen* (light)—were staples of the rhetorical tradition up through the Renaissance. In this tradition, an "ornament" of rhetoric was not a verbal embellishment but a vital piece of equipment; for the fifteenth-century mind, "the hand is a great help and ornament of the body," and a sixteenth-century dictionary listed as "the ornaments of a ship" such things as the rigging and tackling without which it could not sail.

In rhetorical theory from Cicero to the Renaissance, "praise," "honor," and "light" all served as synonyms of "ornament." One could thus refer to the "praise," "honor," and "light" of words or of speech, as if these qualities were actual properties that participated in the life of the realities the words were striving to describe. Ong acknowledges that such a conception of language is too personalistic for the contemporary mind to accept readily. To us, it does not make sense to "treat words as if they are the normal objects of honor and praise, persons." Yet precisely because such associations strike us as implausible, we fail to understand how the medieval mind operated in a world "where the distinctions between persons and objects now made automatically at least by English-speaking persons, are more or less blurred."[23]

The medieval mind had a reason for making such linguistic distinctions, and it went to the heart of the conception of the *Logos*. Because all of reality has been made and is sustained by the Word, language participates in the meaning and being of the realities it presents. In the modern world, we may consider honor and praise to be qualities we bestow on others; on Veterans Day we *give* honor to those who have served our nation in the military, and in our worship we *offer* our praise to God. Yet up to the seventeenth century, the idea would have been that objects themselves "somehow emanate honor and praise, in this way performing a kind of personal role." We take the world to consist of an array of valueless objects to which we as subjects give meaning, but for "the sixteenth- and seventeenth-century mind," Ong says, "the value in the object and the praise elicited by the object tend to be viewed as one whole." Until what Steiner calls "the retreat from the word" begins in the seventeenth century, "the [human] mind does not feel the exterior, objective world and the interior, personal world as distinct from one another quite to the extent that we do. Objects retain a more personal, or at least animistic, glow."[24]

According to Steiner, that glow faded quickly in the early modern era, as a new and powerful language, one that had no discernible connection to the *Logos* tradition, cut off that animistic power at its source. This was the abstract language of mathematical notation, and Steiner argues that with the seventeenth-century development of analytical geometry and calculus, mathematics ceased "to be a dependent notation" tethered to empirical reality. This new language was linked to the technological drive to predict the movement and harness the energy of natural forces, and so it was that mathematics became "a fantastically rich, complex, and dynamic language. *And the history of that language is one of progressive untranslatability.*" As a consequence, from that time to the present day the "most decisive change" in modern thought has been "the submission of successively larger areas of knowledge to the modes and proceedings of mathematics." Mathematical analysis transformed medieval alchemy into the predictive sciences of physics and chemistry, and thus, "by virtue of mathematics, the stars move out of mythology into the astronomer's table."[25]

The story Steiner tells fits within a larger narrative about the modern search for a language of signs that could predict the movement of heavenly bodies and natural objects and subject their forces to human control.[26] Over time, that project acquired a second goal, that being the application to personal, social, and political experience of something akin to the mathematical rigor that had proved so effective in the work of the astronomers. Between 1660 and 1720, Stephen Toulmin explains, few thinkers were content to account for mechanical phenomena alone but pressed a parallel search for mathematical corollaries that could take the measure of the new social practices and politial ideas that seemed to be springing up everywhere in early modernity.[27]

Before nature could be brought under predictable control, the magical forces that had haunted it for centuries needed to be vanquished. Known as the *disenchantment of the world*, this scouring of the animistic world proved to be a long, complicated process that required more than two centuries for its completion. Although the process of disenchantment was driven by mechanistic science, it was propelled by other forces as well, including Calvinist theology, capitalist economics, and nascent forms of political individualism.[28] From the start, disenchantment paid rich dividends, as "the decline of magic co-incided with a marked improvement in the extent to which [the physical and social] environment became amenable to control." Without disenchantment, it is difficult to imagine how long it would have taken for modern medicine, transportation, and communication networks, among other things, to develop as rapidly and completely as they have.[29]

As nature was in the process of being disenchanted, the language used to describe it had to be demystified as well. Gadamer explains that the search for a "system of artificial, unambiguously defined symbols" was born out of this need for demystification. "Only through mathematical symbolism, would it be possible to rise entirely above the contingency of the historical languages and the vagueness of their concepts." Viewed as signs, words become "instruments of communication," and all contingent developments—all the twists and turns, all the startling surprises and gradual changes that accrue to any given language over time—are seen as a nuisance, a "mere flaw in their utility." According to Gadamer, the "exclusion of what a language 'is' beyond its efficient functioning as sign material" became the "ideal of the eighteenth- and twentieth-century Enlightenments," which pressed to discover or create a "language . . . to [which] would correspond the totality of the knowable: Being as absolutely available objectivity."[30]

For such a language, there can be no mystery hidden within the world, nor any divinity dwelling beyond it, for no power can be tolerated that might disrupt the predictable course of matter in motion. (We recall Robert Scholes's structuralist definition of language as a "self-regulating system.") Paul Ricoeur refers to the true mark of "our modernity" as the "forgetfulness of the signs of the sacred, [the] loss of man himself insofar as he belongs to the sacred."

Such "forgetfulness" is the necessary "counterpart of the great task of nourishing men, of satisfying their needs by mastering nature through a planetary technique." The drive for technological mastery has made ours an age in which "our language has become more precise, more univocal, more technical."[31] And the triumph of the sign has become all but complete.

Poetic Romance in a Disenchanted World

For three centuries, theories of literature and poetic language have operated within the contours established by the concept of a language of signs, and from the beginning, the quest for a "precise, univocal" language was taken to be hostile to poetic imagery and fictional invention. In Steiner's words, from the seventeenth century to today, "those of us who . . . imagine the universe through the veil of non-mathematical language inhabit an animate fiction. The actual facts of the case . . . are no longer accessible through the word."[32]

W. H. Auden brings these elements—the disenchantment of the world, the quest for a language of signs, and the isolation of the artist—together, all within the span of a fourteen-line sonnet from a sequence titled *In Time of War*:

> And the age ended, and the last deliverer died
> In bed, grown idle and unhappy; they were safe:
> The sudden shadow of the giant's enormous calf
> Would fall no more at dusk across the lawn outside.
>
> They slept in peace: in marshes here and there no doubt
> A sterile dragon lingered to a natural death,
> But in a year the spoor had vanished from the heath;
> The kobold's knocking in the mountain petered out.
>
> Only the sculptors and the poets were half sad,
> And the pert retinue from the magician's house
> Grumbled and went elsewhere. The vanquished powers were glad
>
> To be invisible and free: without remorse
> Struck down the sons who strayed into their course,
> And ravished the daughters, and drove the fathers mad. (70)

As Auden's poem opens, the process of disenchantment seems to have run its successful course. The "deliverers" have done their work, and all the mythical beasts and magical powers—the giants, dragons, spoors, and kobolds—have been vanquished. The only ones who regret their disappearance are the sculptors and poets, who find themselves stranded in a prosaic world without any dynamic theme to enliven it or any vibrant cast of characters to make it hum. As for "the vanquished powers," they are happy "to be invisible and free." No longer limited by their bodily forms, they can now roam over the earth in the form of neuroses and psychoses that strike down the sons, ravish the daughters, and drive the fathers mad.

Auden's is a skeptical, twentieth-century perspective. In the seventeenth century, not many lamented the disappearance of magic or chafed under the restraints being imposed on language by the ideal of the mathematical sign. Indeed, Thomas Sprat, a founder of England's Royal Society, spoke for a growing number of observers when he railed in 1667 against the "specious *Tropes* and *Figures*" that have brought countless "mists and uncertainties . . . on our Knowledge." Because metaphors and rhetorical flourishes "give the mind a motion too changeable, and bewitching, to consist with *right practice*," they ought to be "banished out of all *civil Societies*, as a thing fatal to Peace and good Manners." Only then might the work of knowledge—of science and reason—proceed on its unimpeded way, as we "return back to the primitive purity, and shortness, when men deliver'd so many *things*, almost in an equal number of *words*." Sprat concludes that the goal of the Royal Society is to "extract from all their members, a close, naked, natural way of speaking . . . [and thus] bring all things as near the Mathematical plainness, as they can."[33]

Some poets quickly sensed there was a danger lurking in the marriage of mathematics and language. William Blake lodged his famous late eighteenth-century protest against the "dark Satanic Mills" that scarred "Englands green & pleasant land," and he prayed, "May God us keep / From Single vision & Newtons sleep." In like manner, John Keats lamented philosophy's and technology's power to "clip an Angel's wings, / Conquer all mysteries by rule and line, / Empty the haunted air, and gnomed mine— / Unweave a rainbow" (226); and in a review touching on the work of Edmund Kean (the great Shakespearean actor), the poet pleaded:

> Kean! Kean! have a carefulness of thy health, a nursing regard for thy own genius, a pity for us in these cold and enfeebling times! Cheer us a little in the failure of our days! for romance lives but in books. The goblin is driven from the hearth, and the rainbow is robbed of its mystery.[34]

Laments and pleas of this kind became standard fare in the romantic tradition, and they fed into a growing sense that poetry was called to counter the reductive, disenchanting powers of the mathematical language of signs.

The romantic poet and critic Samuel Taylor Coleridge sought to resist this seductive power by opposing the symbol to the sign. He was convinced that symbolic language could synthesize the insights of the imagination and make them powerful mediators "between Truth and Feeling." By fusing feeling and fact, he argued, the imagination translates concepts and insights into "terms or symbols persuasive" to the mind and heart.[35]

Symbolic work of this kind is crucial, Coleridge says, because of "the general contagion of . . . mechanic philosophy" and the "unenlivened generalizing understanding" it promotes. The foe of "mechanic philosophy" is the imagination, "that reconciling and mediatory power," which incorporates "the reason in the images of the sense" and organizes "the flux of the senses by the permanence and self-circling energies of the reason," thus giving "birth to a system of symbols, harmonious in themselves, and consubstantial with the truths of which they are the conductors."[36]

Coleridge's use of the word *consubstantial* is instructive. He appropriates the term from the history of Christian doctrine, where it had been used to explain how it was that the three persons of the Trinity could possess distinct identities while being of the same substance. The word was used by theological critics of Martin Luther's interpretation of the Lord's Supper as an occasion in which Christ is present "in, with, and under the in-substance-unchanged bread and wine." *Consubstantiation* contrasts with the Catholic doctrine of *transubstantiation*. The latter holds that in the Eucharist the bread and the wine miraculously become the body and blood of Christ in fact, while for Luther, the elements are transformed into the body and blood through faith but remain bread and wine in fact. In Luther's words, "What is true in regard to Christ is also true in regard to the sacrament. . . . Both natures are simply there in their entirety, and it is truly said: 'This man is God; this God is man.'" To the person who receives the elements in faith, Christ is fully present, while to those without faith, nothing but bread and wine lie before them. "In red-hot iron, for instance," says Luther, "the two substances, fire and iron, are so mingled that every part is both iron and fire. Why is it not even more possible that the body of Christ be contained in every part of the substance of the bread?"[37]

Elements of Luther's effort to solve the sacramental riddle anticipated— and made possible—the later development of romantic poetics and modern theories of language. In Coleridge's *consubstantial* understanding of language, for example, real objects—the otherness of the "bread and wine of natural reality"—could remain discrete and intact, even as the imagination transformed these natural objects into spiritual subjects. In making the idea and the symbol consubstantial with one another, Coleridge secured the rights of material creation even as he trumpeted the supremacy of the spiritual (i.e., mental and verbal) realm. To the material eye it may appear that an absent

God presides over a mechanical world, but through the mystery of spiritual sight, we can detect the workings in human life of "a regeneration, a birth, a spiritual seed impregnated and evolved, the germinal principle of a higher and enduring life, of a *spiritual* life—that is, a life, the actuality of which is not dependent on the material body."[38]

The metaphors Coleridge uses to link spirit and matter were forged on the anvil of sacramental theology in particular and Christian thought in general. As his treatment of the imagination makes clear, the poet's indebtedness to biblical language was deep and pervasive, and of the symbols that are *consubstantial* with the truths for which they serve as *conductors*, he writes:

> These are the *wheels* which Ezekiel beheld, when the hand of the Lord was upon him, and he saw visions of God as he sat among the captives by the river of Chebar. *Whithersoever the Spirit was to go the wheels went, and thither was their spirit to go: for the spirit of the living creature was in the wheels also.* The truths and the symbols that represent them move in conjunction and form the living chariot that bears up (for *us*) the throne of the Divine Humanity.[39]

Coleridge believed the artist "must out of his own mind create forms according to the severe laws of the intellect, in order to generate in himself that coordination of freedom and law . . . which assimilates him to nature, and enables him to understand her."[40] According to W. Jackson Bate, this was not subjectivism, for in speaking of the *symbol*, Coleridge drew on the teachings of eighteenth-century associationism, which held that symbols rise above the "local and temporary" by tapping into "universal principles of human nature." This made symbolism superior to allegory, which depended on arbitrary conventions for its meaning and merely translated abstract concepts into "a picture language." Symbolism, however, performed an essential spiritual work of bringing about the "union and reconciliation of that which is nature with that which is exclusively human."[41]

The romantic theories of language promoted by Coleridge, Blake, Ralph Waldo Emerson, and others were tied together by the slender thread of a singular belief. This belief was that the human imagination had the power to unify nature and spirit, words and things, in such a way that the modern world would see the ancient unity of the Christian *Logos* restored. By this means, the champions of the romantic movement sought to resist the advance of the language of signs in a disenchanted world.

But Charles Darwin would soon cut that thread, and as the nineteenth century wound down, spirit and nature, and word and thing, drifted into a state of separation marked by irreconcilable differences. One of the earliest

Beginning with the Word

forecasts of their eventual divorce can be found in a short piece written in 1873 by Friedrich Nietzsche under the unmistakable influence of Darwin. In a spirit of plaintive mockery, Nietzsche notes "how wretched, how shadowy and flighty, how aimless and arbitrary, the human intellect appears in nature." There is no way to know "the 'thing in itself,'" for it is "quite incomprehensible to the creators of language and not at all worth aiming for." And what about the "truths" we proclaim by way of words? They are nothing but fantasies born of self-deception, for "truths are illusions about which one has forgotten that this is what they are; metaphors which are worn out and without sensuous power; coins which have lost their pictures and now matter only as metal, no longer as coins."[42]

For those who lived in the mythological past—the Greeks of Homer's epoch—or those who live today as primitive poets of a kind—the Benjy Compsons of this world—there is no forgetfulness involved in knowing the truth because for them the unity of word and thing is unquestioned. Yet according to Nietzsche forgetfulness is essential for those of us who dwell within the culture of the sign. Our very belief in truth and our will to live are dependent upon this forgetfulness and the countless illusions it makes possible.[43]

Nietzsche's observations served as an early assessment of the significance of Darwin for theories of language and truth. A century later, the Nobel Prize–winning poet Czeslaw Milosz took a longer view of evolutionary theory's impact on poetry, language, and belief. To Milosz, Darwinian theory represented an "attack . . . aimed indirectly at the meaning of human death." With wanton promiscuity, nature produces the billions of creatures it needs to propagate the species, but it does so with cavalier indifference to the needs of individuals. Once he is wholly "integrated into Nature" through the theory of natural selection, "man also changes into a statistical cipher and becomes expendable." As a result, for a young person being educated in the arts and sciences in the early twentieth century, it was as if "one image of life"—the traditional image that takes the world to be *worded* and ultimately meaningful—"were covered by another one, the scientific," which views life entirely in materialistic terms and considers language to be solely an instrument of adaptation and desire. The sharp contrast between the "traditional" and "scientific" images of life produces, in Milosz's words, "the constant anxiety that arises when the mind cannot cope with contradictions and reproaches itself for inconsistency" (*Witness*, 43).

"The imagination, once visited by the images of the evolutionary chain, is lost to certain varieties of religious belief," Milosz argues. Because of Darwin, "there is no place" in contemporary understanding for a "platonic dualism of soul and body," and the "soulless" vision of life promoted by evolutionary biology offers scant comfort or hope for the human spirit. Until Darwin, it had seemed impossible to deny that life developed according to some form of providential plan, but after him, the whole of life—from the appearance of the first cell in the primordial soup to the prolific generation of billions of creatures—could be seen as unfolding entirely without the necessary assistance, intervention, or presence of God. In the Darwinian scheme of things, human language, whether prosaic or poetic, provides no special insights and offers no unique access to reality or truth. "When poets discover that their words refer only to words and not to a reality which must be described as faithfully as possible," Milosz concludes, "they despair. This is probably one cause of modern poetry's somber tone" (*Witness*, 43, 48–49).

Throughout his life Milosz strove against the spiritual constraints of naturalism, and he represented himself as ceaselessly crying out as "one voice, no more, in the vast theater" of nature and history: "Against closed eyes, bitter lips. / Against silence, which is slavery" ("An Appeal," 270). Yet even as he lodged his protests, Milosz remained keenly and somewhat painfully aware of the power and scope of modern science. He believed that power could not be countered by theories of the symbol and imagination alone, no matter how well intentioned or spiritually earnest they might be.

Darwinian Naturalism and the Structuralist Narrative

Whenever we set out to explore modern views of nature and language, we come upon the fingerprints of Darwin almost anywhere we look. As we have seen, this is the case with both Nietzsche and Milosz, and when the latter speaks of the poets' discovery "that their words refer only to words and not to a reality" beyond them, we find the stamp of Darwinism imprinted upon the structuralist paradigm as well.

With its comprehensive sweep and imperial claims, Darwinian naturalism laid claim to a vast expanse of intellectual territory that included within its boundaries the origins of language as well as the structuralist theory that eventually emerged from the discipline of linguistics.[44] To use a term introduced to us earlier by Alvin Plantinga, with its comprehensive explanation for the whole of biological life—its origin, development, decay, and death—naturalism offered a sweeping *master narrative* for the late modern mind. In light of its materialist presuppositions, structuralism fits squarely within that narrative.

As a field of inquiry, structuralism arose specifically from lectures delivered early in the twentieth century by Ferdinand de Saussure, a distinguished Swiss linguist. To Saussure, linguistics was a part of a "general science of semiology,"

Beginning with the Word

or the study of linguistic signs and symbols. In the lectures that became the book titled *Course in General Linguistics*, Saussure argues that we should consider the study of signs as having to do both with the concept of an isolated system and the idea of an ongoing story. The distinction here between system and story is akin to the difference between looking at a photograph of an extended family and reading a history that documents its complex and often tangled history. The photo provides us with a freeze-frame of the family and its intertwined relationships at a single point in time, while the history seeks to disclose how it was that that family came into being and how it grew and developed, prospered or declined, over time.

Saussure's terms for these separate ways of conceiving of language were *langue* ("language") and *parole* ("discourse"). *Langue* is the total system of a language as it appears at any given time; it envisions language as an infinite web of relationships that radiate from and interlock with an endless variety of centers. To understand a language as *langue* is to see it as a system whose connections have the potential to reveal (and conceal) all that one can know and say about human nature and culture. When we learn a language, it is *la langue* we acquire, as we assimilate a set of forms and a grammatical system developed by speakers working within a language over an extended period of time. The system of language is that historically generated social product that makes possible every individual act of speech we write or utter.

Parole, on the other hand, has to do with all the particular instances of speech and writing in which individuals employ the elements of the system to say specific things. If *langue* is system, *parole* is event. It entails the acts by means of which individuals seek to express their thoughts and achieve their ends. In the main, Saussure proved to be more interested in the universal, systematic study of language than in specific instances of discourse. For him, as for most structuralists, the history of linguistic change is a lesser concern because events are secondary and ephemeral and do little more than disrupt the system.[45]

At the heart of Saussure's thought is a view of language as a system of signs having two primary components: the signifier (*signifiant*)—the word or sign; and the signified (*signifié*)—the concept or reality to which the sign points. In the linguist's words, "the linguistic sign unites, not a thing and a name, but a concept [*signifié*] and an acoustic image [the *signifiant*]."[46] According to Saussure, no intrinsic relationships bind the signifier to the signified because, as a human creation, language has no essential connection to the world as it is delivered to our senses and assimilated into our experiences. Yet at the same time, the study of language does have a real utility, for it can lift the veil and expose those habits of mind and relationships of power that have arbitrarily tethered words to the realities we claim they signify.

In contrast, all theistic theories of natural law or divine revelation (save, perhaps, for some extreme versions of divine command theory) assume that there is a potentially truthful connection between language and the realities of which it claims to speak. If there were no such connection, it would be difficult, if not impossible, for us to understand either the relationships between God, ourselves, and the created order in which we live or the ethical demands and expectations that our creaturely status places upon us. Here as elsewhere, John Paul II has sounded a balanced note. "Faith clearly presupposes that human language is capable of expressing divine and transcendent reality in a universal way," he writes. "Were this not so, the word of God, which is always a divine word in human language, would not be capable of saying anything about God." The interpretation of the word of God cannot go on forever, endlessly referring to one new interpretation after another, without ever arriving at a statement—a use of language—"which is simply true; otherwise there would be no Revelation of God, but only the expression of human notions about God and about what God presumably thinks of us."[47]

To Emily Dickinson, it was an open question whether language could ever capture anything more than "human notions about God" or any other reality. Her skepticism on this point is clear in her poem on botanic classification, which lays before us the crucial issues in the structuralist and Christian differences over language. Her lyric points to the chasm that yawns between us as language users and nature as a wordless breeder of life. It opens with "The Scarlet Flowers" standing in as the "Veins" for all "other Flowers." As far as nature goes, this is sufficient for her purposes, and she has no "leisure" for the "Terms" we use, such as "Branch" and "Jugular," to classify her activities.

"We pass," the second stanza begins; to be human means for each of us to know that we will die individually and that all of us will eventually perish as a species. Nature, however, does not know of her mortality. She simply "abides," even as we employ language to "conjugate Her Skill." We come up with precise terms to classify nature's activities and fool ourselves into believing that our words precisely represent her processes. Yet as Dickinson slyly suggests, while our language games may satisfy our needs, they are no concern of nature's, for "She creates and federates / Without a syllable—" (#798). The terms we assign to her properties and activities are arbitrary signs rather than natural indicators. "Nature folds and absorbs in an enormity of silence, as our syllables cannot 'sound' outside our atmosphere," a critic says of the import of Dickinson's poem, and "our universe's Big Bang beginning was a bang void of whimper or wail."[48]

Just as nature goes on its way "creating and federating" in its wordless world, so does structuralism's linguistic system thrive independently of all of us who use it to accomplish our tasks. That is because for structuralism, the ultimate meaning of a single sentence or entire work is a function of the system's resources rather than a product of a speaker's (or writer's) intentions. For Saussurean linguistics, language represents a complete, self-sufficient system that is sealed off at any given point from all the accidents, incidents, and changes that mark history and the life of individuals. In the words of Frederic Jameson, language for Saussure is "a perpetual present, with all the possibilities of meaning implicit in its every moment."[49] It possesses a coherence that is completely internal to itself and neither requires nor permits any individual agent to alter it. In Saussure's terms, language is the musical score, and we, its users, are the belated performers of that score. "Language is comparable to a symphony in that what the symphony actually is stands completely apart from how it is performed," explains Saussure; "the mistakes that musicians make in playing the symphony do not compromise this fact." In fact, he says, "my definition of language presupposes the exclusion of everything that is outside its organism or system."[50]

To make a connection, then, between language and "everything that is outside its organism"—i.e., nature, history, and human experience as it unfolds in and over time—requires a series of arbitrary actions and decisions. In Saussure's terms, this means that "the bond between the signifier and the signified is arbitrary. Since I mean by sign the whole that results from the associating of the signifier with the signified, I can simply say: *the linguistic sign is arbitrary*."[51] For structuralism, as Saussure defines it, to have the word always means not to have the thing because by its nature the presence of the sign implies the absence of the concept or reality to which it refers. This is Faulknerian wisdom with a vengeance, and if Benjy Compson could grasp the meaning of this claim, he would be devastated by it.

Although the witless wonder of Benjy Compson may be appealing in its own way, it is the savvy wisdom of Ferdinand de Saussure that seems self-evident when they think about language and the truth. Saussure's semiotic theory frustrates all longings for a magical view of language, but it also taps into the energy that drives the modern quest to master nature. If we take the world to consist of objects that have no meanings until we assign them, we are free to try to make of those objects what we wish. We can mine the world for its resources, shape its products to meet our needs, and harness its complex order for whatever purposes or plans we have in view.

Our shaping powers extend to the domains of our own bodies, which have become for many over the past century a prime source of material to be molded and fashioned at will. In the past several decades there have been dramatic shifts, for example, in attitudes toward the surgical and sexual remaking of the body and toward the painting and piercing of it as well. Marking the latest phase in our centuries-long quest to "master nature through a planetary technique," such changes fit perfectly well within the limits of sign theory.[52]

Another reason for the self-evident nature of sign theory can be found in Saussure's claim that signs are arbitrary. That does not mean that a writer's pen is a magic wand that can conjure meanings into being for any words any way or any time we like. (Invented or artificial languages are the fantasy of children and the futility of adults, as even the most avid promoters of Esperanto must realize.) Instead, to say signs are arbitrary is to claim that the only genuine connections between words and things are those that have been established through the force of convention and the forgetfulness of the species. Words mean what they do because they have served the purposes of the powerful who have employed them to their advantage over time.[53]

To any student of modern history, such claims about the arbitrary nature and abusive potential of language ring true. In the past two hundred years alone, words—brazen, brutal words—have been pressed into service to demean, dehumanize, and destroy men, women, and children on an inconceivable scale. In Nazi Germany, Jews became "vermin" fit for extinction, while in antebellum America, black men and women were "chattels" in a system that bought and sold them at will. Repeatedly, in the modern world pernicious *signifiers* have been called into service to enslave or exterminate those *signified* by them.

One can feel the force of the structuralist critique, for example, in the story of Melita Maschmann, who came of age in Hitler's Germany and was swept up in the anti-Semitic passions of the Third Reich. In her memoirs, Maschmann reports that in her secondary school in the early 1930s, one-third of the students were Jewish. She and her Aryan classmates instinctively differentiated their Jewish peers from the mass of "the Jews" in general. Their acquaintances were individuals worthy of affection and respect, but the Jews as a group or a concept "were and remained something mysteriously menacing and anonymous."

Maschmann said it was taken for granted that however one felt about particular Jewish friends, one was utterly and unquestionably "ideologically hostile . . . to *the* Jews" in general. The drumbeat of Nazi propaganda drove home the message that "the misery of the nations was due to the Jews," and even though Maschmann and her peers claimed to find such propaganda juvenile and vulgar, she admits they were deeply shaped by it. "Herr Lewy" or "Rosel Cohn" might be flesh-and-blood persons, but there was only one "bogey-man, '*the* Jew.'" As a consequence, rather than resist the significations that anti-Semitism offered for the Jews, Maschmann says she and her peers chose to embrace them: "The Jews are the enemies of the new Germany. . . . If the Jews sow hatred against us all over the world, they must learn that we have hostages for them in our hands."[54]

What structuralist theory implies and the reality of anti-Semitism amply demonstrates, vis-à-vis the power of language to shape reality, the Psalms corroborate as well. We "love vain words and seek after lies" (4:2); we "do not speak peace" but instead "conceive deceitful words" (35:20); the "words of [our] mouths are mischief and deceit" (36:3); we "utter empty words" (41:6); and our deceitful tongues "love all words that devour" (52:4).

Juliet Capulet and Benjy Compson may both be figments of the authorial imagination, but their questions and longings carry us into the heart of modernity's struggle over the nature of the word. When she asks, "What's in a name?" Juliet has in mind a vision of naming as a fluid, flexible, and arbitrary activity. She points the way to a view of humans as self-constituting agents who strain against unjust practices embedded within the structures of language itself. And there is more than a grain of truth to this view of what it means for us to be creatures of the word.

In like manner, when Benjy Compson howls over and over again in heartbroken amazement at the absence of his sister and his lack of her love, does he not resemble each of us at some point in our lives, when we learn there are things words can never do and persons they can never bring back? Benjy bellowing at the sound of Caddy's name is the other side of the human coin whose face is that of King Lear, a man as sophisticated and complicated as Benjy is naïve and simple. In the end, so little distance separates the howling man at the golf course and the staggering King who bears his lifeless daughter, Cordelia, in his arms:

> Howl, howl, howl! O, you are men of stones.
> Had I your tongues and yes, I'ld use them so
> That heaven's vault should crack. She's gone for ever.
> I know when one is dead, and when one lives.
> She's dead as earth. (V.iii.258–62)

Even though Benjy Compson could neither speak the words nor comprehend the language, is not Lear's sorrow one he shares as a creature who must confront the emptiness to which language points? Lear continues:

> And my poor fool is hanged: no, no, no life?
> Why should a dog, a horse, a rat have life,
> And thou no breath at all? Thou'lt come no more,
> Never, never, never, never, never. (V.iii.306–9)

And yet. All of this truth about the oppressive and heartbreaking powers of words notwithstanding, is there not something missing in a view of language that pictures it exclusively as an instrument of domination or as an agent of tragic wisdom? Is there nothing that we can do with language except use it to expose the contingent nature of our experience and the unjust structures of our social orders? Does language possess a capacity to comfort as well as a power to punish? Is it able to reveal truth as well as conceal it; does it have power to heal wounds as well as inflict them? Can words serve to renew our minds and enchant our hearts?

A Rumor of Angels

In the following chapters, these questions will receive many answers in the affirmative, as we hear from an ecumenical chorus of theological voices. For now, however, we can give a hint of the argument to come with the aid of a great poet and a gifted sociologist of religion.

The poet is Richard Wilbur, whose voice has sounded a note of strong and sober Christian hope throughout a career spanning seven decades. In a poem titled "A Barred Owl," the speaker is a husband who, along with his wife, goes to comfort their daughter one night in her "darkened room." She has been awakened and startled by the booming call of an owl. They tell her not to be afraid, for all the bird was doing was asking an "odd question" repeatedly: "Who cooks for you?" Having offered this reassurance, the speaker of the poem then fashions a general point, which is that while "words" have the power to "make our terrors bravely clear," they "Can also thus domesticate a fear, / And send a small child back to sleep at night."

This parental use of words brings comfort by "domesticating" a fear, but does it do so at a cost? Wilbur hints that it does at the poem's close, when he observes that the words of the mother and father will keep their daughter from dreaming of some animal that has been caught in a "claw" and carried in flight to a branch, where it will be "eaten raw." This is, of course, almost certainly what happened as the owl "Who'd" its way in the darkness toward its prey (29).

In an intriguing study of the role of transcendence in modern religious thought and experience, Peter Berger takes an extended look at a situation very much like the one Wilbur covers in his twelve poetic lines. He asks us to imagine a child awakening in the night from a bad dream. He is "surrounded by darkness, alone, beset by nameless threats." He cries, and his mother comes to comfort him, equipped as she is with "the power to banish the chaos and to restore the benign shape of the world." To accomplish this task, she may sing to her son, cradle him in her arms, or offer words of encouragement: "Don't be afraid—everything is all right." And if all goes well, the son will recover his trust in reality, "and in this trust he will return to sleep."[55]

As Wilbur's poem attests, this is a common scene, but Berger says it raises a fundamentally religious question, "*Is the mother lying to the child?*" In the most profound sense, the answer can be "no" only if there is "truth in the religious interpretation" of human life. "Conversely, if the 'natural' is the only reality there is," the parent is lying, and the words of comfort are hollow and false.[56]

Berger's provocative thesis is that in becoming parents, men and women "take on the role of world-builder and world-protector." They undertake to train their children to "experience trust in the order of reality." But are such experiences mere illusions, and are the ones who promote them nothing but "liars?" If reality extends no further than the natural realm that our reason can grasp, Berger concludes that the comfort is an illusion and that the words we use to instill it are lies. "If there is no other world," he writes, "then the ultimate truth about this one is that eventually it will kill the child as it will his mother." And the final truth our words could proclaim about such a world would be words not of "love but terror, not [of] light but darkness."[57]

To speak of love and light as the final truths about the world is to make a statement of faith that can be neither proved nor disproved. And to believe that words have the power to embody a truth that can comfort, heal, and enchant is to side with the Gospel of John when it affirms the Word that "in him was life, and that life was the light of mankind. The light shines in the darkness, and the darkness has never mastered it" (John 1:4–5, REB). It is time for us to turn our attention to this sense of the word and its power to master the darkness.

3

Picturing the Truth

We used to think, Joseph, when I was an unsifted girl and you so scholarly that words were cheap & weak. Now I don't know of anything so mighty. There are [those] to which I lift my hat when I see them sitting princelike among their peers on the page. Sometimes I write one, and look at his outlines till he glows as no sapphire.

—Emily Dickinson to Joseph Lyman

Well, also he will notice in the course of time, as his reading goes on, that the difference between the *almost right word* and the *right word* is really a large matter—'tis the difference between the lightning-bug and the lightning.

—Mark Twain

I would think how words go straight up in a thin line, quick and harmless, and how terribly doing goes along the earth, clinging to it, so that after a while the two lines are too far apart for the same person to straddle from one to the other; and that sin and love and fear are just sounds that people who never sinned nor loved nor feared have for what they never had and cannot have until they forget the words.

—William Faulkner, *As I Lay Dying*

What is it about words, then, that can astonish or alarm us when we hear them used with clarity and precision? What is the source of their "mighty" power to "glow as no sapphire"? Why do we care so deeply about them, that we strain in our efforts to harness the power of the "*right word's*" lightning bolt?

To account for the transforming potential of language, we require a theory that is both more modest and more mysterious than anything sign theory can offer. By *more modest*, I mean that such a theory needs to temper structuralism's claims concerning the power of language to constitute reality and truth fully; it must try to account for the fact that for the Christian, the truth is not only something that we *make* but also something that we *find*, and that, as the doctrine of revelation would have it, truth is also something that *finds us*. By *more mysterious*, I mean that we require a way of thinking of words that sees them as holding the power to tell the truth of how, "with all wisdom and insight [God] has made known to us the mystery of his will, according to his good pleasure that he set forth in Christ, as a plan for the fullness of time, to gather up all things in him, things in heaven and things on earth" (Eph. 1:8–10).

Between Sign and Symbol: Picturing the Truth

Hans-Georg Gadamer outlines such a theory of words in *Truth and Method* when he seeks to account for the power of language in human experience. Given the foundational role language plays in all our endeavors, he argues, we must think of it as "something other than a mere sign system" that denotes "the totality of objects." A "sign theory" cannot account for the intimacy that thought and language, words and things, have in our experience of the world. "A word is not just a sign," Gadamer explains, but in a legitimately "archaic" sense, "it is also something almost like a copy or an image," for there is a "mysterious connection" between the word and what it images, for the word "belongs to its being."[1]

Although Gadamer gives no evidence of having read the work of Saussure, Joel Weinsheimer believes his denial of the semiotic conception of language makes it logical to contrast his view to that of the founder of structuralism. Since *semiotics* is the study of meaning and *signs* refer to anything meaningful, "there can be no objection to thinking of words as signs. But Saussure's thesis is neither so vapid nor so indubitable," Weinsheimer says, because for the linguist "wholly arbitrary" signs realize better than all others the "ideal of the semiotic process." For structuralism, arbitrariness is not a peculiarity of some signs "but a defining characteristic of all." Saussure acknowledges the difference between a sign and a symbol; the latter is not wholly arbitrary, and

       Beginning with the Word

there is in the symbol a rudimentary connection between *signifier* and *signified*. Weinsheimer quotes Saussure on this point: "The symbol of justice, a pair of scales, could not be replaced by just any other symbol, such as a chariot." To call something a *sign*, on the other hand, implies that in relation to the thing signified, "the signifier is in principle replaceable and interchangeable." Weinsheimer says Gadamer is in complete accord with these "twin Saussurean theses" about symbol and sign. What Gadamer denies is the claim that words are merely arbitrary signs, for he considers a word to be "in one important respect like a symbol."[2]

According to Gadamer, sign theory fails because under its terms "language is taken to be something wholly detached from the being of what is under consideration." To turn language into "an instrument of subjectivity" detached from the world outside the mind is to travel down "a path of abstraction" that carries us far away from the reality of language as we use it. "Language and thinking about things are so bound together," Gadamer argues, "that it is an abstraction to conceive of the system of truths as a pregiven system of possibilities of being for which the signifying subject selects corresponding signs." A word is not something "that one picks up and gives an ideality of meaning in order to make another being visible through it."[3]

Rather than residing in the mind, the "ideality" of a word's "meaning lies in the word itself. It is meaningful already." What Gadamer asserts at this point bears quotation in full because it goes to the heart of both the doctrine of the Incarnation and the Christian tradition's understanding of the word:

> [The word] is meaningful already. But this does not imply . . . that the word precedes all experience and simply advenes to an experience in an external way, by subjecting itself to it. Experience is not wordless to begin with, subsequently becoming an object of reflection by being named, by being subsumed under the universality of the word. Rather, experience of itself seeks and finds words that express it. We seek the right word—i.e., the word that really belongs to the thing—so that in it the thing comes into language. Even if we keep in mind that this does not imply any simple copying, the word still belongs to the thing insofar as a word is not a sign coordinated to the thing ex post facto.[4]

In the words of Hans Urs von Balthasar, "The law of history and that of nature is, ultimately, to be measured by the law of Christ, the final and definitive Logos of the entire creation, for man finds the word that expresses and 'redeems' him only in hearing and vitally responding to the Word of God in Christ."[5] Just as creation is not and never has been *Word*-less, so too is human experience never wordless or senseless; our experiences are not a mass of phenomena and perceptions awaiting arbitrary acts of naming that will make them accessible to us at last as objects of reflection. Instead, experience seeks the right words to express it, and all of creation seeks to praise the Word through whom "all things were made." In the opening paragraph of *Confessions*, Augustine addresses God, telling him that although we humans may be but "a little piece of your creation," we nevertheless long to praise our creator. "You stir man to take pleasure in praising you," he says, "because you have made us for yourself, and our heart is restless until it rests in you."[6]

What Gadamer says about experience *seeking* the right words to express it resonates with what many others have said about the search for the right word. This is the point behind Mark Twain's quip about "the difference between the *almost right word* and the *right word*." That difference really is a "large matter—'tis the difference between the lightning-bug and the lightning."[7] In a similar fashion, Henry David Thoreau speaks in *Walden* of the search for precise and powerful words: "There are probably words addressed to our condition exactly, which, if we could really hear and understand, would be more salutary than the morning or the spring to our lives, and possibly put a new aspect on the face of things for us." Indeed, the book may exist "which will explain our miracles and reveal new ones. The at present unutterable things we may find somewhere uttered." Or as Thoreau's mentor and friend, Ralph Waldo Emerson, wrote early in his career, "By & by comes a word true & closely embracing the thing." The aim of its author "is not to tell the truth" but to "suggest it," and thereby "bring you as near to the fact as he is. For language itself is young & unformed. In heaven, it will be . . . 'one with things.'" The laws of writing, Emerson concludes, are as strict as those of sculpture and architecture. "There is always one line that ought to be drawn or one proportion that should be kept & every other line or proportion is wrong, & so far wrong as it deviates from this. So in writing, there is always a right word, & every other word than that is wrong."[8]

With their passion for the "right word," Twain, Thoreau, and Emerson are in essential agreement with Gadamer when he embraces what Emile Benveniste has called the "speaker's point of view" concerning language: "For the speaker there is a complete equivalence between language and reality. The sign overlies and commands reality; even better it *is* that reality." In fact, "the speaker" and "the linguist" have such different points of view about language and reality, that the linguist's assertion concerning "the arbitrariness of designations does not refute the contrary feeling of the speaker."[9]

From the speaker's point of view, words appear to resemble *symbols*, for when we speak, we take the words we use (the *signifiers*) and the things of which we speak (the *signifieds*) to be all but indivisible. That does not mean we believe words have talismanic powers, nor that we take their relationship to ideas and things to be in all cases clear and unambiguous. Instead, as speakers, we think of words as Gadamer does when he claims that the concept of the symbol derives its power from the experience of the "total coincidence of the apparent with the infinite" that unfolds in religious ceremony. This "coincidence . . . assumes that what fills the symbol with meaning is that the finite and infinite genuinely belong together. Thus the religious form of the symbol corresponds exactly to the original nature of 'symbolon,' the dividing of what is one and reuniting it again."[10] The "coincidence of being and meaning" cannot take place with a sign, whose only function is to stand in for an absent something or someone.[11]

In speaking of the intimate union of the finite and the infinite, Gadamer's understanding of the symbol draws upon the doctrine of the Incarnation and the claim of the Athanasian Creed, that "our Lord Jesus Christ, the Son of God, is God and man. God of the substance of the Father, begotten before the worlds; and man of the substance of His mother, born in the world." Jesus Christ is not a sign pointing to a signified God. As Balthasar observes, when we consider that in Jesus Christ, God became flesh and dwelt among us, "we can by no means speak of 'signs' which, according to their nature, point beyond themselves to something 'signified.'" The "Jesus of history," the man from Nazareth, is not a stunt double who takes risks and suffers pain on behalf of an "invisible 'Christ of faith'" secreted away in the heavenly realms beyond the stars. On the contrary, Jesus Christ is the very "image and expression of God." He is the "indivisible God-man: man, in so far as God radiates from him; God, in so far as he appears in the man Jesus. What is seen, heard, and touched is the 'Word of Life' (1 John 1:1)." Jesus Christ is not an *instrument* by means of which "'someone else' strives for and attains to 'something else.'" He is instead the God-man who serves as the full *expression* of God's presence, grace, and glory.[12]

God told Moses, "you cannot see my face; for no one shall see me and live" (Exod. 33:20). But with Jesus Christ, this is no longer true. "Touch me, and see," the risen Christ tells his disciples, "for a ghost does not have flesh and bones as you see that I have" (Luke 24:39). Or in the pungent words of Emily Dickinson's message of consolation to a grieving friend: "The crucifix requires no glove."[13] In the crucified and risen Christ, not only can we see God, but we may touch him and feel the nail wounds in his hands (John 20:24–28).

The doctrine of the Incarnation is a scandal to sign theory, for in Saussurean semiotics there is no way to conceive of a union of heaven and earth or of word and thing. For structuralism, the "sensible appearance" (of the word) is one thing, and the mental content of its meaning "is quite another, and . . . the two are coordinated" after the fact. The act of meaning is a finite and occasional event, while the meaning itself is neither finite nor situated. "To call a word a sign implies that it consists in an intrinsically meaningless event of utterance connected to an intrinsically disembodied and unhistorical idea," explains Weinsheimer. Things in general—nature, history, the world of appearances—"are meaningless per se. Meaning is a function of mind."[14]

As Weinsheimer describes them, core elements of Saussure's semiotic understanding of language sound uncannily gnostic, in that they posit a radical contrast between the bodily Jesus and the spiritual Christ. To the gnostic, the Word becoming flesh is an "intrinsically meaningless event of utterance," which unfolds while the "intrinsically disembodied" God remains hidden, unsullied by earthly entanglements and untouched by human suffering. In the Incarnation, according to the gnostic line of reasoning, God deigned to be housed briefly within a body so that he might work his will in an alien land. Jesus of Nazareth is the lowly host, God the Father the untainted guest. "When he [Christ] was led before Pilate," one second-century gnostic explained, the "Spirit of Christ set in him was taken away," and "what suffered was [only] the psychic Christ." And this "psychic Christ"? There is need to worry about his purity, for he had only "passed through Mary as water passes through a pipe."[15]

Despite its speculative excesses and heretical conclusions, gnosticism nevertheless "served as a reminder of what the theologians of the church . . . may have been inclined to forget," including such matters as human alienation from the world and the "ineffable greatness of God."[16] In a similar manner, sign theory brings to the fore important linguistic considerations we might otherwise overlook. As a case in point, Weinsheimer observes that sign theory correctly takes ideas and concepts to have qualities that cannot be fully expressed in any particular word. However intimately the word and the thing it symbolizes may appear to "belong together, they are not identical." If a person desecrates the flag as an intentional display of disrespect for his or her country, no one mistakes the flag *for* the country. "No one thinks that the word *is* the thing it means," and because of the nature of language, the symbol never achieves a perfect unity of word and thing but retains in part the properties of a sign. Acknowledging that a symbol is always the same as and different from what it symbolizes, Weinsheimer concedes that "Gadamer overemphasizes the sameness, coincidence, continuity, and unity of the word with what it words." Yet he does this primarily as a corrective, "for 'nobody disputes the arbitrariness of the sign.'"[17]

But if this is the case, what is a *word*, if it is more than a *sign* but less than a *symbol*? To Gadamer, the answer is that the word is most like a *picture*. Like a sign, a picture points beyond itself to something or someone it is meant to indicate, yet like a symbol, it also *re*-presents what it pictures and does so in its form and content alike. It is in the nature of pictures to deal simultaneously with presence and absence, similarity and difference. They stand poised, "as it were, halfway between two extremes: these extremes of representation are *pure indication*, which is the essence of the sign, and *pure substitution*, which is the essence of the symbol."[18]

A picture simultaneously points away from itself and to itself. Consider the case of the portrait. It stands in for the person it represents, and no one will confuse the painted subject for the flesh-and-blood woman or man "behind" the image. At the same time, the picture is not just a sign because in a real sense it participates in the being of the thing it represents. A stop sign is distinct from the action it indicates—the pressure on the brake pedal that brings your car to a halt—but the *Mona Lisa* simultaneously points to the wife of an early sixteenth-century Florentine merchant and stands on its own in its inscrutable mystery. "The difference between a picture and sign has an ontological basis. The picture does not disappear in pointing to something else but, in its own being, shares in what it represents," argues Gadamer.[19]

In the previous chapter we looked briefly at the question of personal names as one way of thinking of the ties that bind words to things. We did so by way of a scene from *The Scarlet Letter*, and to explore Gadamer's view of the word as *picture*, we can look as well at a scene from another imaginative reconstruction of life in seventeenth-century Massachusetts, *The Crucible* by Arthur Miller.

Both Hawthorne's novel and Miller's play work with a strong Protestant dynamic, that being the nominalist view of language first championed by William of Ockham and others in the fourteenth century and brought to prominence in the Reformation two centuries later. As we have seen, the nominalists sought to have language be as transparent as possible in its description of reality, and they had a clear preference for the denotative over the connotative. Denotative terms refer to particular and discrete entities directly, while connotative terms—the language of feelings, values, and relationships—touch on reality indirectly or obliquely.

In theological terms, this meant that for strict nominalists, nature has no symbolic significance that can be detected in its structure, patterns, or workings; instead, nature depends for its order and purpose entirely upon the absolute power of God (*de potentia Dei absoluta*). And we, in like manner, wholly depend on that absolute power for our understanding of the world before us. In pushing to the limit the concept of nature as being utterly contingent upon God's will, the nominalists effectively "desymbolized the universe." In the words of Steven Ozment, "For Ockham, the world was contingent, not necessary, and only concepts, words, and promises bound man to God and to the world. . . . Man too is presently free to organize the world in concepts and terms of his own choosing."[20]

That last point is crucial because one way to read the history of modernity is to see it as the gradual but relentless appropriation by humans of the arbitrary powers of a nominalist God. Take the case of changing one's given name, for example. The freedom to rename has a long history in the American experience, and it is often associated with the promise of regeneration. Until recently, immigrants frequently changed their names upon arriving in the country. My own paternal grandfather did this, shifting from "Peterson" to "Lundin," I am told, in order to stand out from the crowd in the Swedish immigrant community in which he planned to settle and start a business. In the past several decades, name changing has increasingly become a part of the culture's retinue of techniques for self-definition and renewal; the mercurial Ron Artest of NBA fame provides one of the most notorious of recent examples, with his switch to Metta World Peace in late 2011.[21]

In *The Scarlet Letter*, the question of naming has to do specifically with the anguished guilt of Reverend Arthur Dimmesdale. We have seen how Hester Prynne urges him to flee with her and rid himself of guilt by shedding his name. "Preach! Write! Act! Do anything, save to lie down and die!" she pleads with him. "Give up this name of Arthur Dimmesdale, and make thyself another, and a high one, such as thou canst wear without fear or shame" (289).

Dimmesdale agrees to run away with Hester and their daughter, Pearl, but not before he preaches a final sermon. As he makes his way back into Boston, however, he is alarmed to discover that his decision to change his identity has transformed his character in troubling ways. "In truth," explains Hawthorne, "nothing short of a total change of dynasty and moral code, in that interior kingdom, was adequate to account for the impulses . . . [of the] startled minister." At every turn, the minister finds himself "incited to do some strange, wild, wicked thing or other, with a sense that it would be at once involuntary and intentional; in spite of himself, yet growing out of a profounder self than that which opposed the impulse" (306). Dimmesdale's name had been the tie binding him to a complex set of religious beliefs and ethical practices. When he decides to discard his identity and flee with Hester, he finds himself torn from his ethical moorings and buffeted by surging impulses he can neither understand nor master. However arbitrary the name of Arthur Dimmesdale may seem in the abstract, that name and the life story embedded within it mark the identity of the man.

In *The Crucible*, John Proctor comes face-to-face with the deadly power of naming. Condemned to die, this innocent farmer is offered a chance to

Beginning with the Word

save his life by confessing to a crime, witchcraft, that he never committed. Desperate to be reunited with his pregnant wife, Elizabeth, and their children, Proctor confesses. Yet when the authorities put before him a transcript of his confession, he refuses to sign it. Instead, he tells Judge Danforth that he, the judge, is free to report abroad whatever Proctor has confessed but that he, John Proctor, will not sign his name to the document. When Danforth asks him why he refuses, Proctor angrily replies:

> Because it is my *name*! Because I cannot have another in my life! Because I *lie* and sign myself to lies! Because I am not worth the dust on the feet of them that hang! How may I live without my name? I have given you my soul, leave me my name! (90)

Dimmesdale's and Proctor's conflicts testify to the intertwining of language and reality in the lives of all who have the capacity to speak, remember, and imagine. Like the flag as a symbol, a person's name is something less than a full embodiment of that individual but something more than an arbitrary sign pointing to a wordless reality. Neither pure sign nor pure symbol, a name is more like a picture; it simultaneously stands for us and points to us. Our identities are not limited to our histories, but they are rooted in them, and without a past we would have neither a present nor a future. That is another way of saying that for each of us, our identity is bound up with the *story* of who we have been, what we have done, and what we aspire and promise to be. As we will see in the following section, these facts about identity, language, and reality are relevant to our individual lives and our collective histories, to be sure, but they apply supremely to the history of God's redemptive relationship to the human race.

Speaking of God

One pivotal point at which the history of the church and that of language theory came together was the Protestant Reformation of the sixteenth century. In the struggles between the Roman Catholic Church and the early Reformers, and later within the denominational ranks of Protestantism itself, we come upon arguments about symbol, sign, and picture as they are marshaled into service for a series of intense disputes about the central sacrament of the Christian faith.

To see how these arguments developed, we might begin with the idea that words are *symbols*. There are obvious parallels between this theory and the Catholic view of the Mass as a miracle of transubstantiation in which we encounter the Real Presence of Christ, as bread is transformed into Christ's body and wine into his blood. When the first generation of Reformers rejected the Real Presence—the Genevan Confession calls it "a reprobate and diabolical ordinance"—the Council of Trent reaffirmed the doctrine in 1551 in uncompromising terms: "After the consecration of bread and wine, our Lord Jesus Christ, true God and true man, is truly, really, and substantially contained in the august sacrament of the holy Eucharist under the appearance of those sensible things."[22] Four centuries later, John Paul II rearticulated the historic Catholic teaching in the specific terms of modern language theory. In the Eucharist, the Pope explained, "the indissoluble unity between the signifier and signified makes it possible to grasp the depths of the mystery" of revelation's *sacramental* character. "Christ is truly present and alive" in the sacrament at the heart of the Mass, and the word and the thing become one in the Real Presence.[23]

At the opposite end of the theological and linguistic spectrum, we find a number of Reformers who considered the Lord's Supper to be nothing more than a commemorative meal meant to serve as a *sign* of God's grace. Christ is not present in the elements but remembered in the minds of those who partake of them. To Ulrich Zwingli, the thought of consuming and digesting the actual body of Christ seemed "abhorrent to sense," while Johannes Oecolampadius insisted that "there is nothing in this sacrament that either is a miracle or surpasses human understanding." The Dutch humanist Cornelius Hoen spoke of the Lord's Supper in language that echoes the dynamic distinction between word and thing, presence and absence: "Christ, who is recognized by faith alone and worshiped by faith alone [has] withdrawn his presence from us," so that the bread of the communion meal is purely a "sign" of that presence rather than an embodiment of it.[24] In the words of a key Anabaptist document, the Schleitheim Confession, the communion meal is exclusively a "remembrance of the broken body" and "shed blood of Christ."[25]

Martin Luther's view of communion was wedged into the gap between Anabaptist remembrance and Catholic presence. He held that Christ is present in the sacrament but only as a consequence of the grace of God's Word and the promise of God's faithfulness. In the sacrament, writes Lutheran theologian Robert Jenson, God grants to us a "present reality created by a word of God that simultaneously evokes a past event and opens its future, to make it live in the present."[26] For Jenson, the body of Christ consists of the objects that make Christ available to us as subjects. In sacramental terms, through the agency of Christ's works and God's promises, the bread and cup, along with the church whose fellowship is formed around them, represent supreme sacramental realities.

The risen Christ is not present in these objects in a magical way, as though his spirit had infused itself into them. Instead, he is present in the sacraments as a consequence of the faithful nature of God's creative speech. Jenson notes that Christian theology "has often failed to understand the *Logos* as God's utterance and has substituted the notion that he is God's concept." Yet the *Logos* is not God's *concept*—as though he were a structuralist idea or intention needing to be represented by a sign—but is instead God's *utterance*, and "when the Eucharist is celebrated, Christ's promises of the Kingdom and of his presence in it are in fact fulfilled: even though the Kingdom is still future . . . , each celebration is already a wedding feast."[27] In Gadamer's terms, in the Eucharist, Jesus Christ is the *picture* of God's presence rather than a *sign* (*"pure indication"*) or a *symbol* (*"pure substitution"*).

In addition to these Lutheran connections, a second theological corollary to Gadamer's view of language as picture may be found in the Reformed tradition, in a theological line that runs from John Calvin in the sixteenth century to Karl Barth in the twentieth. For Calvin, the relationship of language to truth, of words to things, was anchored in the bedrock of the divine word and will. He believed the "sacraments were dependent on the word of God, apart from which they had no function," and, borrowing a key concept from Augustine, he held that the sacrament is "the word made visible." The bread and wine of communion are nothing more and nothing less than "visible words."[28]

Such an assertion seems to presuppose a series of answers to a set of prior questions: "What makes a word capable of embodying and communicating the will of God?" "Do humans possess a Godlike capacity of some kind that enables them to create and recognize the truth?" "Is there in language some property that equips it to embody truth in a unique, perhaps even magical, manner?" Or as the very root of these separate questions asks, "How is it that human language can bear the truth of God's self-revealing disclosure of himself and his will?"

Questions such as these point to the presence of what theologian Bruce McCormack speaks of as the dominant role played by the concept of the *modern* in our thinking about Christianity. Modern theology emerged as a consequence of theologians having given up on efforts to defend traditional orthodoxy against erosion and having turned instead to a concern with the way in which "the theological values resident in those orthodoxies might be given an altogether new expression, dressed out as new categories for reflection."[29]

In key respects, literary romanticism took the precise form of such a "modern" effort to buttress traditional Christian spiritual formulations and ethics by means of a dramatic recasting of Christian theology. One of the primary ways it did so was by means of romantic theories of the symbol that were intended to describe just how it is that figurative language can discover and embody truth.

Consider, for example, Coleridge and the concept of consubstantiality. In the words of J. Robert Barth, this principle as Coleridge employs it is "clearly akin to the traditional notion of the analogy of all being," a central tenet of Roman Catholic views of natural law and of the relationship of reason to revelation. In a meditation on scriptural language, Coleridge defines the imagination as "that reconciling and mediatory power, which incorporating the reason in images of the sense, and organizing (as it were) the flux of the senses by the permanence and self-circling energies of the reason, gives birth to a system of symbols, harmonious in themselves, and consubstantial with the truths of which they are the conductors." For Coleridge, the imagination and the poetic scriptures it produces are not the only symbols we can read in our search for "consubstantial" truth. We find a second source in "another book, likewise a revelation of God—the great book of his servant Nature." This book "has been the music of gentle and pious minds of all ages, it is the *poetry* of all human nature, to read it likewise in a figurative sense, and to find therein correspondences and symbols of the spiritual world."[30]

Coleridge's doctrine of the symbolic imagination revisits key issues that surfaced in sacramental disputes during the first generations of the Reformation. At the heart of both the Reformation arguments and the romantic theories lay the question of God's use of natural realities and human capacities to reveal his will and convey his grace. What is the source of the power conveyed by the communion elements and baptismal waters? What is it about language and our use of it that makes it possible for words to reveal the truth about nature, our own experience, and God? How are we able, through language, to speak of God, and how, in turn, is he able to speak to us as well?

In good measure, questioning of this kind drove Karl Barth to turn from the liberal Protestant consensus that ruled the theological world of his youth and to embark on a search for an adequate, trustworthy knowledge of God. As he turned away from the nineteenth-century theology of experience and toward a renewed doctrine of revelation, Barth made the theology of the Word and the doctrine of the Trinity the starting points for his thought.[31]

Near the outset of *Church Dogmatics*, Barth writes that we find in trinitarian doctrine the answer to the question, "Who is God?" The Trinity "distinguishes the Christian doctrine of God as Christian" and marks the sharp distinction between a generalized belief in an omnipotent divinity and a Christian trust in a personal God who reveals himself as one who shares in human suffering and has the power to raise the dead. Hidden and inscrutable as he may be, God has nevertheless chosen from the foundation of the world to reveal himself through the Incarnation of the Son and the testimony of the Spirit. "God's presence is always God's decision to be present," Barth argues, and the "form" or means of his revelation "does not take God's place. It is not the form, but God in the form, that reveals, speaks, comforts, works and aids. The fact that God takes form does not give rise to a medium, a third thing between God and man, a reality distinct from God that is as such the subject of revelation." That human language can embody and speak the truth of God is entirely contingent on God's decision to reveal himself to us in and through the forms he chooses (CD, I.1.301, 321).[32]

In his discussion of God's trinitarian revelation of himself and his will, Barth provides a theologically specific context for the matters of language and interpretation that Gadamer treats philosophically. He begins his exposition of the Trinity by affirming that it has "decisive and controlling" power for Christian thought. When we ask, "Who is the self-revealing God?" the Bible's response to that question compels us "to reflect on the triunity of God." When we ask what God can do or when we seek to learn what he accomplishes, we receive "new answers to the first question: Who is He?"

> The problem of the three answers to these questions—answers which are like and yet different, different and yet like—is the problem of the doctrine of the Trinity. In the first instance the problem of revelation stands or falls with this problem. (CD, I.1.303)

What makes this doctrine crucial for our discussion of language and reality is that the Trinity "is distinguished from all other Christian doctrines by the fact that it cannot be made comprehensible as the immediate utterance of Christian self-consciousness" (CD, I.1.304). Any other Christian doctrine—be it that of divine sovereignty, original sin, even redemption—can be developed out of the resources of consciousness and self-reflection. And this is exactly what literature in the romantic tradition has done for two centuries vis-à-vis the Christian faith, as it has sought to sustain by other means—i.e., the powers of consciousness and the imagination—the complex system of values that Judaism and Christianity elaborated over the course of several millennia.[33]

In such efforts to develop a distinctly "Modern Protestantism," Barth detects a deep, widespread aversion to the Trinity. He attributes this hostility to the impossibility of deriving this doctrine from conscious experience, which had become by the mid-nineteenth century, the primary source for our knowledge of God. With its embrace of experience and its indifference to revelation, liberal Protestantism lost interest in the Trinity, for only the self-revealing activity of God can plant the Trinity at the root of Christian thought, and revelation alone can disclose to us "this mystery that governs all mysteries" (*CD*, I.1.303).

If the Trinity is foundational to Christian doctrine and thought, what serves as its root? Barth's answer is, "the biblical concept of revelation." The Trinity "is simply the development of the knowledge that Jesus is the Christ or the Lord" and "does not stem from any other root." To Barth, that means trinitarian doctrine cannot be rooted in what are known as the *vestigia trinitatis* ("traces of the Trinity"). With origins that date back to the early centuries of the Christian era, the *vestigia* tradition has a rich and complex history. At its core, that tradition has operated out of a conviction that because the creation reflects the Creator, we are free—perhaps even compelled—to search "for traces of the triune God (*vestigia Trinitatis*)" within the structures of the created order.[34]

For those who believe they have discovered such traces in various threefold patterns in nature, human consciousness, or historical events, these traces serve as "image(s) of the trinitarian God Himself." Barth quotes Augustine's explanation, in *On the Trinity*, of the *vestigia trinitatis*:

> Therefore, in regarding the Creator, who is known through the things which have been created, we should recognize the Trinity, of which a trace appears in the creature to the extent that is merited. For in this Trinity is the supreme origin of all things and the most perfect beauty and the most blessed delight. . . . Whoever sees this, whether in part or whether through a glass and darkly, should rejoice in knowing God, honor him as God and give thanks; but whoever does not see it should strive through piety toward seeing. (*CD*, I.1. 334)[35]

We might "certainly call the form that God assumes in his unveiling as the Son or Word, the *vestigium trinitatis*," but such christological specificity is not what Augustine and others necessarily had in mind when speaking of the vestiges. Instead of focusing on the special revelation of God in Jesus Christ, the vestiges tradition has searched more generally for objects or relationships that reveal "an essential trinitarian disposition supposedly immanent in some created realities quite apart from their possible conscription by God's revelation." In the structures of reality, that is, "traces of the trinitarian Creator God" are taken to be embedded within nature and human experience in their "pure createdness" (*CD*, I.1.334).[36] One of the best known of all works in the *vestigia* tradition is St. Bonaventure's *The Soul's Journey into God*. Its opening chapter—on the "Ascent into God and on Contemplating Him through His Vestiges in the Universe"—tells us:

> In relation to our position in creation, the universe itself is a ladder by which we can ascend into God. Some created things are vestiges, others images; some

are material, others spiritual; some are temporal, others everlasting; some are outside us, others within us. In order to contemplate the First Principle, who is most spiritual, eternal, and above us, we must pass through his vestiges, which are material, temporal and outside us. This means *to be led in the path of God*. We must also enter into our soul, which is God's image, everlasting, spiritual and within us. This means *to enter in the truth of God*. We must go beyond to what is eternal, most spiritual and above us, by gazing upon the First Principle. This means to *rejoice in the knowledge of God and in reverent fear of his majesty* (cf. Ps. 85:11).[37]

At the close of that introduction, Bonaventure launches into a hymnic celebration of a series of threefold trinitarian distinctions to be found within us and far beyond us in the heavens and earth. He praises the three days' journey into the wilderness (Exod. 3:18), the threefold existence of things in matter, in mind, and in the Eternal Art (Christ as word), as well as the threefold orientation of the human mind: first to material realities, then to spiritual realities, and then to mental realities.[38]

Barth says that if we could actually uncover vestiges of the Trinity within a wide array of physical, mental, and historical phenomena, then their existence would raise the issue "whether we do not have to assume a second root of the doctrine of the Trinity" growing alongside the primary root stemming from biblical revelation. If vestiges can be found throughout nature and human experience, does the biblical revelation do anything more than confirm a knowledge of God that we have already acquired elsewhere, prior to our encounter with the self-revealing God of Father, Son, and Spirit (*CD*, I.1.335)?[39]

These reflections lead Barth to pose a question that strikes at the heart of the structuralist paradigm. Are the vestiges signs of a "Creator God transcending the world?" he asks. Or are they perhaps instead "determinations of the cosmos which must be viewed as strictly immanent and, because the cosmos is man's cosmos, as determinations of man's existence?" If we take this to be the case, we "erase the concept of natural revelation as well as biblical revelation and adjudge the doctrine of the Trinity to be a bold attempt on man's part to understand the world and ultimately himself, i.e., adjudge it to be a myth." The problem of the *vestigia* is of the "greatest importance" because it leads to a questioning not only of the Trinity but also of the grounding of Christian thought in revelation itself. And finally, the idea of a second root for the Trinity calls into question "the meaning and possibility of theology as distinct from mere cosmology or anthropology." Barth then asks:

Do we not have in this idea of the *vestigium trinitatis* an ancient Trojan horse which one day was unsuspectingly allowed entry into the theological Ilium, and in whose belly—so much more alert have certain experiences made us since Augustine's day—we can hear a threatening clank, so that we have every cause to execute a defensive movement—perhaps there is no more we can do here—by declaring, perhaps only very naively, that we do not want to have anything to do with it? (*CD*, I.1.335–36) [40]

A Universe of Words

To some, the *vestigia trinitatis* may seem like an arcane issue situated at a far remove from the concerns of those who love literature and wish to be about the business of plumbing its mysterious depths and studying its shimmering surfaces. Yet in reality, it has remarkable pertinence for any Christian effort to fashion a contemporary theory of literature and language. One way to think of its relevance would be to say that while the search for a *vestigia trinitatis* may have been plausible in the enchanted cosmos inhabited by St. Augustine and St. Bonaventure, such a search would be fruitless in the disenchanted universe of late modernity. For we live, not in the cosmos of Dante Alighieri but the universe of Franz Kafka.

In framing the question in this manner, I draw upon the work of Charles Taylor, who observes that we in the modern world have "moved from living in a cosmos to being included in a universe." The ancient and medieval *cosmos* had the sense of an "ordered whole," and its order was seen to be a "humanly meaningful one." The modern universe, on the other hand, has only that kind of order that can be "exhibited in exceptionless natural laws." The enchanted cosmos of Bonaventure drew on a general understanding of the "things which surround us" as "embodiments or expressions of these [Platonic] Ideas, or as signs of a higher reality which cannot be directly seen." For most people in modern civilization "that whole way of understanding things has fallen away." It is not just that the "cosmos theories" no longer appear believable; "they are even no longer fully intelligible. Seeing physical realities as embodiments or expressions doesn't fully make sense." [41]

This is in good measure the same point C. S. Lewis made half a century ago in a powerful comparison of the medieval and modern understandings of creation. He says that when we look out upon the night sky with modern eyes, we feel that we are gazing "out over a sea that fades away into mist" or peering into "a trackless forest" where there are "trees forever but no horizon." The medieval universe, on the other hand, presented itself to viewers as a great building whose scale we could take in, even though it towered above us. The vastness of space "may arouse terror, or bewilderment or vague reverie," Lewis notes, but "the spheres of the old present us with an object in which the mind can rest, overwhelming in its greatness but satisfying in its harmony."[42]

As long as the argument from design retained its force—as it did until the mid-nineteenth century—vestiges of the Trinity could still conceivably be sought among the connections between the self-consciousness of humans and the patterns of nature. But Darwin and others laid waste to the design argument, and by the end of the nineteenth century, a powerful naturalistic consensus had clamped its grip on all manner of cultural activities, including theories of language and works of literature.

In the post-Darwinian universe as the naturalists envision it, we find ourselves to be orphans living within the imprisoning confines of an immanent universe, and any transcendent truth we claim to believe is merely a myth we have created to pass the time and cushion the blows before we die. This cosmic loneliness is the subject of William Faulkner's *As I Lay Dying*, a passage from which serves as an epigraph to this chapter. It comes from a speech by a woman named Addie Bundren and is delivered after her death, as though it were a letter kept under seal until she slipped away. What Addie says is a clear product of the hardscrabble naturalism she acquired from her father even before she learned it through her experience. "I could just remember," she tells us, "how my father used to say that the reason for living was to get ready to stay dead a long time" (169).

"And so I took Anse," is all she says about the man who was to marry her and father all but one of her children. Addie reports that when she became pregnant with her firstborn, Cash, then "I knew that living was terrible and that this was the answer to it. That was when I learned that words are no good; that words dont ever fit even what they are trying to say at" (170–71).

Words are hopelessly inadequate for Addie, for they can do nothing but expose our needs. With a series of images that seem to sum up two centuries of an ever-expanding cultural anguish over the limits of finitude and the emptiness of language in a disenchanted world, Addie cries out against words: "I knew that . . . we had had to use one another by words like spiders dangling by their mouths from a beam, swinging and twisting and never touching." When she married Anse, and he came to her "in the nights," he "had a word, too. Love, he called it." But by that time, Addie had grown impervious to words. "I knew that that word [love] was like the others: just a shape to fill a lack; that when the right time came, you wouldn't need a word for that anymore than for pride or fear" (172).

Sometimes, when she lay beside Anse in the dark, Addie found herself meditating on his name. "I would think: Anse. Why Anse. Why are you Anse?" She would think about his name until the word became "a shape, a vessel," and he would liquefy and flow into the name and vessel "like cold molasses flowing out of the darkness." When the jar finally stood "full and motionless," it became "a significant shape profoundly without life like an empty door frame," and the name of the jar slipped from her memory. And when she did the same with the names of her sons, "*Cash* and *Darl*," they eventually solidified, died, and faded away, leaving Addie to conclude: "All right. It doesn't matter. It doesn't matter what they call them" (173).

Obsessed by the thought that the members of her family have violated her, Addie remains aloof from them. When her distance and indifference lead a neighbor to tell her that she is not a good mother, Addie says to herself and us, "I would think how words go straight up in a thin line, quick and harmless, and how terribly doing goes along the earth, clinging to it." After a while, the two lines grow "too far apart for the same person to straddle from one to the other" (173). Heaven and earth, height and depth, "air and earth, lightness and weight, all the contrasts point here to an irreducible chasm between word and thing, saying and 'doing.'"[43] Words carry no weight and disclose no truths because they are on the other side of that "irreducible chasm" between language and reality.

Addie's imagery calls to mind Barth's judgment about the *vestigia trinitatis*, those "traces" of the Trinity thought to be found in nature and human experience. Barth believed these "traces" to be "determinations of the cosmos which must be viewed as strictly immanent," and as such they turn the doctrine of the Trinity into a "bold" effort humans have undertaken to explain themselves and their world. Yet if that is the case, Barth says all our efforts to discover the truth by means of language must be "adjudged to be myths," and Addie has it right, when she says our "words go straight up in a thin line," leaving us behind to "cling to the earth."

We hear in Addie's words an undertone of a desperate sadness, for she believes even language has abandoned us to our lot. We stand alone in the midst of creation, left with nothing but the humming efficiency of a "self-regulating system" and the hollow emptiness of our words. No word of grace, no act of power will reach us in our orphaned state. "Our souls are like those orphans whose unwedded mothers die in bearing them," observes Ahab in Melville's *Moby Dick*. "The secret of our paternity lies in their grave, and we must there to learn it" (373). To Addie Bundren as well, we are orphans who have been left to our deeds and have been denied access to the stories that might make sense of them. As she says, musing on Anse and the meaning of words:

> I would lie by him in the dark, hearing the dark land talking of God's love and His beauty and His sin; hearing the dark voicelessness in which the words are the

Beginning with the Word

deeds, and the other words that are not deeds, that are just the gaps in people's lacks, coming down like the cries of the geese out of the wild darkness in the old terrible nights, fumbling at the deeds like orphans to whom are pointed out in a crowd two faces and told, That is your father, your mother. (174)

In sign theory's immanent cosmos, words are as Addie pictures them—"just gaps in people's lacks"—and they are orphans who can do no more than fumble at the deeds that once gave birth to them. As such, they—the words—are powerless and pointless.

The upshot of this is straightforward. No matter how helpful sign theory may be for understanding the limits of language and the lacks of the human condition, it does not have it within itself to sustain a Christian vision of the truth. For that, we require a vision of language that sees words as having the strength to bear the truth and the power to bear witness to it. We need a sense of how our words, like our deeds, may find a place to dwell within the spacious forms of stories.

In the first sermon recorded in the New Testament, the apostle Peter provides such a storied home on the day of Pentecost:

Jesus of Nazareth, a man attested to you by God with deeds of power, wonders, and signs that God did through him among you, as you yourselves know—this man, handed over to you according to the definite plan and foreknowledge of God, you crucified and killed by the hands of those outside the law. But God raised him up, having freed him from death, because it was impossible for him to be held in its power. (Acts 2:22–24)

Every Word at Home

To this point, we have focused largely on the issue of words and how they stand in relationship to the vast world about and beyond us and to the intricate and often unfathomable worlds within each of us. It is time to turn our attention from the idea of the individual word to the reality of sentences and stories. For it is through the agency of stories—and the gift of truths revealed to us by means of them—that our universe begins to take the shape of a dwelling place within which we may learn who we are and what we might become.

In "Little Gidding," the last of his *Four Quartets*, T. S. Eliot imagines such a home in the figure of a perfectly formed sentence. The eschatological setting of the poem as a whole provides the context for his meditation. Written in the early years of the Second World War, at the height of the German bombing campaign against London and other major English cities, the poem focuses on the themes—and reality—of destruction and rebirth, death and resurrection. In this context, the meaning of any event in the stream of time can only be found in the great sea that is its end. And so it is that the fifth and final section of "Little Gidding" begins:

> What we call the beginning is often the end
> And to make an end is to make a beginning.
> The end is where we start from. And every phrase
> And sentence that is right (where every word is at home,
> Taking its place to support the others,
> The word neither diffident nor ostentatious,
> An easy commerce of the old and the new,
> The common word exact without vulgarity,
> The formal word precise but not pedantic,
> The complete consort dancing together)
> Every phrase and every sentence is an end and a beginning,
> Every poem an epitaph. (144)

Of "Little Gidding" in general, critic Denis Donoghue says that Eliot was unwilling to recognize a symbol until he had successfully "imagined its force in the light of death; according to that vision, time is no longer mere *tempus*, one-thing-after-another, but *aevum*, time redeemed in the end and meanwhile lived in the light of that end."[44] It is through sentences that we learn of beginnings and endings and of that end which is, for the Christian faith, the sign of the true beginning, of which God made certain by raising the crucified Christ, thus freeing him and all creation from death, "because it was impossible for him to be held in its power."

4

From Signs to Stories

Language in the Grasp of God

As a matter of fact . . . we have come here in search of an author.

—Luigi Pirandello, *Six Characters in Search of an Author*

LEAR
Dost thou know me, fellow?
KENT
No, sir, but you have that in your countenance which I would fain call master.
LEAR
What's that?
KENT
Authority?

—William Shakespeare, *King Lear*

According to the witness of the New Testament, the world is not abandoned and left to its own devices. God takes it to Himself, entering into the sphere of it as the true God, causing His kingdom to come on earth as in heaven, becoming Himself truly ours, man, flesh, in order to overcome sin where it has its dominion, in the flesh, to take away in His own person the ensuing curse where it is operative, in the creaturely world, in the reality which is distinct from Himself.

—Karl Barth, "The Way of the Son of God into the Far Country"

Near the beginning of Lasse Hallström's film *The Cider House Rules*, there is a brief, heartstring-tugging scene packed with sentiment but also rich in its literary and theological significance. The scene is set at an orphanage on a winter day in the 1930s. As the orphaned boys and girls toss snowballs across the yard, a childless couple emerges from a car at the building's main entrance. It is clear they have come to choose a child for adoption, and the scene fades to the lunchroom a short time later. There the couple works its way down a line of children who are eating at a long table. As the prospective parents move slowly along the row, a staff member calls out a name and provides a brief description of each child they pass.

Many of the children smile shyly at the husband and wife, but those two remain impassive, until they come upon Hazel, a bright-eyed girl of six or seven. We then shift from the table to the yard outside, where the couple and Hazel make their way to the car and head off for the girl's new home. Several of the children left behind gaze wistfully out the window and wave good-bye, and one boy says, with a catch in his throat, "Nobody ever wants me."

That boy's plea strikes a responsive chord in us because it is hard not to sympathize with an abandoned and once-again rejected child. Yet something else is at work in this episode and in the countless stories of orphans we find in the fiction and drama of the past two hundred years. It has to do with a different form of orphaning, one that entails an anxiety many modern people have felt at one time or another. It is the fear of being abandoned—orphaned—by a God who has gone silent, grown distant, or perhaps died. Such an anxiety, bordering on dread, pervades many of Emily Dickinson's poems; it haunts the pages of Stephen Crane's stories; it fills the hearts and minds of Fyodor Dostoevsky's Karamazovs; and it terrifies the madman who cries "God is dead!" in Friedrich Nietzsche's fable.

In either form—as a story of children bereft of parents or as a tale of humans forsaken by God—the orphan theme speaks powerfully of a yearning to belong to a family and to have a role in a drama whose scope might draw us out of solitude and into story. This longing surfaces near the beginning of Shakespeare's *King Lear*, in which an earl by the name of Kent is banished by the king, only to return in disguise to serve his master. When Lear asks the incognito Kent why he wishes to serve him, the faithful gentleman replies that the king's countenance exudes a quality he "would fain call master." When Lear asks, "What's that?" Kent answers with a single word: "Authority."

"Authority," of course, shares its linguistic roots with "author." Both speak of the power to instigate action and to establish contexts in which those actions acquire their meaning. This is, for example, precisely what the six characters are in search of in Luigi Pirandello's provocative play, when they set out to find an author who might fill out the story of their lives.

Whether it manifests itself as the loneliness of the abandoned child, the pain of the anguished seeker, or the desperation of the discarded character, the orphan's dilemma is a particular sign of the general human condition in the immanent cosmos of the structuralists. It is hardly a coincidence that the figure of the orphan moved to the center of nineteenth-century fiction at the same time that Protestant theology was busily at work transforming *the*-ology into *anthro*-pology. Friedrich Schleiermacher and G. W. F. Hegel planted the seeds of this transformation early in the century, and Ludwig Feuerbach harvested the yield at midcentury.

"Existence out of self is the world," wrote Feuerbach in *The Essence of Christianity*. "Existence in self is God. To think is to be God."[1] As Karl Barth notes, Feuerbach did not deny God but only the idea of "an abstract divine Being, divorced from nature and man"—that is, any power situated outside the "self-regulating system" of an "immanent cosmos." Within the confines of that system, Feuerbach was happy to affirm "God's nature as man's true nature," and in denying that there are any differences between God and humans, he was "merely affirming anthropology as the true theology. . . . Religion exists. Religion is possible and necessary. But it is man who is the beginning, the middle and the end of religion—man and man alone."[2]

Once you have reduced God to a projection of human consciousness, however, you have made yourself a parentless child. This is the orphan as parricide, and in the nineteenth century, Dostoevsky and Nietzsche, at least, understood the magnitude of the deed and the consequences of the crime. As the latter wrote in *The Gay Science*:

> The madman jumped into their midst and pierced them with his eyes. "Whither is God?" he cried; "I will tell you. *We have killed him*—you and I. All of us are his murderers. . . . God is dead. God remains dead. And we have killed him."
>
> "How shall we comfort ourselves, the murderers of all murderers? What was holiest and mightiest of all that the world has yet owned has bled to death under our knives: who will wipe this blood off us? What water is there for us to clean ourselves?"[3]

Literature and Religion in an Immanent Cosmos

Since the late nineteenth century, the academic study of religion has been inclined to accept anthropology as the true theology and to embrace human experience as the source of whatever religious authority we may come upon. Stanley Hauerwas analyzes this state of affairs brilliantly in *With the Grain of the Universe* (based on his 2001 Gifford Lectures). His goal in that work is to champion Karl Barth as the proponent of a unique form of natural theology and to privide a sharp critique of the experiential theology that dominates the study of Christianity.

Hauerwas sees that theology of experience as being grounded in eighteenth-century thought. By the time of Immanuel Kant, he explains, nature had become "a self-enclosed causal nexus requiring no explanation beyond itself." Kant's response to this inheritance was to concede the natural world to the sciences and to retreat "to the only place left in which language about God might make sense, that is, to the human" realm of moral experience. By giving priority to ethics over nature as the gateway to God, Kant set the pattern for a century of theological reflection on the relationship of faith in God to the understanding of nature's power and human possibilities. In Hauerwas's words, this "understanding of natural theology left Christian theologians devoid of the resources" they would need to demonstrate that Christian categories can speak with authority about "the way things are." As a result, by the time William James came along to deliver his own Gifford Lectures in 1900, he had nothing much to say about God: "In a world in which theology could no longer pretend to tell us anything significant about the way things are, James attempted, without leaving the world of science, to show how religious experience might at least tell us something about ourselves."[4]

Hauerwas's skeptical approach to the theology of experience offers a useful vantage point from which to consider the recent resurgence of academic interest in religion. For some time now, scholars in English and in disciplines across the humanities have been heralding religion's return to the academy. In essays and books, at conferences and on blogs, observers of all types and stripes have spoken of religion as the Long Repressed Subject that suddenly has become the Hot New Topic. While several prominent public figures—including Sam Harris, Richard Dawkins, and the late Christopher Hitchens—have remained skeptical or openly hostile toward it, many literary critics, philosophers, and social scientists have welcomed religion back to the academy, which is, after all, one of its ancestral homes.

In many cases, however, the invitation to return has come with strings attached and restrictions established in advance. Consider, for example, the boundaries that are set and the fences that are built in the introduction to a recent book on "Literary Culture, Theory, and Post-Secular Modernity." Here we read of "endgame capitalism" and the faltering of "the old promises of secular modernity." In the wake of secularism's failure, claims Simon During, in religious matters the distinctions between "radical conservatism and radical leftism" have been blurred, and "as a result, although *revealed religion cannot be revived in any intellectually respectable way,* new postsecular occasions for leaps of faith appear along with a (skeptical) attention to the history of (defenses of) faith and Church institutions."[5] Christian experience, albeit skeptically considered, can pass muster as a field worthy of study, but the scandalous idea of revelation will never be allowed to take root and flower.

From sharply different angles, Hauerwas and During provide insight into postsecular criticism, the literary offshoot of this recent flowering of interest in religion. Postsecular theory has developed as a result of varied influences, including the rise of Islam and the explosive growth of the Christian church in Central and South America, as well as in Africa and Asia. The growth of Islam and Christianity in the global South has been taken as a refutation of the secularization hypothesis prominent in Western thought since the nineteenth century.

In literary studies, postsecular criticism focuses not on theology or the creeds but on *lived religion,* a way of considering religion rooted in the pragmatism of William James and the cultural anthropology of Clifford Geertz and Victor Turner. In the words of one of its foremost practitioners, the study of *lived religion* deliberately pivots away from matters about which we know a great deal—"the history of theology and (say) church and state"—and toward subjects "we know next-to-nothing about"—that is, "religion as practiced" and reflected in "the everyday thinking and doing of lay men and women."[6]

In shifting the center of religion from profession to practice, postsecular criticism follows the lead of mainstream nineteenth-century Protestantism, which established human experience as the locus of spiritual and moral authority.[7] For a cohort of nineteenth-century thinkers who wished to jettison their specific Christian commitments while retaining the contours of their spiritual identities, experience seemed to provide anchors for values and paths to God. What Scripture, sacrament, and nature could no longer sustain, experience would now yield.

In theology, the twentieth century witnessed a strong, sustained reaction to the nineteenth-century decision to invest so heavily in experience. We have already heard from Stanley Hauerwas on this count, and throughout this book, Karl Barth, Hans Urs von Balthasar, and John Paul II serve as major critics of the experiential tradition. Within the church and within theology as a discipline, they and others have been major conversational partners, yet within the academy they have merited only an occasional mention at the margins of literary and cultural theory. For the better part of a century, the theorists have found little of interest in the theological arguments that marked the twentieth-century turn from experience that Barth and his contemporaries undertook.

The history of doctrine and the creedal affirmations of believers may hold little interest for the postsecular critics, but what does rivet their attention is the stubborn resilience of religious experience in a supposedly secular age. In turn, for some Christian literary scholars, the postsecularist interest in religion appears to override any potential concerns about the attenuated nature of *lived religion*. To be sure, the postsecular critics have a genuine concern for religion, and they often treat religious experience with an appealing mixture of amazement and respect. Still, there are reasons to be cautious, for as historian Darryl Hart suggests, in general "religion does not do well in the hands of academics, whether they are sympathetic to it or not." Because the university lacks any grounds for evaluating dogmatic assertions or any means of judging the authority of revelatory texts—remember that Simon During dismissed revealed religion as not "intellectually respectable"—whatever religion the university is willing to tolerate "tends to be the thin variety that [H. L.] Mencken" called "a row of hollow platitudes as empty [of] psychological force and effect as so many nursery rhymes."[8]

Hart and Mencken have a point. It would be difficult to rest in postsecular criticism's *lived religion*, given its grounding in naturalism and its determination to stay within the boundaries of the strictly immanent cosmos. At the same time, there are lessons to be learned and benefits to be gained from a postsecular approach to modern literature. To get a sense of both the rewards and the limits, we can examine three recent, highly lauded critical studies, each of which explores crucial facets of the postsecular critique.[9]

These three books—written by Tracy Fessenden, Pericles Lewis, and Amy Hungerford—take aim at what is commonly known as the secularization thesis, a theory about modern history that depicts modernity as a drama of irresistible technological, political, and rational progress, with religion cast as an agent of superstition and suppression. Building on the work of Sigmund Freud, Émile Durkheim, and Max Weber, among others, "classical secularization theory argued that the demise of religion was sociologically determined and culturally inevitable." Secularization was seen to be a process of social change and a theory of religious decline that mapped modern history and envisioned a future in which "religion would have little or no public influence . . . or plausible claim to a revelatory authority that in any sense transcended reason."[10]

Charles Taylor calls this view of secularization the "subtraction story." He uses this term to identify those narratives that depict modern history as a drama of "human beings having lost, or sloughed off, or liberated themselves" from the illusions that have long oppressed the human race. In subtraction stories, secularization is an all-but-unqualified good that has gradually enabled long-repressed human capacities to emerge and flourish. "What emerges from this process—modernity or secularity—is to be understood," Taylor says, "in terms of underlying features of human nature which were there all along, but had been impeded by what is now set aside." Against the subtraction story, with its emphasis on supposedly perennial features, Taylor offers a narrative of modern history that focuses on particular developments, surprising inventions, and new forms of self-understanding, which he takes to be the true engines of modern secularity.[11]

For Fessenden, Lewis, and Hungerford, the subtraction story serves as the core of the secularization narrative, and they set out to challenge it by testifying to the enduring vitality of religious experience in modern literature and life. At first glance, the postsecularists' interest in religion could lead one to assume that postsecular theory and Christian theology might reach an accord of sorts on questions of belief, language, and truth. As one sympathetic evangelical critic wrote of Lewis's book, both modern fiction and modern theory develop "ways of understanding residual forms of the sacred in a profane world." Through their exploration of "the magical power of words" and the "mystical character" of "borderline states of consciousness," the modernist theorists and novelists are actually bringing about "a re-enchantment of the world."[12]

Such re-enchantment notwithstanding, these works of postsecular criticism raise as many questions as they answer about the Christian faith. In Fessenden's *Culture and Redemption*, for example, secularization comes off as a pernicious force, not because it stifles religious belief but because it sublimates a specific Protestant ideology within secular structures and thereby provides a surreptitious means for that Protestantism to retain its ironclad grip on American culture. Fessenden complains that the "simplified narrative of secularization" has ironically, even perversely, served "to strengthen the hold of a particular strain of conservative Christianity in American public life." That narrative has gone about its work in a manner simultaneously simple and stealthy. When secularism is taken to consist of the absence of religious faith or indifference to it, Fessenden argues, "then religion comes to be defined as 'Christian' by default, and an implicit association between 'American' and 'Christian'" becomes the norm. As a result, a narrow, "unmarked Christianity" is established as the standard, and the diverse, unkempt reality of American religion is shunted out of sight.[13]

To counter the tacit association of (fundamentalist) Protestantism with America, Fessenden champions a critical approach that ferrets out the dominant and oppressive Protestant presence and floods it with the light of critical scrutiny. The goal is to initiate a "rethinking" of secularity and religion, which in turn will lead to "a newly energized and contestatory pluralism" that prizes religious diversity and releases the grip of "unmarked Christianity" on American politics and culture. The epistemology informing *Culture and Redemption* takes it as a given that all religious beliefs are, in Barth's words, "bold [myth-making] attempts on man's part to understand the world and ultimately himself." In speaking, for example, of "those places where Christianity and secular reason belong to the same constellation of knowledge and power," Fessenden places all Christian truth-claims within a dynamic of power and repression. And pressing her counterargument, she seeks to extend the privileged liberty of self-constituting mythmaking to classes and groups long oppressed by a "Protestant ideology that has grown more entrenched and controlling, even as its manifestations have often become less visibly religious" in American life.[14]

Hungerford offers a less political and more personal treatment of the religious question in *Postmodern Belief*. In a richly textured argument, she claims that we should see the writing and reading of literature as fundamentally religious acts that take place in a world devoid of religious meaning and stripped of divine ends. Although she is fascinated with the question of belief, she refuses to privilege substantial (i.e., doctrinal) belief over gestural (lived religious) practice. As Hungerford tells it, the story of American religion between 1960 and 2010 is one of dual devotional tracks running side by side across the barren prairies of an unbelieving culture. On one track rode the myriad agents and schools that participated in "the strengthening of American religion in the late twentieth century"—the Charismatic movement, Eastern religions, Vatican II reform movements, the renewed literary interest in the Bible, the rise of Pentecostalism, and the revival of evangelicalism. On the parallel track, the major writers of the era glided along in all their agonistic, ironic splendor. They were intrigued by what they saw across the way but also grateful that serious religion always remained Over There, in a distant place where intense belief and passionate practice could play out their dramas without harm to others and without ultimate consequence to anyone.

The value Hungerford finds in this arrangement is that contemporary American literature has been able to trade upon the authority of religion in order to strengthen that of literature. "If literature is a steadily declining source of cultural authority in the postwar mass culture," she explains, "religion is an ever-stronger one." The varied religious movements of the late twentieth century all have "underwrit[ten] the success of the literary bids for authority" made by America's greatest contemporary writers. In turn, those forms of religious belief and practice have buttressed the attempts of American authors to overcome the ironic self-consciousness "entailed in postmodernism as a critical paradigm." The main branch of postmodern theory has looked to economic substructures to explain the ironies, ambiguities, and fractured narratives in postmodern literature. Hungerford turns elsewhere, to religion, for an explanation. "I argue that sincerity overshadows irony as a literary mode when the ambiguities of language are imagined as being religiously empowered. Writers in this mode," she claims, "see fracture and materialism not as ends in themselves but as the conditions for transcendence."[15]

To Hungerford, then, those who believe in God and those who believe in literature are natural allies bound together by the slender thread of a shared opposition to irony and a mutual respect for sincere religious experience. "Lived religion is the kind of religion that deserves our attention—that demands our attention," she suggests, for "what we believe about literature, and about language, underpins our participation in literary culture." Literature relies on religion to underwrite its fading authority, while at the same time fiction turns abstract belief into concrete practice, and in doing so, it does belief a service by revealing "what sort of cultural work belief still can do."[16]

Even more important to Hungerford is the leeway that fiction creates so that religion can be honest about itself. There is in our contemporary world, she says, "a pervading sense of meaninglessness in the face of human suffering," and as a result we face an insoluble "problem of how to be religious in a secular world." For her a "belief in meaninglessness" dwells at the heart of religious and secular people alike, and "its most significant role . . . is to provoke the imagination." There, in the products of our imaginings, we may glimpse flickering images of our condition, as we flit between light and darkness, belief and doubt, meaning and emptiness.[17]

Although he professes "to be 'absolutely unmusical religiously,'" Lewis nevertheless shares Fessenden's and Hungerford's skeptical attitude toward the secularization thesis and subtraction stories. His book focuses on great modernist writers who retained an interest in religious experience even after they had jettisoned the particular commitments of their Jewish, Catholic, and Protestant heritages. The likes of Henry James, Virginia Woolf, James Joyce, Marcel Proust, and Franz Kafka had little interest in explicit beliefs or practices, yet they remained intensely curious about the emotional and aesthetic dynamics of the relics from their religious past. For Lewis, as for Hungerford, there burns at the core of modern fiction a flame of religious intensity that no secularization narrative can ever put out.

Yet an important fact remains: Lewis considers the fuel for this flame to have but a single source, that being the insatiable human yearning to believe in a divine order. We must believe, but we cannot believe, and yet we will go on forever longing to believe. In two passages, Lewis makes this point directly. The first comes from the end of an early chapter titled "God's Afterlife," and in it, Lewis grants that of the authors that he treats, many did not believe in an "unseen order" of any kind. And if one did exist, they were not sure they could adjust to it. Nevertheless, these writers had been sobered by the disappearance of that "unseen order" and by the acting difficulties of living without its support and assurances.

In the second of the two passages, Lewis zeros in on the "fear and desire" that humans have always displayed towards the dead. He attributes to this fear much of the animating power behind religious thought and experience. "The increasingly empty churches of Europe, which Nietzsche called 'the tombs and sepulchers of God,'" hold on to their waning power, because, to quote Philip Larkin, "so many dead lie around." Lewis calls the novels of the modernist masters "their own immense monuments to the dead and to life."[18]

A clear epistemological—or is it metaphysical?—thread runs through the rich tapestry of arguments that Fessenden, Hungerford, and Lewis weave. It consists of the assumption at the heart of what theologian Garrett Green calls the "postmodern turn in religious studies." For those engaged in the study of religion, this postmodern turn involves taking "for granted that all expressions of religion—and all theories *about* religion" are rooted in particular social and historical contexts and thereby "implicated in paradigmatic commitments to certain values, concepts, and methods." It then follows that if theories of religion are to count as genuine, they must "explain the doctrines and practices of a religious . . . community as 'the material products of particular genders, classes, eras, regions, and so on.'"[19]

Fessenden's view of language takes language to be a "material product" that the powerful enlist as a primary agent in a master-slave struggle. Those who acquire power—the masters—employ language efficiently and subtly to secure their status and suppress their opposition, while the servants (and their allies in literary theory and religious studies) see language as a weapon to be used in subverting power and furthering a progressive agenda envisioned as the primary agent of justice. For Hungerford and Lewis, materialist assumptions lead to a focus on what language reveals about our spiritual hunger for meaning and comfort. By definition, the human subject's hunger for God can never find a divine object capable of satisfying it. Instead, it can and must settle for imaginative (i.e., literary) supplements and substitutes that dull our hunger and do not demand our obedience.

Beginning with the Word

God Grasps Language

The issues raised by these books bring us back to the concerns of the previous chapter, where Barth's critique of the *vestigia trinitatis* launched our discussion of the limits that our language and our spirits face in an immanent cosmos. Yet before we return to the Barthian argument about the vestiges, I need to offer a point of clarification. It has to do with the timing and substance of Barth's critique of natural theology, which surfaces powerfully in many different places in his work, including his categorical rejection of the *vestigia* tradition and the thought of a possible *second root* (that is, some source other than revelation) for the doctrine of the Trinity. Why, especially early in his career, did Barth so vehemently reject the possibility of natural theology? Why would he brook no compromises on this front? And if a Christian scholar is to follow Barth's lead on these matters, does that mean he or she is obliged to find nothing of worth or lasting value in books such as those written by Fessenden, Hungerford, and Lewis?

Let us start with the last of those questions. These works on modern literature and postsecular theory are packed with telling insights and make some compelling arguments about particular books and contemporary literary trends. In a number of instances, they have opened for me fresh lines of inquiry or sent me down new paths of discovery and investigation, as I seek to make sense of the literature I teach, the life I lead, and the religious significance of the culture in which I live.[20]

Yet at the same time, these works embrace assumptions that close off in advance the thought of taking seriously the revelation of God in Jesus Christ, the incarnate Word. Operating as they do from the premise that *all* religious truth originates in human practice and experience, they rule out the idea of a transcendent, self-revealing God who holds power over sin and death.

The theology of experience that loosely informs these postsecular studies resembles in many respects the vision of theology and religion that Barth rejected a century ago. Barth was trained in a liberal Protestant tradition that took naturalism and the authority of experience as givens. He began his career, as Bruce McCormack says, with "supreme confidence" in human experience, which he took to be the "ground and motor" of all theology.[21] But that confidence did not last for long. For Barth, the event that precipitated the crisis was the outbreak of World War I. Within a matter of weeks in the summer of 1914, he watched as his theological mentors lined up to support the Kaiser and claim that God was on the side of the Germans. During the same period, in his personal life and pastoral work, Barth was coming up against the limits of experiential theology in dealing with despair and death, sin and meaninglessness.

These disenchanting experiences led Barth to speak of our inability to find either the presence or proof of God within the limits of an immanent cosmos. A world left alone with its experience was an orphaned world, he realized. Like Herman Melville, Fyodor Dostoevsky, and Emily Dickinson, Barth in his early writings seemed to cry out: "Wretched man that I am! Who will rescue me from this body of death?" (Rom. 7:24).

Barth developed his theology as an exegesis of God's decision from all eternity not "to hold aloof" from such cries but to go instead "into the far country" where men and women live in bondage and cry out for release (CD, IV.1.158). If Jesus Christ does not make this journey into our far country, who will rescue us from "this body of death"? We certainly are not capable of saving ourselves through the exercise of those mythmaking powers that *religion*, be it lived or theoretical, generates from the depths of the "self-sustaining" cosmos:

> Precisely this capacity to be in the world and to be human is, as man's own capacity, identical with the capacity to devise and fashion gods and to justify and sanctify himself. . . . A real crisis of religion would have to strike at this capacity too, and in fact to do so at the outset and decisively. . . . Only from a place outside the magic circle of religion, along with its place of origin—that is, only from a place outside of man—could this real crisis of religion break in. Only in an opposition wholly other than that between religion and the religious capacity, only from the standpoint of faith, could the verdict 'faithlessness, idolatry, works-righteousness' strike at this whole sphere, and thus at the whole man, in such a way that he could no longer flee from one refuge into another. In God's revelation this does happen, to be sure.[22]

Barth never yielded in his opposition to natural theology, but he did modulate his critique over time. Among other things, he developed in the *Church Dogmatics* a line of theological argument meant to acknowledge and account for the revelatory potential of the created order and human experience. His most extensive argument along these lines can be found in one of his last works, "The Doctrine of Reconciliation." In that section of the *Church Dogmatics* (IV.3.1), Barth examines "the prophetic office of Jesus Christ" (the *munus propheticum Christi*). In Catholicism, the *prophetic office* had been employed to justify the authority of the magisterium, or teaching office, of the church; in Protestantism, it referred to the mediating functions of the Bible and proclamation (preaching). For Barth, the theme of the "prophetic office" also provides a means of dealing with a perennial question facing the Christian church: What capacity does pagan thought have to discern and disclose truths about God's world?

Within the tradition of natural theology, the long-standing answer to this question was an anthropological one. Men and women can know truth

Beginning with the Word

independent of direct revelation because God has planted evidence of his existence within the orders of creation and the structures of the human mind. As profoundly as they differed on major theological points, on this question, the likes of Augustine, Aquinas, Calvin, and Jonathan Edwards were in essential agreement. Barth famously held back on this point, arguing that it was only through the power of the self-revealing presence of Christ that humans could find evidence of God in creation. "Where Calvin speaks of the human *mind* being invested with 'excellent talents'" that enable it to discover truth, George Hunsinger explains, "Barth prefers to speak instead of human *words* being invested and adorned, miraculously, with a capacity they do not intrinsically possess."[23]

As an epigraph for his treatment of the prophetic offices of Jesus Christ, Barth quotes the first sentence of the Barmen Declaration, published in 1934 as a call to theological arms against the Nazi affiliations of the German state church: "Jesus Christ as attested to us in Holy Scripture is the one Word of God whom we must hear and whom we must trust and obey in life and in death." Barth said that "a very concrete and threatening situation" had prompted the writing of the Declaration, which rejected the pro-Nazi "German Christian" movement and its glorification of Adolf Hitler as a "prophet" (*CD*, IV.3.1.86).

What a clash with specific historical forces had called for, however, was not what a general doctrine of reconciliation required, and for that reason, Barth turns his attention in the final volume of the *Church Dogmatics* to "the real lights of life and words of God" to be found in the "outside sphere" where witness to Jesus Christ "does not take place" and his "impulses are not seen." He calls these truths from nature and human experience "witnesses" to the Word and "secular parables of the kingdom." The church should be grateful for such words whenever they "illumine, accentuate or explain the biblical witness in a particular time and situation, thus confirming it in the deepest sense by helping to make it sure and concretely evident and certain" (IV.3.1.96, 115).

What Barth says in the language of systematic theology, Gerard Manley Hopkins asserts in the bracing images and tensile rhythms of a tribute to the Son, who "plays" before "the Father through the features of men's faces":

> As kingfishers catch fire, dragonflies draw flame;
> As tumbled over rim in roundy wells
> Stones ring; like each tucked string tells, each hung bell's
> Bow swung finds tongue to fling out broad its name;
> Each mortal thing does one thing and the same:
> Deals out that being indoors each one dwells;

Selves—goes itself; *myself* it speaks and spells,
Crying W*hát I dó is me: for that I came.*

I say móre: the just man justices;
Keeps gráce: thát keeps all his going graces;
Acts in God's eye what in God's eye he is—
Chríst—for Christ plays in ten thousand places,
Lovely in limbs, and lovely in eyes not his
To the Father through the features of men's faces. (51)

"Christ plays in ten thousand places"—this is a *winsome* image, in the ancient sense of the word in which to be winsome is to be a gracious and merciful source of joy. Hopkins depicts in these lines a trinitarian God who takes pleasure in dwelling within us as Spirit, playing among us as Son, and delighting in us from beyond as Father.

Similarly, for Barth, Christ speaks through myriad voices in the play of human experience and in the dazzle of the divinely created order. Whether we come upon the truth in the lucid intricacies of postsecular theory or in the astonishing array of objects that meet our eyes at dawn, we are called to bear witness to what we discover. As Richard Wilbur writes in "Lying," one of the finest Christian poems of the past half century:

In the strict sense, of course,
We invent nothing, merely bearing witness
To what each morning brings again to light:
Gold crosses, cornices, astonishment
Of panes, the turbine-vent which natural law
Spins on the grill-end of the diner's roof,

. . . .
                    All these things
Are there before us; there before we look
Or fail to look. (83)[24]

With this background in mind, we can understand why Barth took the *vestigia trinitatis* to be a weighty matter. Of the repeated efforts—undertaken by Augustine, Anselm, Aquinas, Luther, and others—to elaborate such a doctrine, Barth concludes "there must be 'something in' the connexion between the Trinity and all the 'trinities' to which reference is made here. Why should there not be something in it? The only question is what?" To Barth, the answer has to do with language. Theology, the church, and the Bible "speak no other language than that of this world," and both the form and content of that language are shaped by the realities of the world and the limits of human nature. As a result, when God reveals himself to us in language, he is using the same medium we humans use to wrestle "with the world as it encounters" us and as we strive to comprehend it (CD, I.1.339).

God and his witnesses in the church appropriate human language and employ it to disclose revelation, give witness, and proclaim the good news of Jesus Christ. This must mean, Barth says, that something profoundly significant can be made of language, for with it we have the potential to do miraculous things. But everything depends on one crucial question:

> The only question is whether this possibility is to be understood as that of the language and consequently of the world or man, or whether it is to be regarded as a venture which is, as it were, ascribed to the language, and consequently to the world or man, from without, so that it is not really the possibility of the language, the world, or man, but the possibility of revelation, if in the form of concepts and ideas that exist elsewhere and independently, in correspondence with the created world and the capacity of man as he attempts an understanding of this world, we really come to speak of revelation and therefore of the Trinity, of the remission of sins and eternal life, i.e., of things for which man's speech as such has no aptitude whatever. Now it cannot be said that the discoverers of *vestigia trinitatis* have made this distinction. As we make it, we are brought back to a realization that the true *vestigia trinitatis* is the form assumed by God in revelation. (CD, I.1.339)[25]

When we ask "what makes such speech about God's revelation possible," we move "beyond the horizon of the problem of a hermeneutic oriented to the relation of indication between sounds, words and things; beyond, that is what is essentially a hermeneutic of signification."[26] Such a hermeneutic is based upon the foundational distinction between *signum* (sign or word) and *res* (thing) that we have explored in depth during our discussion of the structuralist paradigm. There is a rupture—a gap—between word and thing, and humans are powerless to bridge the distance, but according to Barth, the self-revealing power of the trinitarian God spans the gap. With the development of the doctrine of the Trinity, the early church "found for the first time, not that the language could grasp the revelation, but that revelation, the very revelation correctly and normatively understood in the formulated dogma, could grasp the language" (CD, I.1.340).[27]

In the early history of the church, men and women were eager "to talk about the Father, Son, and Spirit," writes Barth, so "they opened their eyes and ears" and found themselves driven to refer to "spring, stream and lake" and other worldly analogies to make sense of the great trinitarian mystery. It was not that these analogies were "in and of themselves suitable" for the task, but they could be "adapted to be appropriated or, as it were, commandeered as images of the Trinity" to give men and women a way of speaking about God's revelation in Christ and in the Scriptures. There would have been "nothing in it" if they had sought to say that "source, stream and lake" were related to each other in the very same way as "Father, Son, and Spirit." But there was "something" to it when they claimed the relationship of the Father, Son, and Spirit resembled that of source, stream, and lake. According to Barth, it "was not a matter of apologetics but polemics." That is, the purpose was not to prove the possibility of revelation to "the world of human reason." Instead, the goal was that "of establishing the actual possibilities of the world of human reason as the scene of revelation" (*CD*, I.1.340–41).[28]

Something bold to the point of foolishness appears to be at work in all this talk of God "grasping" language and revelation "commandeering" words to express the mysteries of God's self-disclosure, but this is foolishness as Paul defines it in 1 Corinthians: "Jews demand signs and Greeks desire wisdom, but we proclaim Christ crucified, a stumbling block to Jews and foolishness to Gentiles" (1:22–23). To use Barth's language, Paul is asserting that in the crucifixion of Jesus Christ, God commandeered a barbarous form of Roman punishment and made it the agent of his reconciling mercy. The cross was a stumbling block to Jews because they rejected the concept of a crucified and risen messiah, and to Greeks because they expected rulers to overcome their enemies rather than submit to them. In a similar fashion, for contemporary naturalism the stumbling block is the audacious claim that a self-revealing God has the power to employ ordinary language to tell us how he is healing the deepest wounds of creation and reconciling us to himself.

Even to such a generous and open-minded critic as Amy Hungerford, the debate is over and the case closed as far as the question of truth and revelation is concerned. For her, as for Pericles Lewis and Tracy Fessenden, naturalism and the "hermeneutic of signification" are to have the last word. The opening paragraph of Hungerford's book champions the move Ralph Waldo Emerson made almost two centuries before to promote a view of religion that shuns "the content of doctrine" and embraces the "critique of institutional religion and its discourses of doctrine and theology." Hungerford considers the naturalist critique of religion to be self-evident and so deeply engrained in modern culture that the only way we can sustain the religious impulse is by promoting "belief in meaninglessness" as the essence of religion.[29]

The postsecular critics conclude that it is impossible to square with naturalism the claim that God grasps language for his purposes. In a strictly immanent cosmos, nothing is more difficult to imagine than the idea that the God who made the world and all things in it—that is, every teeming thing within the

Beginning with the Word

structural system—did so through the agency of a personal Word who became flesh, dwelt among us, and suffered death, death on a cross, so that at his name every knee would one day bow, and every tongue confess, that Jesus Christ is Lord. Who would have ever thought such things to be possible? Who, indeed!

Yet whatever the state of religion may be in the literary studies branch of the immanent cosmos, the task of rigorous reflection remains before Christian students of literature. David Jeffrey offers incisive reflection on the task before us in an analysis of Augustine's theory of language that provides us with a helpful corollary to Barth's theory of the divine commandeering of language. To comprehend how it was that God did "come to us . . . in mortal flesh," Augustine says:

> It is as when we speak. In order that what we are thinking may reach the mind of the listener through the fleshly ears, that which we have in mind is expressed in words and is called speech. But our thought is not transformed into sounds; it remains entire in itself and assumes the form of words by means of which it may reach the ears without suffering any deterioration in itself. In the same way the Word of God was made flesh without change that He might dwell among us.[30]

Jeffrey calls this an "imperfect analogy" because the Word of God and human words are anything but identical. We speak with words, while God speaks through natural phenomena, through persons and events in time, and supremely so through the "event of the Incarnation."[31]

As Jeffrey explains, Augustine's theory of language (signs) is grounded in the distinction between *use* and *enjoyment*. The trinitarian God is the one thing meant to be enjoyed by us, and "those things which are to be enjoyed make us blessed." Everything else is meant to be used, and those things to be used "sustain us as we move toward blessedness." All of creation—Augustine calls it "the whole temporal dispensation"—was made by God "for our salvation." All that is in that world "we should use" but with a "transitory" rather than an "abiding love." That love and delight should be like the pleasure we take in a "road or in vehicles," which are "those things by which we are carried along for the sake of that toward which we are carried."[32] In a term echoing Barth's view of God's appropriation of human speech, Jeffrey concludes that Augustine's theory of language has a "Christocentric" focus, which shows us that language's work of signifying receives its fullest meaning only in and through the story of the Word that became flesh and dwelt among us. It is not that language enables us to understand the Incarnation, but that "the theology of the Incarnation" provides us with unique insights into the way that language itself operates.[33]

That is, when God employs the world's languages to reveal himself, he marshals the metaphorical capacities of those languages to deepen and transform them for his purposes. Eberhard Jüngel explains that God's being is "brought to speech" out of the history of God's coming into the world, and "intrinsic to this history as its decisive moment is the cross." The cross provides the ground for all metaphors appropriate to God, and these metaphors have the "function of bringing about a turning around, a change of direction." Through the revelation of God in the Scriptures and in Jesus Christ, the Christian faith "brings to expression more than the actual and yet equally engages with actuality." In fact, "the language of faith sharpens" our sense of reality by addressing us with truths that communicate more deeply than the actual in itself could ever say.[34]

Incarnation: The Author Enters the Drama

In the opening chapter, we began by considering the wounding breach that splits words at their core. As we saw, the separation between word and thing reaches into the depths of our most intimate experiences, and it has worked its way into the core of our understanding of words and their relationship to reality. Centuries before the time of Christ, the shift from *icon* to *sign* gave birth to philosophy as we know it, and in early modernity the search for a perfect language of signs propelled the scientific and technological revolutions that have transformed our world. In addition, we have seen how over the 150 years, sign theory has played a key role in fostering the naturalist consensus that has become the tacit creed of contemporary life.

In *Church Dogmatics*, Barth struck at naturalism, root and branch, with a theory of language grounded in the trinitarian life of God. He thereby sought to shift the debate about language from its primary framework of signification, with its dialectic of *sign* and *thing*, and place it within a narrative frame, one that tells of God's power to grasp language for the purposes of telling the story of his eternal covenant with us through Jesus Christ.

The contours of this story—of the God who enters the world and reveals himself through deeds and word alike—fit within the grand narrative of the Incarnation. For Hans-Georg Gadamer, that doctrine has great relevance for the history of language and thought, regardless of whether or not one considers it to be true. (To Gadamer, there was no truth to Christianity in any metaphysical sense, as explained to Jens Zimmermann in his final interview: "It is human not to know, he said. "It is inhuman to turn this into church.")

It is in the final section of *Truth and Method* that Gadamer puts the Incarnation to work to assist him in his reflections on "the being of language." He begins by distinguishing a Christian understanding of Incarnation from the Greek concept of divine embodiment. In Greek myth, the gods assume those bodily forms whenever doing so serves their purposes, but the process never involves *becoming* a human. "God does not become man" in Greek theories of embodiment, but like the divine spirits depicted in early Christian gnosticism, the gods appropriate human bodies to accomplish superhuman tasks, and then they discard them and retreat to their Olympian glory.[35]

Everything changed with the Incarnation, which Gadamer calls the "cornerstone of Christian thought" and which he says "is closely connected to the problem of the word." From the beginning of Christian history, "the *mystery of the Trinity*" was bound up with the question of "the relationship between human speech and thought." Not surprisingly, for Gadamer the foundational text for plumbing the depths of that relationship was the prologue to John's Gospel.[36]

Gadamer argues that even though *Logos* is a distinct Greek concept, its development acquired a dramatically different trajectory when the early church pressed it into service to explain the work of Jesus Christ. (Gadamer's argument about the appropriation of the *Logos* is a variation on Barth's theme of the divine *commandeering* of human language.) "Philosophy won through John a dimension closed off from Greek thinking," Gadamer claims.

> If the word becomes flesh and the actuality of the spirit fulfills itself only in the incarnation, so likewise the Logos is released from its spirituality, which signifies equally its cosmic potential. Hereupon the uniqueness of the redemptive event introduces historical being into Western thought, allows the phenomenon of language to escape from its submersion in the ideality of meaning, and offers itself to philosophical consideration. For as distinct from the Greek logos, the word is pure event.[37]

To understand what Gadamer is asserting here, it may be helpful to think in terms Barth used to define the atonement. "The atonement is history," he writes, "the very special history of God with man, the very special history of man with God." The key to the doctrine of reconciliation, according to Barth, is that in the Incarnation, God "does something unnecessary and extravagant, binding and limiting and compromising and offering Himself in relation to man by having dealings with him and making Himself his God." That is, John's prologue claims that from all eternity God had chosen to become the Word made flesh; in the Incarnation, God "humbled himself, but He did not do it by ceasing to be who He is. He went into a strange land, but even there, and especially there, He never became a stranger to Himself" (*CD*, IV.1.157–58, 180).

In transposing this pattern into philosophical language, Gadamer says that "the Logos is released from its spirituality," and language is thereby enabled "to escape from its submersion in the ideality of meaning." By "ideality of meaning," Gadamer has in mind the Greek idea that language is not a necessary condition for thought, which is able to conduct its business in silence through the workings of a purely mathematical rationality. In the logic of Greek myth, embodiment, while useful in certain situations, is hardly a condition a god would readily seek or relish, but in the Christian Scriptures it is something God the Son deliberately accepts (Phil. 2:1–11).

Barth makes a similar point, when he says that God reveals his genuine divinity by demonstrating that he is "capable and willing and ready" to undergo the condescension of the Incarnation, the entry into the world and the suffering that leads to death. What distinguishes God from all the "false gods" is his eagerness to undertake this "act of extravagance, this far journey. . . . In their otherworldliness and supernaturalness and otherness, etc., the gods are a reflection of the human pride which will not unbend, which will not stoop to that which is beneath it. God is not proud. In His high majesty He is humble" (*CD*, IV.1.159).[38]

John Arthos observes that one might ordinarily associate binding the soul to the body with an act of enslavement, but "Gadamer wants to reverse" this view of things, as he uses the doctrine of Incarnation to recast our thinking about thought's relationship to language. "God sacrificed himself in order that we may be free," is the way Arthos describes the Incarnation. "So God's gift, the ultimate sacrifice . . . is in the economy of salvation the opposite of itself, freedom rather than enslavement." As a consequence of this Incarnational freedom, "the Logos is released from its spirituality," Gadamer concludes and "the uniqueness of the redemptive event introduces historical being into Western thought."[39] Through his act of obedience, that is, the Son of God fulfills the eternal will of God, which is to travel, as Barth says, "into the far country" to redeem his "unfaithful people to whom He gives and maintains His faithfulness" (*CD*, IV.1.171).

With its embrace of the God who entered history and became a subject within it, Christianity transformed the possibilities of thought and revolutionized late antiquity's view of history. The uniqueness of the life, death, and resurrection of Jesus will never be repeated and will leave nothing unchanged. That means history is no longer an endless cycle but a singular story in which events unfold and new realities emerge. Analogously, Arthos says of Gadamer's treatment of the Incarnation, language is not a static system of ritualized formulas and meanings but a constantly developing process in which ideas—and words—are always being nourished by the concrete realities of embodied life.

Thereby, "something new is always being created as we find words to come to terms with the world."[40]

To understand what it means to create new realities through our efforts "to come to terms with the world," we might enlist the aid of Paul Ricoeur and Paul the apostle. While Gadamer may show no familiarity with Saussure and Barth never mentions him, Ricoeur directly engages the Saussurean project and in doing so arrives at a position strikingly similar to what Gadamer and Barth conclude. In an essay titled "Structure, Word, Event," Ricoeur acknowledges that structuralism does a remarkably efficient and fitting job of providing inventories for the elements and units of language; for a fixed corpus of texts and artifacts—things "already constituted, finished, closed, and . . . dead"—structuralism works just fine. But it does so at the expense of providing any understanding of the "acts, operations, and processes" that constitute discourse, i.e., our human use of language.[41]

Ricoeur notes that in its understanding of language, structuralism "breaks entirely with the naïve idea that the sign is made to stand for a thing." The true definition of a sign understands it only by way of its dynamic "relation of opposition to all other signs" and in the internal distinction between the signifier and the signified. The isolation and systematizing of words makes a science of signs possible, but it does so at the cost of neglecting or suppressing the act of speech and the reality of historical change. It also overlooks what Ricoeur aptly terms "the primary intention of language, which is to say something about something."[42]

The one who says "something about something" is, of course, the speaker or writer, and the essential tool for saying anything is the sentence. The sentence is a remarkable unit of expression that can take an infinite number of forms yet still be immediately comprehensible to both the speaker and the hearer (or the writer and the reader). The parts of speech, including nouns and verbs, take the individual word and place it, by means of the sentence, into human discourse. And "more particularly," Ricoeur writes, "the noun and the verb are parts of speech thanks to which our signs are . . . 'returned to the universe' under the aspect of space and of time." In "completing the word as noun and verbs, these categories render our signs capable of grasping the real and keep them from closing up in the finite, closed order" of the structuralist system.[43]

There are lovely buried metaphors contained in what Ricoeur has to say about discourse. The image of the sign being freed by the noun and verb to return to the universe of space and time is a variation on the theme of the Word become flesh (John 1) and the Son of God who "did not regard equality with God as something to be exploited, but emptied himself . . . and became obedient to the point of death—even death on a cross" (Phil. 2:6–8). And just as the word is to Ricoeur the unit that moves out of the system of signs and into the reality and history of discourse, so too is Jesus Christ the Son of God who leaves the security of heaven to make his way into the dangerous far country of earth.

This story of the God who humbled himself and took on human form to suffer on behalf of his people and, through his suffering, to redeem them—this is what the church from the very beginning sought to say in its proclamation of the gospel. This is what Paul felt he had to speak about, as he waited in Athens for Silas and Timothy. We are told he was prompted to do so by the sight of a city "full of idols." So, to tell the story of the crucified and risen Christ, Paul debated with Jews in the synagogue and with gentiles in the marketplace.

The Epicureans and Stoics, believers in the world as a closed system, were both baffled and intrigued by his preaching on "Jesus and the resurrection." To learn more, they brought him to the Areopagus and asked him to say more about these "foreign divinities" and the "rather strange" things being claimed and proclaimed on their behalf. Paul took up the challenge by drawing Greek philosophy and poetry into the conversation. The "unknown God" mentioned on an Athenian altar Paul had seen is really the revealed God, the Lord of heaven and earth who has "fixed a day on which he will judge the world in righteousness by a man whom he has appointed; and of this he has given assurance to all by raising him from the dead." Some scoffed at the thought of the resurrection, while others lingered to hear more and eventually "joined him and became believers" (Acts 17:18–34).

The loneliness of a closed world system and the anxiety of chasing after an unknown God—these things that vexed the first-century Athenians also assail the characters in Luigi Pirandello's *Six Characters in Search of an Author*. "We have come here in search of an author," one of them informs the director of a play onto whose set he and his forlorn companions have wandered. The characters have been forsaken by their author, who refuses to set them within a drama that possesses a plot, a conflict, and a resolution. The author will not give them a role, Pirandello acknowledges, because he cannot abide the thought that his characters, born of his mind, "were already living their own life, a life that was not mine." He thus punishes them by denying them the one thing they most desire: "What was I denying them? Not themselves, clearly, but their drama, which interested them most." But there is no drama that belongs inherently to life, the director has concluded. His characters believe plots exist, but "if anyone were to tell them" that their belief in meaning is a fantasy, "they would not believe it; it is impossible to believe that the sole ground of our life is the pain which seems unjust and inexplicable to us."[44]

Within the Christian doctrine of the Incarnation, the dilemma of Pirandello and his abandoned characters is addressed directly through the sacrificial power and mercy of a God who is not only the author of the universe but an actor in its divine drama. Of the many theologians who have picked up on this motif in the past century, none has made more daring and effective use of it than Hans Urs von Balthasar, who fashioned a multivolume systematic theology around the theme of "theo-drama," which is "theology and drama" or "theology as drama."[45]

There are what Balthasar calls "two cycles of theme" to this drama. One involves the story of a mighty God who stands as the author of creation and the finisher of eschatological faith. The other has to do with "God, who cannot lose himself in the world play and yet puts himself gravely at risk." Has God "'staked his all' on this play?" What does it mean to speak of "God's history" and to claim that in Jesus, God emptied himself, or that the Son of God died? All of these questions come together to pose a most significant challenge: "Where is the path that leads between the twin abysses of a systematics in which God, absolute Being, is only the Unmoved before whom the moving world plays out its drama, and a mythology which absorbs God into the world and makes him to be one of the warring parties of world process?"[46]

The trail that threads its way between these "twin abysses" is the one blazed by the Son of God on his way to the far country. And down a similar path, Balthasar and Barth, Gadamer and Ricoeur would argue, our view of language must travel, as it wends its way between the Scylla of the structural system and the Charybdis of arbitrary naming and the isolated individual.

The great "miracle of language," writes Gadamer, is to be found not in the belief that the "Word becomes flesh" and takes on an "external being, but that that which emerges and externalizes itself in utterance is always already a word." The trinitarian claim that "the Word is with God from all eternity" rules out any idea of the Son of God being subordinate to the Father, and it also means that we cannot view the *word* as being either secondary or superior to the *thing*. Because the Son of God became a man and dwelt among us, the word can never be solely a sign:

> The mystery of the Trinity is mirrored in the miracle of language insofar as the word that is true, because it says what the thing is, is nothing by itself and does not seek to be anything. It has its being in revealing. Exactly the same thing is true of the mystery of the Trinity. . . . The human relationship between thought and speech corresponds, despite its imperfections, to the divine relationship of the Trinity. The inner mental word is just as consubstantial with thought as is God the Son with God the Father.[47]

Gadamer's incarnational view of the word and the thing provides a powerful theory of language, but the problem posed by Benjy Compson remains. We may acknowledge a bond between thought and language, we may celebrate the power of words to embody thought and truth, and we may be convinced by the incarnational claim that human words and thoughts "illuminate" the fundamentally incomprehensible "mystery of the Trinity."[48] Yet because of sin and death, until the end of time—until the coming of the kingdom of God—language will always bear for us the marks of absence as well as those of presence, and as we use it, we will consistently feel the pangs of loss as well as the delights of promise.

These are losses and lacks that words cannot overcome on their own. Only words that have been pressed into the service of a larger vision—words "commandeered" for God's redemptive and revelatory purposes—can bring good news to the oppressed, bind up the brokenhearted, and proclaim liberty to the captives and release to the prisoners (Isa. 61:1). These words become more than the sum of their parts, when they are gathered into sentences by one who wishes to say something with them and to do something by way of them. A dictionary may give the meanings of *wolf, goat, child, graze, cobra, adder, holy, waters*, and *sea*, but only a speaker of language can offer prophesies and make promises that speak of a peace we can barely imagine, of a dream so beautiful it may break our hearts:

> The wolf shall live with the lamb,
>   the leopard shall lie down with the kid,
>   the calf and the lion and the fatling together,
>   and a little child shall lead them.
> The cow and the bear shall graze,
>   their young shall lie down together;
>   and the lion shall eat straw like the ox.
> The nursing child shall play over the hole of the asp,
>   and the weaned child shall put his hand on the adder's den.
> They will not hurt or destroy
>   on all my holy mountain;
>   for the earth will be full of the knowledge of the LORD
>   as the waters cover the sea. (Isa. 11:6–9)

Such use of language takes words to be pictures that represent the world's realities, even as they point beyond them to possibilities we have and promises God has made. In a rich study of Barth's view of revelation and language, Eberhard Jüngel speaks of the Incarnation as the "interruption of the secularism of life in the world." To all of us who live within the immanent cosmos of naturalism, this interruption reveals Christ, the Word through whom we have been created and by whom we are sustained. "Prior to being conceived as the correspondence of mind and reality," truth must be understood "christologically as the event of a *saving interruption* of the actual connectedness of life." Like the disciples on the road to Emmaus, when Jesus Christ enters our world, we are illumined and enabled "to grasp that the world *holds together* at the deepest level, though not through itself." The "saving interruption" of the Word who became flesh and dwelt among us "makes *more possible* in the actuality of the world than that actuality is capable of granting to itself."[49]

5

Modern Times

Literature and the Patience of God

> There are in our existence spots of time,
> That with distinct pre-eminence retain
> A renovating virtue, whence, depressed
> By false opinion and contentious thought,
> Or aught of heavier or more deadly weight,
> In trivial occupations, and the round
> Of ordinary intercourse, our minds
> Are nourished and invisibly repaired.
>   —William Wordsworth, *The Prelude*

> These are only hints and guesses,
> Hints followed by guesses; and the rest
> Is prayer, observance, discipline, thought, and action.
> The hint half guessed, the gift half understood, is Incarnation.
>   —T. S. Eliot, "The Dry Salvages"

It is one thing to affirm a belief in the "saving interruption" (Jüngel's phrase) of God's incarnational presence in our midst, and another thing entirely to try to chart the relationship of God's redemptive acts to our cultural endeavors. How are we to draw connections between our belief in the revelatory power of God and our knowledge of what we do when we link incident to incident to tell a story? What do the stories we invent have to do with the grand story we claim God is telling in and through human history? How do we reconcile our modern conceptions of freedom and self-formation with a doctrine of divine providence?

A Christian effort to answer such questions is complicated by a fact of literary and cultural history. I am referring to a project begun more than two centuries ago at the height of the romantic movement in literature, politics, and theology. It involved a concerted effort to salvage core Christian concepts and values by reinterpreting them and assimilating them within a broader secular, naturalized framework. In the words of literary historian M. H. Abrams, romantic writers self-consciously undertook "to save traditional concepts, schemes, and values which had been based on the relation of the Creator to his creature and creation, but to reformulate them within the prevailing two-term system of subject and object, . . . the human mind or consciousness and its transactions with nature." By displacing the central themes and language of the Christian faith from a supernatural to a natural framework, the romantic writers believed they could sustain the core values of the Christian story by turning it into a drama of human inwardness and development.[1]

These romantic literary attempts to reinterpret and recuperate the Christian tradition tracked with similar efforts under way in theology during the same period. "Across the theological spectrum," Hans Frei has argued, a "great reversal had taken place" in the early modern period. It involved the overturning of the "precritical" practice that had governed scriptural interpretation from the early church up to and through the Reformation. For this precritical hermeneutic, the Bible provided the narrative from within which all human experiences and natural phenomena were to be interpreted. One was to begin one's thinking about experience and nature by considering them to be part of a divine drama embedded and enacted in Scripture and sacrament.

Under pressure on a number of philosophical, political, and economic fronts, the precritical framework began to buckle in the seventeenth century and collapsed entirely by the end of the eighteenth. In its place a series of "mediating theologies" sprang up across the hardscrabble landscape of the nineteenth century. As the name implies, these approaches sought to reach across the gulf between the ancient and modern worlds, and they did so by giving priority not to the biblical account but to "an antecedent . . . religious context"—that is, personal experience and the religious capacities of human nature—in terms of which the Bible itself was now to be read. Mediating theologies reversed the direction of biblical interpretation from what it had been so that the biblical texts "now made sense by their inclusion in a wider frame

Beginning with the Word

of meaning." As a result, by the end of the eighteenth century, interpretation had become "a matter of fitting the biblical story into another world with another story rather than incorporating that world into the biblical story."[2] In 1841, Ralph Waldo Emerson offered in "Self-Reliance" a brilliant and pithy description of the nineteenth-century drive to internalize the whole of human life, from the scriptural stories to history itself: "History is an impertinence and an injury, if it be any thing more than a cheerful apologue or parable of my being and becoming" (270).

This move to internalize the sources and resources of the Christian faith established an alternative method for the use and interpretation of Christian language. This new approach was meant to supersede a model that had been established by the labors of the apostolic age, sustained throughout the patristic era, deepened by the church East and West through the Middle Ages, and then expanded (and fragmented) by the explosive energies of Protestantism and the modern era. Within this diverse group of theological perspectives, disagreements abounded and schisms sometimes resulted, but in the main the church continued to read the symbolic and storied language of the Christian Scriptures and tradition as the record of a self-revealing God and his relationship with his creation.

In contrast, the internalizing method deliberately established the needs and nature of the self as the frame of reference and final arbiter for biblical interpretation. Under its influence, the languages of Scripture and sacrament were found increasingly to apply to the development of the self rather than to God and his acts of mercy, judgment, and self-disclosure. And as we have seen, in this scheme of things, theology was gradually transformed into anthropology.

Thus, in both its German philosophical and theological varieties and its English literary forms, romanticism represented an ambitious effort to provide a more secure foundation for belief by grounding the Christian tradition's images and narratives in the dynamics of the human mind and experience. In this chapter, we will examine some consequences of the romantic enterprise as it has coursed its way through the literature and experience of the past two centuries. Our journey will begin with William Wordsworth, but we will also encounter such nineteenth-century figures as Emily Dickinson and Charles Darwin, before we move on to the twentieth century. The final stage of this literary journey will return us to Faulkner and *The Sound and the Fury*, which will allow us to interact with several critics, artists, and theorists—from C. S. Lewis and Wallace Stevens to Jean-François Lyotard and T. S. Eliot—who grappled with the romantic legacy in the twentieth century.

Moving as it does from the romantic period to the recent postmodern past, this survey of modern literature and modern views of time will raise questions about a Christian understanding of God's relationship to the vastness of astronomical and biological time. In turn, those questions will bring to the fore issues at the heart of modern views—Christian, post-Christian, and otherwise—of the nature of stories. Up to this point, we have focused on the mysteries of language and the wonders of the word, but it is time now to shift our attention to the storied orders that we make, as well as the story God tells, by taking up those words and saying something with them.

Spots of Time

Near the close of *The Prelude*, his epic poem that details the "Growth of a Poet's Mind," William Wordsworth offers a stirring tribute to the intense, evanescent experiences that he calls "spots of time":

> There are in our existence spots of time,
> That with distinct pre-eminence retain
> A renovating virtue, whence, depressed
> By false opinion and contentious thought,
> Or aught of heavier or more deadly weight,
> In trivial occupations, and the round
> Of ordinary intercourse, our minds
> Are nourished and invisibly repaired;
> A virtue, by which pleasure is enhanced.
> That penetrates us, to mount,
> When high, more high, and lifts us up when fallen.

What is a "spot of time"? To Wordsworth, it marks a point at which our experiential stars fall into alignment, if only briefly, and the cacophony of our lives becomes, if but for a moment, the music of the spheres. According to the poet, such incidents of intense experience are "scattered everywhere" along the trail of our lives. Both in the midst of these experiences and through our later reflection on them, we may gain what Wordsworth calls the "profoundest knowledge." It is that "the mind is lord and master—outward sense / The obedient servant of her will" (479).[3]

The spots of time break upon us suddenly and depart from us without warning, but they nevertheless disclose depths of meaning that endure. Long after the experience passes, the memory of it dwells within us and buoys our spirits when we fall under the weight of "trivial occupations." Under the influence of romanticism, these phenomena came to be known in the nineteenth century as "epiphanies," that term having been appropriated from the ecclesiastical

Beginning with the Word

year. Like the manifestation of the Christ child to the gentiles, the spots of time are meant to witness to a merciful power at work within our experiences and beyond them. At a time when a number within the Christian church had begun to harbor doubts about the adequacy and authenticity of the scriptural narrative, many romantic artists cast their lot with the human imagination and its ability to divine in epiphanic moments a new story of the spirit.[4] "God most often acts," Samuel Taylor Coleridge explained in a reflection on prophetic inspiration, "by a potenziation of existing, or the awakening of inherent, tho' dormant or latent Faculties of Human Nature—not by suspending or overwhelming the natural Powers and reducing the Seer or Prophet into a passive Automaton, or mere Camera Obscura."[5]

For a time in the nineteenth century, the romantic investment in the spots of time looked as though it was going to pay handsome dividends. Great promise seemed to flow from a view of the self as a fount of inspiration and a fathomless source of revelation. As Ralph Waldo Emerson declared in "The American Scholar," "The one thing in the world, of value" is "the active soul." The Bible possesses no power on its own, he argued, for it is only a dead-letter record of a once lively spiritual perception. The prophets, the Gospel writers, and the apostles were adept chroniclers of their own revelatory spots of time, but their experiences carry no lasting weight for us. Moses, Isaiah, and St. Paul may *show* us the inspired imagination at work, yet they cannot *tell* us truths that have binding power or enduring authority. On the contrary, if we are to receive revelation, we must generate it within ourselves by imitating what Emerson called "the scholar of the first age," who had the courage and creativity to receive the world and impart to it through his perceptions "the new arrangement of his own mind." And forever anew, this pattern repeats itself in the minds of genuine scholars and artists:

> It came into him, life; it went out from him, truth. It came to him, short-lived actions; it went out from him, immortal thoughts. It came to him, business; it went from him, poetry. It was dead fact; now, it is quick thoughts. It can stand, and it can go. It now endures, it now flies, it now inspires. Precisely in proportion to the depth of mind from which it issued, so high does it soar, so long does it sing. (56)

As nineteenth-century history wore on, however, the investment in the imaginative powers seemed to pay ever-smaller dividends. In a perceptive analysis of Hegel's philosophy, Karl Barth describes the problem the post-romantic era faced. He quotes a passage from Hegel's *Lectures on the Philosophy of Religion*: "God is this, to distinguish oneself from oneself, to be object to oneself, but to be completely identical with oneself in this distinction." For the philosopher, Barth writes, the "living God . . . is actually the living man," no more and no less. Yet because Hegel declares rational thought to be the essence of human life, this "living man" may be no more than a figment of the imagination, an "abstractly thinking man . . . who is merely thought" and not real at all. If that is the case, "it is possible that this living God, too, Hegel's God, is a merely thinking and merely thought God, before whom real man would stand as before an idol, or as before a nothing. At all events he would stand in boundless loneliness, 'without a God in the world.'"[6] And when this occurs, we find ourselves orphaned once more, driven back within the confines of the immanent cosmos within which we stand alone in the void.

Thus it proved to be the case that the more the romantics banked on the "powers of the active soul," the less they were able to detect any presence of the "divine in nature." Fed by the vast claims made on its behalf, the human mind gradually supplanted nature as the primary source of values. It was able to accomplish this task because nineteenth-century science and philosophy were steadily siphoning the spirit from nature, until the latter became, in Tennyson's memorable phrase, "red in tooth and claw." For Darwin, nature was a fertile, destructive, and mindless sower of life and agent of death, while for Karl Marx, nature stood as the power of necessity from whose grip humans had to free themselves. After Darwin and Marx, if humans wished to discover an "expressive unity between man and the natural and social world," they could no longer hope to *discover* it but would have to *create* it by using their own powers to reshape nature and society.[7]

For political millennialists such as Marx, there was much to relish in the prospect of transforming the world in such a manner as to bring it into line with human desire. To them, if nature stood as a system of necessity operating in accordance with a set of inexorable laws, then history could be celebrated as a neutral domain in which the human spirit would be liberated from oppression and set free to remake the world. As Marx wrote in 1845, "The philosophers have *interpreted* the world in various ways; the point however is to *change* it."[8] Charles Taylor explains that for the author of *The Communist Manifesto*, "because expressive fulfillment came with the radical freedom to shape nature, it could be combined with the most far-reaching Enlightenment aspiration to dominate the natural and social world through science and technology."[9]

To others, however, there was something profoundly unsettling about the very thought of an impersonal natural necessity. For all its modern and romantic trappings, Wordsworth's theory of the spots of time had remained loosely tethered to the *Logos* tradition and the sense it had of language and reality—words and things—participating together within a larger frame of

Beginning with the Word

reference and a more expansive story. For Wordsworth, spots of time arise out of our experience in nature and point to truths that God has woven into the fabric of spirit and nature alike. To dwell on the spots of time and to discern the patterns within them was to unveil truths that had depth and staying power.

But what would happen if it turns out that nature has no secrets to reveal and our experience contains no hidden wisdom waiting to be revealed? What are we to do if we come to suspect or learn with certainty that in our encounters with nature and our own experience, we discover nothing more than what we have projected out of the "boundless loneliness" of our condition? If we lack the capacity either to find the truth or to receive it—if we dismiss both natural law and revelation as sources of knowledge—do we have any recourse other than to fabricate the truths we need, if we are to get by?

Such a conclusion makes for a genuine problem. How can the human heart possibly place its trust in an illusion that it knows it has conjured up from within itself? How can we stake our lives on promises we know to be fabricated? How can a pilgrim muster the will to set off on a journey, knowing in advance that it has no destination and will arrive at no place of rest? Questions such as these set the philosophical and literary agenda for the late nineteenth century and beyond. They informed the Christian existentialism of Søren Kierkegaard, the radical perspectivalism of Friedrich Nietzsche, and the supple pragmatism of William James; and they burrowed their way into the core assumptions of literary modernism in the twentieth century.[10]

Emily Dickinson felt the force of those questions keenly. A number of her poems serve as imaginative forays into a new cultural ground of unbelief. How does one live, if one's mind is divided between a fortifying belief in divine order and purpose and a desolate sense that the mind alone has the power to fabricate the order it needs and desires? In one poem, written shortly before she died, Dickinson employs an image of the mangled stump of a dismembered deity to describe her longing to believe in God and her fear that he may no longer exist:

> Those—dying then,
> Knew where they went—
> They went to God's Right Hand—
> That Hand is amputated now
> And God cannot be found—
>
> The abdication of Belief
> Makes the Behavior small—
> Better an ignis fatuus
> Than no illume at all— (#1581)

Deprived of heaven as its destination, and devoid of any sign of the hand of God at work in the world, the modern people depicted in this poem grope their way through life by means of a series of small behaviors. Given the starkness of their condition, the speaker concludes it would be better to follow a "fool's light" (an *ignis fatuus*) than to admit that darkness has descended upon us all.

In a world in which belief has abdicated its position of authority, how is the soul to find its way to God? In such a world, is it even possible to consider human life as a journey with a divinely appointed end? With deadly seriousness, Dickinson toys with a provisional answer to these questions in a late poem. Its speaker spies a distant "traveller on a Hill" who is ascending "to magic Perpendiculars" on a moonlit night. The image calls to mind the ascent to God—a common theme of the devotional tradition—but the poem can envision nothing concrete about the journey, and we are left with an awareness of the utter indefiniteness of God's dwelling place. The traveler is "terrene"—that is, he is earthly and secular rather than heavenly and sacred—and the "shimmering ultimate" that represents his destination remains completely "unknown" to him. Yet even though he is a man on a mission to who knows where, he still "indorse[s]" the "magic Perpendiculars" because they "shimmer" with a "sheen" that somehow draws him onward and propels him upward:

> The Road was lit with Moon and star—
> The Trees were bright and still—
> Descried I—by—the gaining Light
> A traveller on a Hill—
> To magic Perpendiculars
> Ascending, though terrene—
> Unknown his shimmering ultimate—
> But he indorsed the sheen— (#1474)[11]

"To shimmer" means "to shine with a tremulous or flickering light" and "to gleam faintly," and this is precisely the function the "fool's lights" serve for the benighted souls who live in the shadow cast by an abdicating God. Dickinson lauded those who had the wherewithal to believe in an *ignis fatuus* or the foolhardy courage to chase after the "sheen" of terrene fantasies, yet she found it difficult to do such things herself. She longed to believe in God but could not trust or rest in him. The best she could do was to assert her wavering conviction that human consciousness itself is immortal:

> Though the great Waters sleep,
> That they are still the Deep,
> We cannot doubt.

No vacillating God
Ignited this Abode
To put it out. (#1641)[12]

Buoyed by her stubborn belief in personal immortality, Dickinson sought to reconcile herself to the fact that she lived at a time when spots of time no longer opened upon a divine drama in which we and our language participate. Instead, in her poems, moments of epiphany appear, only to vanish without warning, leaving behind a trace of their presence and the weight of their absence:

> In many and reportless places
> We feel a Joy—
> Reportless, also, but sincere as Nature
> Or Deity—
>
> It comes, without a consternation—
> Dissolves—the same—
> But leaves a sumptuous Destitution—
> Without a Name—
>
> Profane it by a search—we cannot—
> It has no home—
> Nor we who having once waylaid it—
> Thereafter roam. (#1404)

The speaker in this poem cannot "report" whence this joy came or whither it has fled. All she knows is that she has been left behind with "a sumptuous Destitution— / Without a Name—." Her present state is "sumptuous" because of the richness of memory, and it is "destitute" because of the poverty of reality. Memory shelters a *signifier* that points our broken hearts toward the thing *signified*, which is the joy that "Dissolves" and drifts away. Yet even though that joy has fled, and she is left to grieve the loss of it, the speaker in the poem knows better than to "Profane it by a search," for it "has no home—." Nor do we, "having once waylaid it—," have any place to dwell, for we have lost our own heavenly bearings and "Thereafter roam." The foxes have holes, and birds of the air have nests, but like the Son of Man, we modern men and women have nowhere to lay our heads (Matt. 8:20).

Dickinson's is a poetry of homeless devotion. The speakers in her poems routinely doubt the trustworthiness of the Bible, and they generally consider its story of sin and redemption to be a fantasy. "The Bible is an antique Volume—," after all, and it was "Written by faded Men / At the suggestion of

Holy Spectres—" (#1577). There is only "one favor" that we can ask of God, and that is "that we may be forgiven." Of course, we don't know for what because "the Crime, from us, is hidden." All we know is that we spend our lives "reprimand[ing] the Happiness" we feel. Why? Because it "competes with Heaven" too powerfully for our own good (#1675).

Thus, for Dickinson, to be human is to discover that we are stranded on the earth, alone with "Silence, some strange Race / Wrecked, solitary, here—" (#340). We tell each other stories to break the silence, to lighten the load, and to give us the illusions we need to make us take life's pointless journey. But like many who were to come after her, Dickinson believed that while such stories clearly reveal our longings, they have nothing clear or certain to say about whether those longings can or will ever be satisfied.

The Life of Stories, the Life in Stories

In a witty yet harrowing story by the Argentine writer Jorge Luis Borges, a desultory medical student comes across a Bible while idling away his time at an isolated ranch. He decides one evening to read the opening of the Gospel of Mark to the illiterate ranch foreman and his family. As he reads he feeds off their excitement, and it occurs to him "that throughout history, humankind has told two stories: the story of a lost ship sailing the Mediterranean seas in quest of a beloved isle, and the story of a god who allows himself to be crucified on Golgotha" (400).

They might quibble a bit about the number Borges offers—perhaps it's three rather than two, or maybe we tell versions of five different tales—but most students of narrative would agree with his basic point. The stories we tell have common shapes and fit our experience into orderly forms, and the number of different types of stories is limited. Stories differ dramatically in their details, but each in its own way speaks of beginnings and ends, of rises and falls, of confusion that befuddles and disclosures that make things clear at last. Stories take the seemingly random facts of our experience and place them within a larger context; they make prominent what we take to be vital, and they dispense with things we consider trivial. Stories channel the aimless flow of time and turn our wanderings into quests. They have the power to cast us into dark despair, and just as quickly, they may flood our experience with illuminating clarity.

What we make of the stories we tell depends in good measure on what we take our own roles to be in the stories we live. In *After Virtue*, a classic study of moral theory, Alasdair MacIntyre argues that cultures are like certain forms of drama—"Japanese Noh plays and English medieval morality plays are examples"—that have a set of stock characters whom audiences recognize immediately. To a considerable degree, these characters limit and define the possibilities of plot and action. In understanding them, MacIntyre says, we find a way of interpreting the behavior of the actors who play them "because a similar understanding informs the intentions of the actors themselves," and other actors define their own roles in relationship to the central characters.[13]

The same holds true for cultures, which produce their own limited stock of characters whose actions provide insight into the core values of the culture. Such characters represent a "special type of social role," in that they have "a certain kind of moral constraint" placed on their actions; understood in this sense, *characters* have both moral and dramatic associations. To explain the distinction between roles in general and characters in particular, MacIntyre asks us to consider the difference between a dentist and a garbage collector, on the one hand, and a bureaucratic manager, on the other. The former are not characters in the way the latter is, and the reason has to do with the way characters embody central moral assumptions of their age and "are, so to speak, the moral representatives of the culture." Through characters, the crucial ethical and metaphysical ideas of a culture are enabled to assume "an embodied existence in the social world. *Characters* are the masks worn by moral philosophies." The bureaucratic manager is a mask of contemporary moral values in a way that the dentist and garbage collector never can be.[14]

To MacIntyre, the dominant characters of contemporary postindustrial culture are the Rich Aesthete, the Therapist, and the Manager. Rich Aesthetes see the social world as "nothing but a meeting place for individual wills" and an arena in which they may pursue their own satisfaction; for the Aesthete, the last and greatest enemy is boredom. The Therapist represents more than a branch of psychology and medicine, for the concept of the therapeutic has entered fully into the mainstream of modern culture. To MacIntyre its prevalence is seen in the manifold ways in which psychological effectiveness has supplanted truth as a value. And, finally, the Manager represents the triumph of bureaucratic control over interest groups whose values conflict. In the culture of the Manager, authority has little or nothing to do with questions of truth and value, for "bureaucratic authority is nothing other than successful power."[15]

For our understanding of modern literary culture, I would add a fourth character to MacIntyre's list—we might call this character the Daring Warrior. This is a figure that any student of the literature and philosophy of the past 150 years will readily recognize. He or she is the one who has the courage to face unflinchingly the hardest truths of the modern condition. The Daring Warrior does not do battle against any human foes but struggles against the twin spirits of hostility and indifference that appear to divide between them the rule of the world.

The Daring Warrior has taken to the stage in an endless number of the dramas played out in the literature, visual art, and music of our time. She is the patient, saintlike heroine of George Eliot's novels; he is the man who bravely demonstrates grace under pressure in the stories of Ernest Hemingway; and they are the women and men of popular music—from Jim Morrison to Kurt Cobain to Amy Winehouse—who do what they can to defy the nihilistic demons before they are themselves done in. "We picture the world as thick with conquering and elate humanity," says the narrator of Stephen Crane's "The Blue Hotel":

> but here [on the prairie], with the bugles of the tempest pealing, it was hard to imagine a peopled earth. One viewed the existence of man then as a marvel, and conceded a glamour of wonder to these lice which were caused to cling to a whirling, fire-smote, ice-locked, disease-stricken, space-lost bulb. The conceit of man was explained by this storm to be the very engine of life. One was a coxcomb not to die in it. (822)

Courageous human conceit as the engine of life—this is the bravery of the Daring Warrior, and we are called by Crane to ponder the moral significance of such daring. Crane clearly finds there to be "a glamour of wonder" in our willingness to face the hostile loneliness of our lives on this "space-lost bulb" and to refuse to be cowed by it. Such an attitude is superior to a naïve desire to believe in God or a foolish willingness to hope for the future. The Daring Warrior would easily pass what F. Scott Fitzgerald famously defined as "the test of a first-rate intelligence," which "is the ability to hold two opposed ideas in the mind at the same time, and still retain the ability to function. One should, for example, be able to see that things are hopeless and yet be determined to make them otherwise."[16]

As a social role and character, the Daring Warrior draws on several philosophical sources, one being a modern version of ancient Stoicism and the other an offshoot of the naturalistic materialism that came to the fore in the late nineteenth century. The Stoic tradition counseled individuals to live in accord with nature and to submit themselves to the providential plan underlying all of reality, including human experience. Nineteenth-century naturalism accepted the Stoic call to endurance, but it was *nature as mechanism* to which it submitted, not *nature as Logos-bearer*. As a result, the constraints of the Daring Warrior's role required the lonely individual to oppose all suggestions that a personal God might be the creator, ruler, and reconciler of the world as we know it. To live without the comfort of belief in such a God became the sine qua non of one brand of modern heroism.

The code of the Daring Warrior differs sharply from that of a more ancient Christian ethic, and that difference shows itself clearly if we set side by side paragraphs from two books by twentieth-century writers. The first passage comes at the very end of *The First Three Minutes*, a study of the origins of the universe written by the Nobel Prize–winning physicist Steven Weinberg. In it, he moves far beyond the confines of science to face what he takes to be the ultimate question:

> As I write this I happen to be in an airplane at 30,000 feet, flying over Wyoming en route home from San Francisco to Boston. Below, the earth looks very soft and comfortable—fluffy clouds here and there, snow turning pink as the sun sets, roads stretching straight across the country from one town to another. It is very hard to realize that this all is just a tiny part of an overwhelmingly hostile universe. It is even harder to realize that this present universe has evolved from an unspeakably unfamiliar early condition, and faces a future extinction of endless cold or intolerable heat. The more the universe seems comprehensible, the more it also seems pointless.[17]

The second passage serves as the opening of C. S. Lewis's 1941 sermon "The Weight of Glory":

> If you asked twenty good men today what they thought the highest of the virtues, nineteen of them would reply, Unselfishness. But if you asked almost any of the great Christians of old he would have replied, Love. You see what has happened? A negative term has been substituted for a positive, and this is of more than philological importance. The negative ideal of Unselfishness carries with it the suggestion not primarily of securing good things for others, but of going without them ourselves, as if our abstinence and not their happiness was the important point. I do not think this is the Christian virtue of Love. The New Testament has lots to say about self-denial, but not about self-denial as an end in itself. We are told to deny ourselves and to take up our crosses in order that we may follow Christ; and nearly every description of what we shall ultimately find if we do so contains an appeal to desire. If there lurks in most modern minds the notion that to desire our own good and earnestly to hope for the enjoyment of it is a bad thing, I submit that this notion has crept in from Kant and the Stoics and is no part of the Christian faith. Indeed, if we consider the unblushing promises of reward and the staggering nature of the rewards promised in the Gospels, it would seem that Our Lord finds our desires, not too strong, but too weak. We are half-hearted creatures, fooling about with drink and sex and ambition when infinite joy is offered us, like an ignorant child who

wants to go on making mud pies in a slum because he cannot imagine what is meant by the offer of a holiday at the sea. We are far too easily pleased. (25–26)

To Weinberg, the only authentic story that can be told about our world is one in which the primary agent of action is mindless matter spinning in pointless motion. All our other accounts of life that we might offer are nothing more than fabulous fictions that may shelter us, but only briefly, from the cold, brutal fact of our plight. For the more that we learn about the "overwhelmingly hostile universe" we inhabit, the less we are able to believe it has any meaning intended for us. The wise thing for us to do is to renounce our desires for assurance and, like a sheriff facing down a scoundrel, look this terrible truth in the eye with courage and without flinching.

Lewis draws an opposite lesson about our desire to believe in meaning and reward. By nature and through the grace of God, he explains, our lives and the world in which they unfold are enfolded within an order that God has created and continues to sustain in love. If we are prone to consider deprivation and meaninglessness as our heroic lot in an indifferent universe, it may be that we do so because we mistakenly prize unselfishness more than love. We have come to believe that self-denial is our highest calling and that it is more virtuous to renounce our needs than to hope for their fulfillment.

On this matter, Lewis links up with MacIntyre through their emphasis on the *virtues*, those moral goods and ideals that, according to Aristotle and Aquinas, God has woven into the fabric of creation. To believe in such virtues is to acknowledge that God has established certain ends for human life and the created order. When, for example, Augustine cries to God at the start of the *Confessions*, "Our hearts are restless, until they find their rest in Thee," he is testifying to his conviction that however aimless our strivings and longings may seem to be, they point to a story-shaped form that God has written into the cosmos and inscribed upon our hearts.

To Weinberg, such a belief is incomprehensible in light of what we know about the impersonal laws that generate and regulate all of life, including that curious, self-reflective, language-saturated form of life that only we humans know. The steely resignation Weinberg promotes is rooted in a Stoic view of virtue as freedom from passion achieved through self-mastery. To embody this virtue in late modernity, we are called to align our wills with nature and to resign our hearts to its sublime indifference.

It is in this context that Lewis suggests that if we believe it wrong to long for our own good, such a "notion has crept in from Kant and the Stoics and is no part of the Christian faith." He rejects what he calls the "negative ideal of Unselfishness" and says that if we consider "the unblushing promises of reward" as well as their "staggering nature" as Jesus describes them in the Gospels, it would appear "our Lord finds our desires, not too strong, but too weak." We would prefer to conclude, that is, that our lives are stories of desiccation and decline than believe the unblushing promise of a staggeringly happy ending. When it comes to telling and hearing the story of our destiny in a world ruled by the risen Word, we do indeed seem, as Lewis said, to be "far too easily pleased."

The First and the Last

Our discussion to this point has highlighted two powerful but countervailing tendencies the modern mind displays when it tries to divine the meaning of time. One is the romantic ideal of the epiphanic moment, those spots of time that are assumed to reveal the deep patterns buried within our seemingly random experiences. This view, as we have seen, draws upon the *Logos* tradition of the Christian faith but dispenses with the particular substance of Christian belief. The other tendency, involving the courage of the Daring Warrior, also taps into the *Logos* tradition, in this case through its deep debt to Stoicism. In this instance, the emphasis is not on discovering the pattern of the *Logos* that emerges in the spots of time; instead, it involves aligning one's desires with the natural order of things in a disenchanted universe.

Perhaps not surprisingly, in the literature of late modernity these two impulses—the drive to be illuminated and the determination to endure—clash repeatedly. This is the case, for instance, in *The Sound and the Fury*, where the sections belonging to the Compson brothers read like case studies in epiphanic failure. The brothers remain clueless about the meaning of their experiences, and none comes close to detecting any pattern in the larger scheme of things. As we have seen, this is especially true of Benjy Compson, whose opening section consists of an endless string of disconnected impressions. Above all else, Benjy can neither find nor fabricate a storied order in the strictly immanent cosmos that is the only home he can know or imagine.

Benjy's section is followed by an equally disjointed narrative fashioned by his brother, Quentin. If reading Benjy's chapter is like watching a series of disconnected images flit before our eyes, to read Quentin's narrative is to stumble through a darkened maze with no light or exit in sight. In an interior monologue that he delivers on the last day of his life, Quentin repeatedly circles back to key conversations with his father, a heartbroken man and besotted cynic whose maxims have a talismanic power over his son.

Like Weinberg, Mr. Compson (the father) considers the universe to be pointless, and his reasons have to do with the meaninglessness of time. At one point in Quentin's monologue, the son remembers a speech his father had delivered as he gave him a watch: "I give you the mausoleum of all hope and desire. . . . Because no battle is ever won he said. They are not even fought. The field only reveals to man his own folly and despair." There is no meaning embedded within time, no truth revealed about it from beyond, and no promised end for which it might be bound. For as Mr. Compson tells Quentin, "Christ was not crucified: he was worn away by a minute clicking of little wheels" (76–77).

Benjy may not be able to discern any difference between word and thing, but his Harvard-educated brother cannot conceive of the two as being related in any way. The promiscuity of their sister, Caddy, haunts Quentin, as does his failure to have defended her honor. Whenever he dwells on that muddled situation, he finds thoughts of incest and eternal punishment running together in his mind, as he fantasizes about the permanence of hell. If only he and Caddy were imprisoned together in a state of eternal torment, then time and change and loss would come to an end, and the two of them could endure forever: *"If it could just be a hell beyond that: the clean flame the two of us more than dead"* (116).

Quentin has confided in his father about his fantasies and fears, but in response, the elder Compson offers only a brusque dismissal and a series of cynical quips: "Women are never virgins. Purity is a negative state and therefore contrary to nature. It's nature is hurting you not Caddy." Quentin says, "That's just words and he [Mr. Compson] said So is virginity." When Quentin shoots back, "You dont know" [that it is "just words"], his father replies, "Yes. On the instant when we come to realise that tragedy is second-hand." Mr. Compson's point is that *when* we realize everything in life is "just words," then we know that all of life's seriousness—its *meaning*—consists merely of a string of conclusions others have reached based on experiences we never had (116).[18]

In another conversation that Quentin recalls, Mr. Compson tells his son, "Man is the sum of his misfortunes." Quentin is desperate to believe suffering will come to an end at some point, but "time is your misfortune Father said. A gull on an invisible wire attached through space dragged." Earlier in his section, Quentin had made note of the hands of a clock in a Cambridge jewelry store window. To him they looked "like a gull tilting into the wind" (104, 85). As we are dragged through time on that wire, we can make no sense of what strikes us or sails by as we glide toward death. Quentin is haunted by the thought that each tick of the clock drives the present we cannot retain into a past we cannot retrieve. In his mental world, both our memory of God's faithfulness and our trust in God's promises are taken to be fantastic and groundless. As Cleanth Brooks observes, "Any Christian solution is meaningless to this

Beginning with the Word

intense, sad, and terribly honest young man," who concludes that death alone can free him from time's ironclad grip.[19]

Another Compson brother, Jason, narrates the third and final section of *The Sound and the Fury*. Neither as witless as Benjy nor as tormented as Quentin, he nevertheless is as shallow and ruthless as one could imagine a person to be. His section pulses with the beat of indignation and flames with the fury of self-righteousness. After the confusion of Benjy's impressions and the convolutions of Quentin's reflections, Jason's storytelling seems disarmingly transparent. Yet despite its clarity, his account reveals his obliviousness rather than his wisdom, for "Jason's is a shallow mind essentially and he often does not understand what he thinks he understands perfectly."[20]

As his brothers do, Jason Compson also becomes hopelessly tangled in the web of time. He never seems to have enough time and never seems to be in the right place at the right time. Jason doesn't understand this fact about himself, but others do. One day, Old Man Job, who works at the hardware store where Jason is also employed, tells the Compson brother:

> "I wont try to fool you," he says. "You too smart fer me. Yes, suh," he says, looking busy as hell, putting five or six little packages into the wagon. "You's too smart fer me. Aint a man in dis town kin keep up wid you fer smartness. You fools a man whut so smart he cant even keep up wid hisself," he says, getting in the wagon and unwrapping the reins.
> "Who's that?" I says.
> "Dat's Mr Jason Compson," he says. (250)

Jason's monologue contains more than a hundred references to time, and each event in his section has to do with his inability to manage or master its flow. In every race Jason is always a step or two behind, for every appointment just a few minutes late. Whether he is pursuing his niece (Caddy's daughter) and her boyfriend, or frantically checking the tickertape as he plays the market, or trying to fool his boss about where he has been and what he has done, Jason is always slightly out of sync. Like Benjy and Quentin, he lives a life full of sound and fury signifying nothing. The Compsons have neither the confidence to believe in revelatory spots of time nor the stoic courage to bear the sound and fury of pointless time.

Stories of Sacred and Profane Time

As has often proved to be the case in modernity, poets such as Dickinson and novelists such as Faulkner trace the contours of the future long before they theoreticians arrive on the scene to fill out the arguments and systematize the insights. As a case in point, consider the overlap between Dickinson's and Faulkner's depictions of the fracturing of stories, secular and sacred alike, and the assessment Jean-François Lyotard offers of narrative in his highly influential 1979 book, *The Postmodern Condition*. Commissioned as a study of technology by the government of Quebec, this work almost single-handedly introduced the term *postmodern* into the philosophical lexicon. In its opening pages, Lyotard speaks of the "transformations which, since the end of the nineteenth century, have altered the game rules for science, literature, and the arts." These transformations are evidence of a fundamental "crisis of narratives" that marks the human experience of reality in the postmodern world.[21]

To Lyotard, the history of early modernity may be characterized as the drama of a relentless struggle between the stubborn particularities of scientific fact and the falsifying comforts of generalizing stories. "Science has always been in conflict with narratives," he claims; from the early sixteenth to the late nineteenth century, it undertook a sustained effort to measure narratives by a scientific yardstick and thereby prove "the majority of them . . . to be fables." Because "science does not restrict itself to stating useful regularities" but makes the grander claim that it "seeks the truth," it was forced to devise a means of legitimating its own enterprise. To that end, Lyotard says, science invented a "discourse called philosophy." He defines as "modern" any science that seeks legitimacy through "reference to a metadiscourse . . . making an explicit appeal to some grand narrative."[22]

The metanarratives developed by modern philosophy took many forms, depending on the enterprises they were meant to legitimate. Some trumpeted "the dialectics of Spirit," others "the hermeneutics of meaning." For some, the fundamental story of modernity involved "the emancipation of the rational . . . subject," while in other instances the dominant narrative had to do with "the creation of wealth." In what Lyotard calls the central "Enlightenment narrative," we find a "hero of knowledge" who "works toward a good ethico-political end."[23] Indeed, where would most of the literature and philosophy of the nineteenth century be without such ethical heroes of knowledge—without Frederick Douglass and Jane Eyre, without Hester Prynne and Huck Finn, without Dorothea Brooke or David Copperfield, or without Henry David Thoreau's and Walt Whitman's respective conceptions of their own selves?

According to Lyotard, the second half of the twentieth century witnessed a sudden upsurge of skepticism concerning the narratives of modern philosophy and "the validity of the institutions governing the social bond." It was this crisis of legitimacy that gave birth to the phenomenon we call postmodernism. "Simplifying to the extreme," Lyotard concludes, "I define *postmodern* as

Beginning with the Word

incredulity toward metanarratives." He takes it for granted that the Christian metanarrative lost its focus and power several centuries ago, and he claims its secular successors have been undermined, as well, over the past century. As the metanarratives have decayed and collapsed, the narrative function in general has lost its central "functors" (operators) along with "its great hero, its great dangers, its great voyages, its great goal." The elements that had long been linked together within narratives are now "being dispersed in clouds of narrative language elements." Within each cloud we find "pragmatic valencies [combinations] specific to its kind," and all of us today live at the "intersection" of any number of discrete clusters of meaning and association.[24]

By Lyotard's standards, we in the postmodern world resemble Benjy Compson, as we struggle to bring facts and perceptions together to form a plausible story that might speak truthfully of the world and our history within it. We find it difficult to establish "stable language communications," and the ones we do "establish are not necessarily communicable." The driving force of storytelling in the postmodern world, concludes Lyotard, "is not the expert's homology"—his or her discovery of family relationships—"but the inventor's paralogy"—his or her willingness to refuse to conform to the rule of precedent or logic. We value the inventive irruption into the dominant narrative far more than we do the synthesizing power of new narrative accounts.[25]

But what might be the practical or theological significance of Lyotard's assertions concerning the collapse of metanarratives in the postmodern world? I'd like to suggest that one way to answer such a question might be to consider the changing roles that public monuments have come to play in modern culture. Consider, for example, two events and their memorial sites—the battle of Gettysburg (1863) and the death of Diana, Princess of Wales (1997)—that provide us with a picture of dramatic changes in the late modern understanding of narrative. In the decades after the Civil War, more than twelve hundred separate monuments and markers were erected on the Gettysburg battlefield to commemorate the heroism, sacrifices, and tragedies that marked the three bloodiest days in American history. These historical markers pay tribute to countless different military units and individuals, from the Union and the Confederacy alike. But even though each is anchored in a strong sense of individuality and region, the separate monuments are meant to blend together into a single, grand, and complex narrative about the "War Between the States." Given the intensity of the conflict and the depth of division between the sides, it might be more accurate to say a majority opinion (Union) and a minority opinion (Confederacy) find expression in this collection. Yet the overall impression is of a series of private witnesses to a shared public event with a discernible narrative significance.

In the weeks after Lady Di's death in the summer of 1997, memorials sprang up in Paris near the crash site and in key locations across England, particularly in front of Kensington Palace, her London residence. Where the Gettysburg memorials focus on the narrative valorizing what Lyotard calls the "great hero, great danger, great goal," the makeshift tributes to Diana displayed "a heterogeneity of elements," including thousands of flowers—piled many feet deep at Kensington Palace—countless teddy bears, photos, and notes of sorrow and worshipful admiration.

The palace memorial in particular was considered a form of protest, an effort to break the silence of the royal family in the wake of the death of the woman Tony Blair named "the People's Princess." The pressing concern of the memorializers of Princess Diana had little to do with the past or future glories of the British Empire and virtually everything to do with the private aspirations and associations of people whose primary connection to Diana had come through the transmission of cultural symbols and video images.

The disparate objects, photos, and flowers piled up in front of Kensington Palace call to mind a line near the end of T. S. Eliot's *The Waste Land*. Having finished offering more than four hundred lines of personal, literary, religious, and historical images in a dazzling, densely packed poem, Eliot concludes, "These fragments I have shored against my ruins" (50). At this point in history (1922), the poet took as given the collapse of both the Christian metanarrative of redemption and the secular metanarrative of progress. All one could hope for, according to the speaker at the poem's close, was to patch together bits and pieces from a "heterogeneity of elements" to stave off ruin, if only for a while.

Whether the spots of time served to restore Wordsworth's spiritual powers or to provide access to a mysterious source of divine illumination, for him they hinted at a storied completeness embedded deeply within human experience. The spots of time drew from individual experience, yet their focus was ultimately on underlying patterns that spoke of a wholeness whose true home was in the world—and in a divine power—beyond the human mind. The Diana memorial and *The Waste Land*, however, are products of what Stephen Spender has called the modern "psychological" view of the imagination, for which "poetry is a means of arranging the order of our internal lives by making a harmonious pattern of extremely complex attitudes, *once thought to refer to an external order of metaphysics* but now seen to be a symbolic ordering of our inner selves."[26] With the metanarratives of public life—be they political, ethical, or religious—called into question, only the symbolic ordering of the inner life seems justified or legitimated.

A number of writers, including Eliot, were profoundly troubled by the thought that all stories were pastiches of personal emotions and private

Beginning with the Word

associations. For when narratives are pulverized into a series of fragmented incidents and perceptions, time becomes flattened, and all experiences appear equally valid and equally useless. In Eliot's "The Love Song of J. Alfred Prufrock," the neurotic speaker has time for everything but finds meaning in nothing. "There will be time, there will be time," he sighs, "To prepare a face to meet the faces that you meet," just as "There will be time to murder and create," and even time "for a hundred indecisions, / And for a hundred visions and revisions. / Before the taking of a toast and tea" (4).

Prufrock comes from a long line of time-wearied modern figures at the head of which stands Shakespeare's Macbeth, whose "sound and fury" speech reads like a charter document for our culture of ennui. Before its "tale told by an idiot" flourish at the close, that speech laments the manner in which "Tomorrow, and tomorrow, and tomorrow / Creeps in this petty pace from day-to-day / To the last syllable of recorded time" (vv. 20–22). Macbeth's weariness is a product of the moral anarchy his murderous actions have produced. Yet by the time we reach Prufrock in the twentieth century, the sense of time's futility stems from an epistemological perception more than from a moral flaw.

That change in perception had to do with what Charles Taylor describes as the emergence of a sense of profane, secular time, a view of time in which all events are seen to exist on a single plane, and there is no distinction between a past series of sacred founding events and the present extension of mundane time. Sacred, or higher, time gathers and reorders all that unfolds in secular time; an event in one era—say, the sacrifice of Isaac—is a prefiguring of another event, the crucifixion of Christ. The two separate occurrences are linked together within the divine plan, which is to say "they are drawn close to identity in eternity, even though they are centuries (that is, 'aeons' or 'saecula') apart." *Secular* time, on the other hand, is time as we have come to know it in late modernity; it is "ordinary time, indeed, to *us* it's just time, period. One thing happens after another, and when something is past, it's past."[27] This shift from *sacred* time to *profane* time bears directly on a Christian understanding of narrative, so it is crucial to note several key distinctions between the conceptions.

To explain the concept of sacred time, literary historian Erich Auerbach points to medieval practices of storytelling, which were based on the concept of *figural interpretation*. Patterned on the New Testament's appropriation of the Hebrew Bible, figural interpretation established connections between events separated by vast expanses of time. In figural practice, the first event or person is taken to signify "not only itself" but also a second that comes after it, so that the second "involves or fulfills the first." Because it affirmed both the validity of the individual incident and the storied relationship of a vast series of events, the figural method had proved crucial to the efforts a number of church fathers made to bring large frames of reference, particularly Roman history, into harmony with a Judeo-Christian theology of history. Figural interpretation linked these distant and disparate episodes by portraying the two poles of the figure—the past anticipation and the contemporary fulfillment—as being separated in time yet bound together through God's redemptive history of promise and providential care.

For figural interpretation both the past and the present flow within the same stream of historical experience. It is only the revealing, and the seeing, of the connection between them that constitutes a spiritual act. In and of themselves, they stand apart as discrete phenomena. In the Hebrew Bible, for example, the sacrifice of Isaac is a distinct event in the history of Israel; yet in the New Testament, that sacrifice also becomes a prefiguring of Christ's crucifixion. Isaac's story announces and anticipates Christ's sacrifice, which fulfills the promise contained within the earlier event. The connection between the two events, Auerbach observes, cannot be established by reason "in the horizontal dimension" but only vertically through the revelatory words and deeds of God.[28]

The figural method requires us to practice something similar to what Fitzgerald had in mind with his test of a "first-rate intelligence." In Auerbach's words, figural interpretation holds that "earthly life is thoroughly real, with the reality of the flesh into which the Logos entered," but it also considers that reality to be only a shadow of "the real reality that will unveil and preserve the *figura*." Each event in time is substantial in its own right and cannot be explained away or dismissed as insignificant. Yet at the same time, "the individual earthly event is not regarded as a definitive self-sufficient reality, nor as a link in a chain of development in which . . . events perpetually give rise to new events." Instead, discrete events are seen as elements vertically related to "a divine order which encompasses" them and establishes their ultimate meaning. "In the eye of God and in the other world," the comprehensive reality of all events is timelessly present. For us within history, however, everything remains a matter of partial understanding, which is sustained by the hope for fulfillment and the promise of revelation.[29] In the words of St. Paul, "For now we see in a mirror, dimly, but then we will see face to face. Now I know only in part; then I will know fully, even as I have been fully known" (1 Cor. 13:12).

The figural method had a pervasive influence on the New Testament, on early Christian history, and on medieval Christianity. That influence extended well into the modern period, through the covenantal theology of Calvinism, the typological practices of the New England Puritans, and the nineteenth-century elaboration of the concept of Manifest Destiny. Only with the emergence

Beginning with the Word

of the modern conception of profane time in the eighteenth century did the figural method's hold on interpretive activity begin to slacken dramatically.

To describe the importance of profane time, political theorist Benedict Anderson contrasts it specifically with Auerbach's analysis of figural interpretation. Anderson notes that time in the figural system involves a "simultaneity of past and future in an instantaneous present." He says we might call this a "conception of simultaneity-along-time." Over the past two centuries such a conception of time has gradually been replaced by the idea of "'homogeneous, empty time' in which simultaneity is, as it were, transverse, cross-time, marked not by prefiguring and fulfillment, but by temporal coincidence, and measured by clock and calendar."[30]

In Anderson's words, the shift from a sacred to a profane view of time "has been a long time in the making," but events near the close of the nineteenth century hastened the process and propelled it quickly toward its logical end. At the midpoint of that century, scientific discoveries dramatically extended our understanding of the vast stretches of developmental time that lay behind geological formations and biological transformations. A child born in the early nineteenth century would have come into a world thought to be a scant six thousand years old. Yet by the time that person reached adulthood, the earth had grown older by a factor of millions.

There is no denying the impact of this dramatic extension of time. Emily Dickinson captured the feel of it in an ironic and heartbreaking poem about the dead, who are depicted as meekly awaiting, in their graves, the promised resurrection. While they linger in their tombs, the glacial wheels of time continue to grind away above them:

> Grand go the Years,
> In the Crescent above them—
> Worlds scoop their Arcs—
> And Firmaments—row—
> Diadems—drop—
> And Doges—surrender—
> Soundless as Dots,
> On a Disc of Snow. (#124)

It takes an interminable length of time for a galaxy to scoop an arc in the sky and a firmament to row its way across the heavens. Within a matter of decades in the mid-nineteenth century, it seemed to Dickinson that humans had gone from serving as microcosms of a cosmic order to becoming silent dots adrift in a vastly expanding universe.

At the same time that the sense of astronomical, geological, and biological time was undergoing this revolution, the social orders of the North Atlantic countries were also experiencing tumultuous changes, as industrialization packed the cities and shifted the center of production from home and farm to factory and office. Women were all but shut out from the latter spheres and left to bide their time in the home, which had suddenly been transformed from a site of production into a scene of consumption. In many of these homes, boredom seemed to lurk in every corner, as a foreign observer noted in an 1840 survey of London life. Flora Tristan found the lives of English women to be "unbelievably monotonous, sterile and drab," for there was never a change in the oppressively uniform quality of their "days, months and years." As a result, Tristan noted, "time has no meaning for them," and there being few things they can do to pass the time, "they plunge headlong into the reading of novels."[31]

Some of the most dynamic, driven characters of late nineteenth-century literature—Gustave Flaubert's Emma Bovary, Henrik Ibsen's Hedda Gabler, Kate Chopin's Edna Pontellier—suffered from an ennui that had settled over the middle-class home and seeped into the hearts of many who dwelt there and had nowhere else to go.[32]

This domestic sense of endless time dovetailed with the new ways of measuring time that were needed to meet the demands of modern commerce and transportation in the late nineteenth century. Railroads and shippers had to impose a uniform system of time on the provincial and chaotic world of local time, which lacked precision and conformed to no standards save the needs of individual communities. In 1870, if a traveler from Washington to San Francisco had reset his or her watch in every town that traveler passed through, there would have been more than two hundred adjustments to make along the way. In 1883 the railroads imposed centralized time zones on America, and in the following year Greenwich, England, was established as the zero meridian, and the world as a whole was divided into twenty-four time zones.[33]

The standardizing of time marked a distinct shift from premodern understandings in which time had been taken to be multidimensional. The myths and epics of traditional societies told of extraordinary founding events that had taken place at a higher level and in a sacred time. Gods and heroes mingled, warriors clashed at Troy, and Greek culture was born; Aeneas led the vanquished Trojan remnant on a divine mission, and the seeds of the Roman Empire were planted. The founding events had taken place *then*, in a sacred age and on a lofty plane, but this is *now*, a profane period playing itself out on a flattened earth situated at a point far from the sacred origins and the divine destinies alike.

Beginning with the Word

In myth and liturgy, sacred times have distinct rhythms and vary one from the other, but all derive their meaning from the divine framework that gives them an origin, an order, and a destiny. In profane time, there is only a single dimension. On this plane, all moments are of equal value, and they extend infinitely into all directions—past, present, and future alike.[34]

Space, Time, and the Patience of God

We have seen how the prospect of endless time and its infinite possibilities had bedeviled T. S. Eliot's J. Alfred Prufrock, an emblematic man for the age of profane time. Prufrock has time "for a hundred indecisions, / And for a hundred visions and revisions," but he has no idea of how to make use of time, and its weight threatens to crush him. In looking at the time that stretches ahead of him, it is as though he has experienced everything before it happens because, with all time being equal, there is nothing distinctive to mark any particular event or moment: "For I have known them all already, known them all:— / Have known the evenings, mornings, afternoons" (5). For Eliot, "time becomes a collection of individual parts," and to know "all" in advance is to feel impotent in the face of a time that is not full "but paradoxically empty, constituted as it is by pure repetition."[35]

Eliot himself was unable to solve the riddle of time or heal the wounds inflicted by it until he returned, in his late thirties, to the practice of the Christian faith and the pursuit of Christian virtues. The fullest poetic expression of those renewed beliefs can be found in *Four Quartets*, a series of long poems written between 1935 and 1942. A brief focus on the first of them, "Burnt Norton," will give us a sense of how a troubled Christian artist grappled with the new and shocking views of time that had swept in during the final decades of the nineteenth century.

Burnt Norton was a manor house in the Cotswolds, which Eliot visited one day in the mid-1930s in the company of Emily Hale, a woman he had fitfully courted during his years as a Harvard undergraduate. Out of the circumstances of that place and visit—the deserted gardens, the feel of autumn (the *fall*), and the reunion with a woman whose love he had once known and lost—Eliot fashioned an intricate opening meditation on "the what might have been" of the road not taken, the door not opened, the choice never made.

> Footfalls echo in the memory
> Down the passage which we did not take
> Towards the door we never opened
> Into the rose-garden. (117)

As the meditation builds toward its close, one of Wordsworth's spots of time breaks open for the speaker. With imagery that evokes both intricate order and sensuous fullness, Eliot and his companion are drawn into the "heart of light." They stand entranced, but only for a moment, before their spiritually saturated experience fades, and they are sent out of the timeless garden and back into the flow of profane time.

The closing lines of "Burnt Norton" return to the imagery and themes of its opening, as the speaker breathlessly tracks the "shaft of sunlight" and the "hidden laughter of children in the foliage," which appear and disappear in an instant. That their radiance is brilliant but momentary only deepens the melancholy pall of the ordinary time that extends before and beyond them forever:

> Sudden in a shaft of sunlight
> Even while the dust moves
> There rises the hidden laughter
> Of children in the foliage
> Quick now, here, now, always—
> Ridiculous the waste sad time
> Stretching before and after. (122)

For Eliot, Wordsworth's spots of time remained, but they had become in and of themselves discrete and fleeting glimpses of an unnamed glory. What power can such momentarily illuminating experiences have, if a "ridiculous waste sad time" stretches "before and after" them into infinity?

Eliot wrote "Burnt Norton" after his publicly announced conversion to Anglo-Catholic Christianity. The poem makes only glancing references to the Christian faith, but it does set the stage for the three, more theologically explicit poems to come. In the third of the *Four Quartets*, "Dry Salvages," Eliot returns to the spots of time by way of the Incarnation and a Christian understanding of time's arc. He revisits "Burnt Norton's" garden and classifies these "moments in and out of time."

> These are only hints and guesses,
> Hints followed by guesses; and the rest
> Is prayer, observance, discipline, thought and action.
> The hint half guessed, the gift half understood, is Incarnation.
> Here the impossible union of spheres is actual,
> Here the past and future
> Are conquered, and reconciled. (136)

The spots of time can only hint and guess at life's secret, which is the Incarnation, the gift by means of which eternity is reconciled to time. The moments are still fleeting, but when they vanish, we can begin to "hint and guess" at their meaning during the "waste sad time." Eliot says it is natural for us to make those guesses when the moments come and go, but the rest of our life—all the hours and days and months we spend in what the liturgical year calls "Ordinary Time"—is made up of "prayer, observance, discipline, thought and action."

As we pray, think, and act in our free but fitful ways, we do so as creatures who enjoy the liberty of God's children and the promise of God's patience. This latter theme is important to consider when we think of time and narrative because divine patience offers a way of making theological sense of our new awareness of profane time. Unless one believes in a seven-day creation that took place a mere six thousand years ago, a Christian must find a way to conceive of what it means that some 13.7 billion years have led to this point, to this coming Sunday—which will be October 7, 2012, as I write this—when hundreds of millions of men and women will eat the body and drink the blood of Jesus Christ, the crucified and risen Lord.

In considering the astonishing changes that have overtaken our understanding of biological time and astronomical space, the distinguished Catholic critic Walter Ong posed a series of questions in a brief essay published shortly before his death. What are we to make, he asks, of the dramatic growth in our knowledge of the age and immensity of the universe? Does our knowledge give us a new or different undertsanding of God's relationship to us? How long will it be before we have assimilated our knowledge of God's special revelation to our understanding of his universe. And "without this assimilation how, or how long, can Christian faith survive?"[36]

In his treatment of the doctrine of creation, Lutheran theologian Robert Jenson provides us with a means of creatively addressing questions such as these. Jenson defines time as God's way of making "narrative room in his triune life for others than himself; this act is the act of creation, and this accommodation is created time." As we have seen, the crisis modern literature addresses is one in which time is felt to extend out from the self's present back to a seemingly infinite past and forward into an endless future. Instead of thinking of time as an extension of finite consciousness, Jenson suggests, we should consider its "stretching out" to be a matter of its being contained within the "infinite enveloping consciousness" of God. We are players and participants, that is, in a drama that takes place "within the divine life."[37]

The same holds for space, which Jenson describes as the means by which "God opens otherness between himself and us" and thereby creates "present room for us." In this space, God allows us to live and develop in our otherness from him. He celebrates that otherness and delights in our human ability to participate in the creator's divine life without us having to sacrifice our identities as creatures. Jenson quotes a maxim of John of Damascus—"God is his own space"—and says this can only be the case if God posits an other "from which he is at a *distance*." That is where we stand, in created space at a certain remove from God. Since we are in fact creatures, our "otherness from God establishes that God is one place, and creation is spatially located by not being *at that* place. God is one place and creatures another, and just and only so there is created space."[38]

Jenson links a modern understanding of time and space to God's willingness to allow creation to develop in accordance with its intrinsic logic and the time span that entails. For Karl Barth, such willingness reveals God's patience, a human virtue or divine attribute about which we rarely speak at present. But the Bible, and particularly the Old Testament, points everywhere to God's patience—Barth cites Exodus 34:6; Joel 2:13; Jonah 4:2; Nehemiah 9:17; and Psalms 86:15; 103:8; 145:8—a quality long synonymous with a willingness to be *long-suffering* on behalf of others.

"Patience exists where space and time are given with a definite intention," Barth writes, "where freedom is allowed in expectation of a response. God acts in this way" and thereby "makes a purposeful concession of space and time. He allows this freedom of expectancy." Yet things could be otherwise. Barth explains that "God could be gracious and merciful in such a way that His love would consume His creature." He could do so by taking our distress so fully "to Himself" that we would no longer have any "opportunities in space and time" and would find ourselves stripped of both, with God having destroyed our "perverse and tortured wills" and substituted his "own good will as the sole effective reality." In other words, from a certain perspective, would it not be more merciful for God to bring an end to human consciousness—to human life itself—by obliterating the distinction between himself and us? For "is not the very existence of all that is other than God identical with its suffering, its suffering with its existence?" And if that is the case, "could not eternal death" as a consequence of divine wrath be "eternal peace," a state in which we live "unviolated and in fact inviolable by all the assaults and torments . . . bound up with space and time" (*CD*, II.1.408–9)?

As he discusses divine patience in these terms, Barth strikes a deep nerve in modern literature and experience. That nerve registers the pain many in our world feel when they compare the wearying futility of self-conscious awareness with the blissful contentment of unconscious existence (or non-existence). For example, consider a poem Emily Dickinson wrote in 1863:

Beginning with the Word

Of Course—I prayed—
And did God Care?
He cared as much as on the Air
A Bird—had stamped her foot—
And cried "Give Me"—
My Reason—Life—
I had not had—but for Yourself—
'Twere better Charity
To leave me in the Atom's Tomb—
Merry, and nought, and gay, and numb—
Than this smart Misery. (#581)

For the speaker of this poem, the God who has promised to answer prayers
in general has turned a deaf ear to hers in particular. In its last four lines,
the poem grows dark, as its speaker dreams of "the Atom's Tomb." There
she could have remained, in Barth's words, "unviolated and inviolable." She
would have been "merry" because she would have been "nought" (nothing),
and she would have been "gay" (happy), for she would have been "numb" to
the pain we all come to suffer through experience.

The love of death and the longing for an oblivion that will bring suffering
and consciousness to an end—these are themes whose roots dig deep into
naturalism's rocky soil. They are notes sounded in John Keats's aside in "Ode
to Melancholy": "Now more than ever seems it rich to die, / To cease upon
the midnight with no pain" (206); we hear them in Walt Whitman's sensuous
embrace of "the low and delicious word death" (393); we feel their pulse in
the "sensuous, soft, close embrace" of the sea that envelops the naked and
weary Edna Pontellier at the close of *The Awakening* (654); and we see them
in motion in the deadly embrace to which Gustave Aschenbach opens himself
in Thomas Mann's *Death in Venice*:

> Then he raised his head, and with both hands, hanging limp over the chair-arms,
> he described a slow motion, palms outward, a lifting and turning movement,
> as though to indicate a wide embrace. It was a gesture of welcome, a calm and
> deliberate acceptance of what might come. (39–40)

In this version of postromantic apocalyptic, a vexed human consciousness
dreams of being obliterated and absorbed into the all, that otherness which
is death. This involves a strange reversal of things, as the free and finite self
spurns life and suffering and seeks instead a blissful apocalypse of nonbeing.

Barth links this longing for death to a modern hopelessness about time. If
there is no story of transformation to be told—if there is no healing for the

wound at the core of life—why endure the endlessness of time? The theology of God's patience responds by setting the vast extension of time and space within the drama of God's long-suffering solidarity with his creatures. In summarizing his argument, Barth defines "God's patience as His will, deep-rooted in His essence, . . . to allow to another . . . space and time for the development of its own existence." God grants to us "a reality side by side with His own," and mercifully fulfills his will toward us "in such a way that He does not suspend and destroy [his creation] as the other but accompanies and sustains it and allows it to develop in freedom." Unlike Pirandello's author, God neither abandons his creation nor aborts his creatures. Instead, he enters into their lives—our lives—and walks beside us, suffers on our behalf, and patiently allows us to develop in our full and fallen freedom (*CD*, II.1.409–10).

We return at our chapter's close to its beginning. There we explored spots of time as William Wordsworth defined them and the romantic tradition developed them. Trading on centuries of the Christian reflection on the doctrine of the *Logos*, the romantic era pinned its hopes on the power of the imaginative and illuminated self to renew the ancient but now lagging faith. The romantic writers considered that self to have the capacity to uncover foundational truths in the intimate relationship between the human spirit and the natural world.

For a time, the romantic ideal embodied in the spots of time appeared sufficient for the grand task set before it. But that time proved to be short, and by the mid-nineteenth century, these moments of intense illumination drifted free of the narrative framework that had given them depth, resonance, and enduring meaning. As we saw in a poem by Emily Dickinson, those illuminations became furtive visitors who arrive without warning and "dissolve the same." They cannot be pieced together into some larger story of the spirit, and when they depart they leave behind nothing but a "sumptuous Destitution / Without a Name—."

Dickinson's poetry and Faulkner's fiction were seismographs registering the shock waves that new perspectives on time sent rippling through ancient views of narrative for more than a century. In image and story, these writers reported how things felt on the ground, as tremors of profane time rolled through their world. And as has often been the case in modernity, their imaginative insights anticipated many of the key arguments that theorists would belatedly come to articulate.

Dickinson, for example, observed in 1882, that "the abdication of Belief / Makes the Behavior small." A century later, Jean-François Lyotard would make a similar point in *The Postmodern Condition*, his 1979 work that defined the "*postmodern* as incredulity toward metanarratives." The stringent skepticism that Lyotard notes concerning narratives went hand-in-hand with the move from sacred time to profane time that Dickinson and Faulkner, among many others, struggled to understand.

One consequence of the shift to profane time involved the collapse of figural interpretation. Stripped of the resources provided by that practice, Christian theology in the twentieth century was forced to rethink questions of providence, history, and the nature of the stories that the Christian faith is called to proclaim in a secular age.

In this chapter, we examined the response Christian theology has made to these challenges, and again, an imaginative writer led the way into the discussion. In this instance, it was T. S. Eliot, whose *Four Quartets* provide both a brilliant critique of the romantic celebration of spots of time and a creative picture of Christian witness carried on within the depths of profane time.

The theological arguments we drew on, from Robert Jenson and Karl Barth, stressed God's respect for the otherness of creation and his patient willingness to allow it to develop according to the logic of its own potentiality and freedom. Barth's treatment of this question combines theological rigor and pastoral passion. As we bring this discussion to a close, we can let Barth have the final word:

> That Jesus Christ is very God is shown in His way into the far country in which He the Lord became a servant. For in the majesty of the true God it happened that the eternal Son of the eternal Father became obedient by offering and humbling Himself to be the brother of man, to take His place with the transgressor, to judge him by judging Himself and dying in his place. But God the Father raised Him from the dead, and in so doing recognized and gave effect to His death and passion as a satisfaction made for us, as our conversion to God, and therefore as our redemption from death to life. (*CD*, IV.1.157)

6

"I Will Restore It All"

Christ, Fiction, and the Fullness of Time

In him we have redemption through his blood, the forgiveness of our trespasses, according to the riches of his grace that he lavished upon us. With all wisdom and insight he has made known to us the mystery of his will, according to his good pleasure that he set forth in Christ as a plan for the fullness of time, to gather up all things in him, things in heaven and things on earth.

—Ephesians 1:7–10

In recent weeks this line has been running through my head over and over: "Calm your hearts, dear friends; / whatever plagues you, / whatever fails you, / I will restore it all." What does that mean, "I will restore it all"? Nothing is lost; in Christ all things are taken up, preserved, albeit in transfigured form, transparent, clear, liberated from the torment of self-serving demands. Christ brings all this back, indeed, as God intended, without being distorted by sin. The doctrine originating in Ephesians 1:10 of the restoration of all things—*recapitulation* (Irenaeus)—is a magnificent and consummately consoling thought.

—Dietrich Bonhoeffer, *Letters and Papers from Prison*

Literary modernism—that sprawling, dynamic cultural movement of the early twentieth century—rose to prominence in good measure as a reaction to the advent of profane time. Startled by the vast expanse of empty time that had now suddenly stretched before them, many poets and novelists set off in search of ways of making art tame the unruliness of time.

Few worked at this task with as much passion as did Wallace Stevens, an American poet of the highest order. A craftsman of lyrics that were often simultaneously witty and weighty, Stevens sought to fashion in his art structures of beauty that could frame the formlessness of time and fill the emptiness of space. In his words, "The major poetic idea in the world is and always has been the idea of God," yet what has marked "the modern imagination" has been its clear "movement away from the idea of God." Having originally brought the idea of God into being by means of the imagination, poetry must now make a decision, Stevens suggests. It must either adapt that idea of God "to our different intelligence, or create a substitute for it, or make it unnecessary." We have no choice but to fabricate illusions to live by, and as long as the human race exists, we will require surrogates and successors to the discredited gods of theism.[1]

To Stevens, the lesson to be drawn from the story of God's decline is simple: "After one has abandoned a belief in god, poetry is that essence which takes its place as life's redemption" (*Adagia*, 901). To explain what that redemptive power is, the poet promotes a version of the *ignis fatuus* ("fool's light") argument Dickinson had reluctantly embraced. If we want meaning, we must create it, and we must do so knowingly: "The final belief is to believe in a fiction, which you know to be a fiction, there being nothing else. The exquisite truth is to know that it is a fiction and that you believe in it willingly" (903).

In the intellectual climate of the mid-twentieth century, Stevens appeared to make it possible to recuperate the value of religiously inflected narratives—and metanarratives—in an intellectually acceptable fashion. (Reading Stevens, one feels permitted to be simultaneously savvy and sentimental on the question of belief.) His theory of fictional beliefs and believable fictions held a special appeal for critics who combined within themselves an affection for biblical language with a suspicion of biblical claims.

This was true of Northrop Frye, an ordained minister in the United Church of Canada who employed Stevens's insights in a series of influential works linking the Bible to literary history.[2] And it was also the case with Frank Kermode, a distinguished British critic whose output spanned six decades. Although he held no discernible religious beliefs, Kermode recognized the need for language and literature to furnish something akin to the metaphysical assurance that Christian belief has provided for two millennia.

In an influential 1967 study, *The Sense of an Ending: Studies in the Theory of Fiction*, Kermode suggests what it is that the art of Stevens can impart to the world of Saussure. He goes about this task by articulating a narrative theory that assumes the arbitrary relationship of word and thing, and extends that arbitrariness to stories and their relationship to time. As an epigraph for a pivotal chapter in *The Sense of an Ending*, Kermode quotes Stevens on "the nicer knowledge of / Belief, that what it believes is not true." The longer poem in which these lines appear ("The Pure Good of Theory") opens with a blunt declaration about the irresistible force of time, as we moderns understand it:

> It is time that beats in the breast and it is time
> That batters against the mind, silent and proud,
> The mind that knows it is destroyed by time.
>
> Time is a horse that runs in the heart, a horse
> Without a rider on a road at night.
> The mind sits listening and hears it pass. (289)

For Kermode, fiction represents the mind's effort to harness time and to impart to us the illusion that we are headed somewhere, as we ride on its back toward oblivion. "Fictions meet a need," he writes. "They seem to do what Bacon said poetry could: 'give some show of satisfaction to the mind, wherein the nature of things doth seem to deny it.'" Central to his argument is a sharp distinction between two Greek words for time, *chronos* and *kairos*. The world as a finely calibrated, heartless mechanism—the world as reason takes it to be—is ruled by *chronos*, which measures the endless succession of moments that flow past us with each tick and tock of the clock. This is time as Prufrock and the Compson brothers know it, and it is time as Macbeth and Stevens's riderless horse render it. *Chronos* time has no place for stories of divine love or human salvation, for those are airy fancies spun with words, not hard facts grounded on the rock of reality.[3]

Unlike human reason, which renders time as alien, relentless, and indifferent to human needs, the imagination is able to offer the satisfactions of *kairos*. Following the lead of Oscar Cullmann and others, Kermode considers *kairos* to carry with it a sense of climactic time. It speaks, that is, of a point in time at which something crucial for the whole of time occurs. In the New Testament, it is "a divine decision that makes this or that date a *kairos*, a point of time that has a special place in the execution of God's plan of salvation."[4] Not every segment of ordinary time has redemptive significance, but only those specific moments or points of time—the *kairoi*—that God makes a part of redemptive history.

In the Gospel of Mark, the first saying of Jesus uses *kairos* to announce the decisive turning point of history: "The time is fulfilled, and the kingdom of God has come near; repent, and believe in the good news" (1:15). In the Letter to the Ephesians, Paul employs the term to detail God's plan of redemption made known to us "in the mystery of his will, according to his good pleasure that he set forth in Christ, as a plan for the fullness of time, to gather up all things in him, things in heaven and things on earth" (1:9–10). *Kairos* time is pregnant with meaning, and it represents human experience and history as possessing a God-given, story-shaped form. "Thus we see," explains Cullmann, "that in the past, the present, and the future there are special divine *kairoi*, by the joining of which the redemptive line arises."[5]

Kermode secularizes the concept of *kairos* and applies it to the illusion of meaning that stories create for us. Within the structured orders of fiction, we are enabled to pretend that our profane lives have sacred origins and ends. Situated as we are, "in the *middest* [the midpoint of time's succession], we look for a fullness of time, for beginning, middle, and end in *concord*."[6]

"Concord fictions" provide us with a frame that establishes boundaries for the boundlessness of time as we experience it. Few writers have evoked the disorienting effects of boundless and formless time as hauntingly as Ralph Waldo Emerson does in the opening paragraph of "Experience":

> Where do we find ourselves? In a series of which we do not know the extremes, and believe that it has none. We wake and find ourselves on a stair; there are stairs below us, which we seem to have ascended; there are stairs above us, many a one, which go upward and out of sight. But the Genius which, according to the old belief, stands at the door by which we enter, and gives us the lethe to drink, that we may tell no tales, mixed the cup too strongly, and we cannot shake off the lethargy now at noonday. (471)

We live in a fog of confusion, situated somewhere within a series whose "extremes" we cannot know. So, to bring order to our confusion, we create myths about our origins and fabricate dreams about our ends. For Kermode, these are things we must do if we are to bear the weight of our formless world, but he would have us never lose sight of the fact that the *concord* we discover in our stories is not something established in our lives. After all, significance is something our imagination *makes*, not something our reason *finds*.

Before the modern period, Kermode asserts, it was easy to believe in time's "significance," which was considered to be "a simple property of the interval" between life's sacred origin and its heavenly end. But here in late modernity, where we doubt or deny our divine destiny, the meaning of time seems beyond

Beginning with the Word

our reach. If we are to have meaning, Kermode says, "we have to provide it" for ourselves, and we can do so by means of fiction, with its story-shaped plots and resolutions: "We still need the fullness of it, the *pleroma*; and it is our insatiable interest in the future (towards which we are biologically orientated) that makes it necessary for us to relate to the past, and to the moment in the middle, by plots." In Kermode's vocabulary, all stories that supply our sense of time's fullness are *fictions*, which may shower us with significance but reveal no fruitful connection between our bountiful desires and our arid destinies.[7]

The First and the Last

With this discussion of *chronos* and *kairos*, we return for a final time to Faulkner and *The Sound and the Fury*. In the terms employed by Kermode and embedded in classical myth and Christian history, the beleaguered Compson brothers are creatures of *chronos* who stand helpless in the face of time. Only one major character in the novel understands the fullness of time as *kairos*, and her story is not told until the fourth and final section of the novel. Her name is Dilsey Gibson, and she is an African American woman whose family has served the Compsons for decades. Although Dilsey does not narrate the final section of *The Sound and the Fury*, as the Compson brothers do theirs, she nevertheless serves as its dramatic center.

A suffocating air of confusion permeates the stories the Compson brothers tell, but Dilsey's section is marked by a brisk and bracing lucidity. The difference becomes obvious in the first sentence, whose beginning strikes a note of clarity hitherto unsounded in the novel: "The day dawned bleak and chill, a moving wall of gray light out of the northeast" (265). As the narrator describes the entry to Dilsey's cabin, the reader feels as though he or she has been released from the prison of the Compson mind and returned at last to a solid world rendered on a recognizably human scale: "The earth immediately about the door was bare. It had a patina, as though from the soles of bare feet in generations, like old silver or the walls of Mexican houses which have been plastered by hand" (266).

The contrast between the brothers' narratives and Dilsey's section is striking. Faulkner establishes the opposition through his depiction of an Easter service that Dilsey attends, along with Benjy and members of her own family. Before they leave for church, Benjy sits on the cellar steps, wailing, "again, hopeless and prolonged." It is as though he has tapped into some abysmal cosmic sorrow. "It was nothing. Just sound. It might have been all time and injustice and sorrow become vocal for an instant by a conjunction of planets" (288). On this climactic day of Holy Week, as on every other day of the year, waves of anguish wash over Benjy, and he can only bellow in response, as he struggles against being swept away by the tides of his wordless grief.

The guest preacher for Easter is the famed Reverend Shegog, who delivers a mesmerizing sermon on "the recollection and the blood of the Lamb" (294). Shegog's sermon moves from the exodus from Egypt to the "blastin, blindin sight" of Calvary: "I hears de weepin en de cryin en de turnt-away face of God: dey done kilt Jesus; dey done kilt my Son!" The Reverend says that he "can see de widowed God shet His do," just as he "sees de whelmin flood roll between" and "de darkness en de death everlasting upon de generations" (296). And what is the final thing Reverend Shegog spies on the horizon? "What I see? Whut I see, O sinner? I sees de resurrection en de light; sees de meek Jesus saying Dey kilt me dat ye shall live again. . . . I sees de doom crack en de golden horns shoutin down de glory, en de arisen dead whut got de blood en de ricklickshun of de Lamb!" (297).

Carried along by a chorus of voices calling out their praise and buoyed by a crowd of swaying hands and bodies, "Ben sat, rapt in his sweet blue gaze. Dilsey sat bolt upright beside, crying rigidly and quietly in the annealment and the blood of the remembered Lamb." As they walk home after the service, Dilsey's daughter Frony is embarrassed by her mother's tears and asks her to stop crying because "we be passin white folks soon." Dilsey's response is simple and all-encompassing: "I've seed de first en de last. Never you mind me." When Frony asks, "First and last what?" Dilsey replies, "Never you mind. I seed de beginnin, en now I sees de endin" (297).

By means of this Easter service, Faulkner traces a path out of the maze in which the members of the Compson family seem to wander endlessly. The sermon Shegog preaches and the faith Dilsey professes anticipate a miraculous future in which men, women, and children "will hunger no more, and thirst no more; . . . and God will wipe away every tear from their eyes" (Rev. 7:16–17). It is one thing, however, to admire such a vision from a distance, another thing entirely to embrace it as one's own. As far as Shegog's densely textured Christian understanding is concerned, Faulkner remains on the outside looking in, for he "makes no claim for Dilsey's version of Christianity one way or the other." Yet at the same time, he finds it "moving and credible" as an expression of our longing to be freed from our misery and mortality.[8]

The blend of admiration and skepticism that marks Faulkner's attitude toward Christianity relates to the key distinction Kermode makes between myth and fiction. For the theorist, fictions are illusions in which we take comfort even as we recognize them to be illusions, while myths are fictions whose origins we have forgotten or repressed. (Remember Wallace Stevens's definition of "final belief": "The exquisite truth is to know that it is a fiction and that you believe in it willingly.") In Kermode's terms, Dilsey and Shegog live with the false assurances of myth, while Quentin is denied even the fleeting consolations of fiction. Fictions survive and prosper on the narrow ground between mindless belief and mindful unbelief. Like Stevens, Faulkner takes fictions to be useful "for finding things out, and they change as needs of sense-making change. . . . Myths call for absolute, fictions for conditional assent." Myths dream about a lost wholeness or a promised glory, but fictions seek only to "make sense of the here and now."[9]

As useful as they may be to academicians and aesthetes, fictions as Kermode defines them would have been luxuries Reverend Shegog and his congregation could not afford. With the exception of Benjy Compson, all the worshipers at Dilsey's church would have been former slaves and their descendants. They would have experienced bondage as a fact or known it as a tangible memory in their families' lives. Their parents and grandparents had recounted the sorrows of slavery in story and song, and its legacy remained palpable in the Jim Crow laws of the segregated South. For Dilsey and the others who heard that Easter sermon, the story of the crucifixion and resurrection of Jesus Christ resonated with the whole of their experience, as it recapitulated that experience and placed it within a story of redemption and release.

In Reverend Shegog's sermon and in their worship, Dilsey's black church was sustaining (in the late 1920s) a tradition of suffering, longing, and hope established more than a century before in the slave culture of the antebellum South. For the slaves of that day, as for Shegog and the worshipers of a later era, the resurrection of Jesus built upon a foundation and followed a pattern set long before by the exodus of the Israelites from Egypt. Both were stories of bondage and deliverance, and in them, African American slaves found a way to appropriate a promise of liberation and the prospect of freedom in God. In the words of Albert Raboteau, as they identified with the Exodus narrative, the slaves "created meaning and purpose out of the chaotic and senseless experience of slavery. . . . The sacred history of God's liberation of his people would be or was being repeated in the American South."[10]

The move the slaves undertook, to tie the events of Israel's suffering and deliverance to the drama of the crucifixion and resurrection, had clear precedents in Christian history. For as Colin Gunton argues, the church has long believed that with the crucifixion and resurrection of Christ, "the promise God made to Abraham, on which the meaning of history depends, has been fulfilled." In the "justifying action" of "the life, death and resurrection of Jesus, all significant human groupings, Jews first and then Gentiles, have been together brought into the community of praise." Citing Romans 8:21—"the creation itself will be set free from its bondage to corruption and obtain the freedom of the glory of the children of God"—Gunton explains that Christian hope encompasses the suffering that sets Benjy to wailing, for that suffering is not "a foretaste of death" but resembles instead "the suffering of a woman about to give birth, a promise and foretaste of life."[11]

To affirm an intimate connection between suffering and deliverance, as St. Paul and Gunton do, is also to claim that the record of God's faithfulness constitutes a story, in which he reveals himself to be a forgiving Lord who suffers alongside his people and pledges to set them free. To speak of life's sacred origin, its meaningful duration, and its holy end is to trust in the promises made by the One who raised Jesus from the dead. "Do not fear," says the One "who created you, O Jacob" and "who formed you, O Israel":

> For I have redeemed you;
> I have called you by name, you are mine.
> When you pass through the waters, I will be with you;
>   and through the rivers, they shall not overwhelm you;
> when you walk through fire you shall not be burned,
>   and the flame shall not consume you.
> For I am the LORD your God,
>   the Holy One of Israel, your Savior. (Isa. 43:1–3)

The *end*—the telos—for which the Holy One has created us "is life and not death," writes Gunton. "The Spirit who hovered over the face of the waters of creation and raised Jesus from the tomb is indeed the bearer of eschatological life," and it is the crucified and risen Christ who will speak the last word about the meaning of creation. Our private dramas and public spectacles, as well as the vast cosmic theater in which we play them out, all "will take their final meaning from the one who entered history" as a child two thousand years ago and now reigns as the "crucified man [who] will one day return to sum up all things, things in heaven and things on earth."[12]

As it weaves together remembrance and promise, a Christian narrative of redemption makes truth-claims of a kind that the fictions of Kermode could never countenance. As he and Wallace Stevens conceive of them, fictions are therapeutic agents that provide a way of coping with the burdens of what the eighteenth-century naturalist the Comte de Buffon called "the dark abyss of time." Paul Ricoeur finds in Kermode a Nietzschean suspicion that fiction is a "form of trickery" meant to console us in the face of death. "A divorce is thus established between truthfulness and consolation," he writes, and this leaves Kermode "ceaselessly oscillat[ing] between the inescapable suspicion

Beginning with the Word

that fictions lie and deceive, to the extent that they console us" and an "equally invincible conviction that fictions are not simply arbitrary, inasmuch as they respond to a need over which we are not masters, the need to impress the stamp of order upon the chaos of existence."[13]

Fictions are sanctioned in Kermode's Nietzschean world because they cast a flickering fool's light (Dickinson's *ignis fatuus*) into the abyss and let us live, briefly, with the illusion that the darkness has been dispelled forever. But we face great trouble if we forget that our consolations are fictions and then begin to believe the lies we tell. If we ever come, for example, to believe that a real and divine "light shines in the darkness, and the darkness has never mastered it" (John 1:5), that means our fictions have hardened into myths, and we have deceived ourselves. In pressing this argument, Kermode is hardly alone, for like the arbitrariness of word and thing, the distinction between myth and fiction has become a theoretical given of contemporary cultural criticism.

Philosopher Louis Mink makes the implications of this distinction clear in an essay on fiction and historical understanding. In that work, he criticizes claims made by literary critic Barbara Hardy, who argues that "narrative, like lyric or dance, is not to be regarded as an aesthetic invention used by artists to control, manipulate and order experience, but as a primary act of mind transferred to art from life." Fiction does not invent meaning out of whole cloth but "merely" heightens and analyzes "the narrative motions of human consciousness." Narrative, Hardy says, is a natural part of the human experience, and its order is not something we force upon an otherwise chaotic experience: "Inner and outer storytelling . . . plays a major role in our sleeping and waking lives. For we dream in narrative, daydream in narrative, remember, anticipate, hope, despair, doubt, plan, revise, criticize, construct, gossip, learn, hate, and love by narrative."[14]

Mink thinks Hardy has it wrong because on its own and in itself, life possesses neither an intrinsic order nor a storied form. "Stories are not lived but told," Mink asserts, for "life has no beginnings, middles, or ends." Affairs begin and partings unfold, but only in the stories we create and not in the lives we lead. Hopes and plans exist, as do battles and ideas, "but only in retrospective stories" do we find our hopes fulfilled or discover out battles to have been decisive. "So," Mink concludes, "it seems truer to say that narrative qualities are transferred from art to life."[15] This is, once again, the story of the arbitrary relationship of word and thing, as we have heard it being made by everyone from Rorty and Saussure to Stevens and Kermode.

In *After Virtue*, Alasdair MacIntyre directly challenges this line of thought. "What are we to say to this?" he asks concerning Mink's claim that life has neither beginnings nor endings. "To someone who says that in life there are no endings, or that final partings take place only in stories, one is tempted to reply, 'But have you never heard of death?'" MacIntyre's own "central thesis" is that in our actions, as well as our fictions, we humans are essentially "story-telling animals." Through our histories, we become storytellers who "aspire to truth," and the only way we can begin to think about how we should act is to answer the question, "Of what story or stories do I find myself a part?" We enter our conscious lives with imputed characters—"roles into which we have been drafted"—and we must learn what those are before we can begin to learn what we are to do. "Deprive children of stories," he explains, "and you leave them unscripted, anxious stutterers in their actions as in their words."[16]

As a Catholic philosopher, MacIntyre states here in general terms a point that Hans Urs von Balthasar elaborates in a more theologically explicit manner in his *Theology of History*. The crux of Balthasar's argument is that the only thing that makes history possible, in all its storied variety and complexity, is the space created by "an opening within the utter freedom of God." This divine freedom in turn grants "space and scope" to human freedom, but since the space "belongs to Christ," we should not consider it to be empty. Instead, it is "shaped and structured and completely conditioned by certain categories." We cannot "fall out of this space which is Christ's, nor out of the structural form created by his life."[17]

To Balthasar, the implications of this are clear for our understanding of stories. Each of us is born within a narrative framework established by the freedom, judgment, and mercy of Jesus Christ. We do indeed wake to "find ourselves on a stair," as Emerson heartbreakingly observes, but it is not that the "series" of human experience has no "extremes"—no purposeful beginning or end. Instead, "all existences, both before him and after him, receive their meaning from Christ's existence." We are not random threads in an unraveling universe, but we are instead people whose "destinies are interwoven; and until the last of us has lived, the significance of the first cannot be finally clear."[18] Or in the terms of moral philosophy, as MacIntyre argues:

> I spoke earlier of the agent as not only an actor, but an author. Now I must emphasize that what the agent is able to do and say intelligibly as an actor is deeply affected by the fact that we are never more (and sometimes less) than the co-authors of our own narratives. Only in fantasy do we live what story we please. In life, as both Aristotle and Engels noted, we are always under certain constraints. We enter upon a stage which we did not design and we find ourselves part of an action that was not of our making. Each of us being a main character

in his own drama plays subordinate parts in the dramas of others, and each drama constrains the others.[19]

If we are to consider our lives as being contained within the "structural form" created by the life, death, and resurrection of Jesus Christ, we must swim against the currents of late modernity, for on the question of human identity, modern thought flows in a single direction, out to the boundless sea of self-constituting freedom. Liberty for us in the modern world means not only freedom of choice but also freedom of framework; we believe in our right to create the context, write the story, and determine the ends of our experience. With good reason, political philosopher Michael Sandel identifies "the idea that freedom consists in the right to choose our own ends" as an unarguable assumption of modern "politics and law. Its province is not limited to those known as liberals rather than conservatives in American politics; it can be found across the political spectrum."[20]

In theological terms, we have become thoroughgoing Arminians, in that we believe that human dignity requires an unfettered freedom of the will. In turn, that conviction goes hand-in-hand with a belief in the essential neutrality—or outright innocence—of that will. Almost two centuries ago, for example, Alexis de Tocqueville sought to explain "how democracy suggests to the Americans the idea of man's infinite perfectibility." He pictured the democratic citizen marching "indefatigably on toward the immense grandeur that he can but dimly make out at the end of the long road that mankind has yet to travel."[21] In the words of a great romantic poem from the early twentieth century—William Butler Yeats's "A Prayer for My Daughter"—this self-constituting individual is a "self-delighting" person who is free to seize the "radical innocence" that is her birthright:

> Considering that, all hatred driven hence,
> The soul recovers radical innocence
> And learns at last that it is self-delighting,
> Self-appeasing, self-affrighting,
> And that its own sweet will is Heaven's will;
> She can, though every face should scowl
> And every windy quarter howl
> Or every bellows burst, be happy still. (92)

The romantic belief that we are free to choose our own ends is a reality of our cultural lives, just as it is a touchstone of our political theories and economic systems. This is a development whose broad implications Christians need not resist out of hand and cannot overturn in toto. Even if we sought to dispense with self-determining freedom, we would do so as people already powerfully shaped by the ideal. Half a century ago, literary critic Robert Langbaum rightly observed that even those who arrive at what they take to be an objective position on matters of truth and values "do not reverse but fulfill the direction of romantic thought." This is the case because any intellectual or moral position "remains within the romantic tradition as long as it has been chosen." For the distinguishing mark of the "romanticist . . . is the subjective ground of his commitment, the fact that he never forgets his commitment has been chosen."[22]

What Sandel and Langbaum argue is undeniably true about our experience, but it is not, as MacIntyre argues, the whole of the story. Those "certain constraints" of which he speaks and the "structural form" that Balthasar describes cannot be dismissed or destroyed. The drama of our lives does not begin or end with us. We may improvise within our parts and contribute our bit to the script, but what we can do with our role remains circumscribed. That is another way of saying that before we can know who we are, we first must learn who we have been and imagine what we might become.

The Compson brothers have no context for their self-understanding— Benjy because he cannot comprehend the meaning of time and the difference between words and things, Quentin because he is overwhelmed by time and sees nothing but a vast gap between words and things, and Jason because his self-absorption enslaves time. Only Dilsey can stand back and see her own suffering and the Compsons' folly as belonging within the story of "the first and the last" that is being told by the Alpha and Omega who is "the author and finisher of our faith" (Heb. 12:2 KJV).

"Time is God's way of keeping things from happening all at once," observes an anonymous graffito spotted not long ago by the English cosmologist John Barrow. For Dilsey, faith provides a saving means of keeping time's distinctions straight and her hope intact, but for the Compson brothers, things do indeed appear to "happen all at once." In their lives, past and present events race through their minds as a series of immediate impressions, with past, present, and future all blended together as an indistinguishable present. In contrast, Gunton suggests that if we are to understand time, we must accept that we cannot possess the world in its fullness *now*. Wisdom prods us to recognize "the limits of human agency" as well as the futility of seeking to have "things happen all at once." Within the "structural form" provided by the lordship of Jesus Christ, the present is a gift from the past that comes to us "through Christ and the Spirit" and is drawn "to its true end" by God, the maker of heaven and earth and the creator and redeemer of time.[23]

Gathering Up the Past

"The aim of creation is history," writes Karl Barth at the beginning of his treatment of the doctrine of creation. "This follows decisively from the fact that God the Creator is the triune God who acts and reveals Himself in history." God has created the world and all who dwell within it "for the sake of his Son or Word and therefore in harmony with Himself; and for His own supreme glory and therefore in the Holy Spirit." Both the doing of these things and the recording of them constitute what we know as "history. What is meant is the history of the covenant of grace instituted by God between Himself and man; the sequence of the events in which God concludes and executes this covenant with man." In Barth's words, "from all eternity" God has determined to reconcile himself to the world through Jesus Christ. And this means that he has willed the centrality of history, which Barth defines as "the sequence of the events for the sake of which God has patience with the creature and with its creation gives it time—time which acquires content through these events and which is finally to be 'fulfilled' and made ripe for its end by their conclusion. This history is from the theological standpoint *the* history" (*CD*, III.1.59).

To Barth, the urge to find patterns within history and evidence of God within nature remained secondary to the primary reality of God's covenant. God created the cosmos for the sake of his covenantal relationship with us, and "the object of heaven and earth and all creation . . . is to be the theater of His glory."[24] The "theater" imagery comes from Calvin, and for Barth it means that creation's purpose is not intrinsic to it as a quality but imparted to it as a gift. The universe is good *because* it is the theater within which God's glory is enacted and proclaimed. In the drama of that glory, we serve both as audience and as actors.

In key respects, Barth's Reformed view of human and divine ends dovetails with MacIntyre's Catholic defense of story. Both see narrativity as a structured reality of the created order, with MacIntyre working out of natural theology and Barth relying on Christology to arrive at this conclusion. In a perceptive recent study, William Dowling describes how Paul Ricoeur, a French Protestant, arrives at a parallel conclusion without recourse to specific Christian assumptions. For Ricoeur, the key is Aristotle's theory of dramatic *catharsis*, that purging of pity and terror brought about by our having accompanied a tragic hero through the process that leads to his or her moment of *anagnorisis* (recognition).

According to Ricoeur, the experience of catharsis and recognition discloses the *teleological* structure of narrative. To explain what the philosopher means by this, Dowling offers the example of reading *Pride and Prejudice*. As we read, we move forward along with Elizabeth and Darcy "as they proceed through a long series of misunderstandings and willful misprisons." The difference between us and them, however, is that as readers we understand that we are in the hands of a narrator who knows the story's end, the *telos* toward which it is moving. In the words of Dowling, "*Telos* thus becomes a movement toward that moment of *anagnorisis* or recognition when those following the story will have revealed to them what the narrator has known from the outset."[25] In theologically explicit terms, John Paul II defines history as "the arena where we see what God does for humanity." The plot is there for all to see and read:

> Now, in Christ, all have access to the Father, since by his Death and Resurrection Christ has bestowed the divine life which the first Adam had refused (cf. Rom. 5:12–15). Through this Revelation, men and women are offered the ultimate truth about their own life and about the goal of history. As the Constitution *Gaudium et Spes* puts it, "only in the mystery of the incarnate Word does the mystery of man take on light." Seen in any other terms, the mystery of personal existence remains an insoluble riddle. Where might the human being seek the answer to dramatic questions such as pain, the suffering of the innocent and death, if not in the light streaming from the mystery of Christ's Passion, Death and Resurrection?[26]

Catholic and Protestant views of narrative have much in common, but we ought not overlook a key distinction between them on the relationship between nature and grace. Pope John Paul II offers a forceful summary of the Catholic understanding of that relationship. "Thomas [Aquinas]," he writes, "had the great merit of giving pride of place to the harmony which exists between faith and reason." Because both come from God, they cannot be thought to be in contradiction. "Faith therefore has no fear of reason," the Pope explains, for "just as grace builds on nature and brings it to fulfillment, so faith builds upon and perfects reason." The pattern here is one of initiation and completion, with nature and reason mapping the initial stages of the journey to truth, until grace and revelation step in to provide the guidance and sustenance needed by the mind and soul if they are to reach their destined end in God.[27]

Barth draws a sharp distinction between such an understanding and his own, as he focuses on what we might call the sequential order of creation and covenant. As we have seen, Barth posits as the foundation of creation the decision made by God from all eternity to reconcile humanity to himself through Jesus Christ. According to Keith L. Johnson, this commitment entails a reversal of the Roman Catholic view, and for Barth "there can be no true knowledge of God or the human through reflection upon human existence or the created order in and of itself." Barth argues that what humans are *intrinsically* remains always a function of their *extrinsic* relation to God in Jesus Christ. Only through the revelation of Christ can the relationship of human nature and divine order be understood.[28] "What *we* consider to be the truth about the created world is one thing," explains Barth. "Quite another is the covenant of grace, the work of Jesus Christ, for the sake and in fulfillment of which creation exists as it is" (*CD*, III.1.370).

To Barth, human life and the created order have a narrative arc because God has imparted to them a storied order through his acts of creation, redemption, and reconciliation, all of which he has accomplished through the work of Jesus Christ, the incarnate Word. Of time in particular, Barth says it is "not a something" alongside other things, a "creature with other creatures." Instead, time is "a form of all the reality distinct from God, posited with it, and therefore a real form of its being and nature." Time is nothing less than "the form of the created world" that God has "ordained to be the field for the acts of God." There is no such thing as "time in itself, rivaling God and imposing conditions on Him," Barth concludes. "There is no god called Chronos. And it is better to avoid conceptions of time which might suggest that there is" (*CD*, III.2.438, 456).

As the *theater* of God's glory and the *field* in which God acts, time as an ordering of reality has a spatial dimension as well as a temporal core. The metaphors of theater and field provide the space in which the drama of creation and covenant can be acted out to its eschatological end. Yet as the Compson brothers discover, it can be terrifying to consider that drama from the vantage point of the present, a place Barth describes as being "midway between the vanished" past and the "unknown future" that awaits us. With both past and future lying beyond our ken, "what is our present but a step from darkness to darkness?" Unless we have recourse to "secret borrowings from theology" or choose to live by illusions, there is no way for us to think hopefully about the lostness of the past, the uncertainty of the future, and the evanescence of the present. If we work out of the framework of a general picture of the human condition, Barth argues, we will always come up against the riddling and ruthless limits of human temporality. Quentin Compson and J. Alfred Prufrock know this to be true, as do Frank Kermode and Steven Weinberg (*CD*, III.2.513–14).

For Barth, Jesus Christ provides no line of escape from time. On the contrary, only "the existence of the man Jesus in time is our guarantee that time" is willed, created, and given to humans by God. This alone makes time "real." Because Jesus Christ entered and suffered in the stream of time, time is not "the abyss of our non-being, however perverted and corrupt we may be in it" (*CD*, III.2.520–21). Instead, it is the God-given form of our existence, and because of the Incarnation and the covenant, our past is not lost, our future is secure, and our present is steeped in the storied significance of salvation history. "The existence of the man Jesus means that God became man, the Creator a creature, eternity time. It means, therefore, that God takes and has time for us; that He Himself is temporal among us as we are" (CD, III.2.519).

Barth's emphasis on the christological nature of time received a forceful reiteration by Dietrich Bonhoeffer in a letter written to Eberhard Bethge in December 1943. In that letter, the imprisoned pastor speaks openly of the intense homesickness he has felt during his first months in jail. After detailing the steps he has used to fight against loneliness and lethargy, Bonhoeffer says that above all, he refuses to give way to self-pity, and he does so by affirming "that this poor earth is not our own."[29]

Yet as soon as he has quoted this line from a hymn, Bonhoeffer says that while "that is indeed something essential, . . . it must come last of all." In the meantime, he tells Bethge, "I believe that we ought so to love and trust God in our *lives*, and in all the good things that he sends us, that when the time comes (but not before!) we may go to him with love, trust, and joy." Until then, "to put it plainly, for a man in his wife's arms to be hankering after the other world is, in mild terms, a piece of bad taste, and not God's will." Instead of spurning the blessings and pleasures of the present moment, setting them at naught in light of heavenly glory, "we ought to find and love God in what he actually gives us." We ought not to reject a present happiness in the name of a future sorrow, for to do so is simply to try "to be more pious than God." Bonhoeffer quotes Ecclesiastes 3, with its well-known "to everything there is a season" passage, and concludes with the assertion, "God seeks again what is past." He tells Bethge he suspects these final words "mean that nothing that is past is lost, that God gathers up again with us our past, which belongs to us." Because God does so, when we are seized by a longing for our lost past, we can be sure that these "hours" are what "God is always holding ready for us." In turn, we ought not to seek the past through our own efforts but only with God.[30]

Although he writes at this point, "enough of this," it is clear that Bonhoeffer is not finished with this theme, which he picks up again as he completes the letter the following day. He reports to Bethge that two lines from a Paul Gerhardt hymn have continued to run through his mind during his imprisonment: "Let pass, dear brothers, every pain; / What you have missed I'll bring again." That nothing is ever lost in Christ—these are words of comfort to the imprisoned pastor, who is also a son, a brother, and a fiancé. Everything is "taken up in Christ," and "it is transformed" in the process, made clear and free of sin and selfishness. "Christ restores all this as God originally intended

Beginning with the Word

it to be, without the distortion resulting from our sins." Bonhoeffer finds the sources of this doctrine of "the restoration of all things" in the first chapter of Ephesians and in the second-century theology of Irenaeus of Lyons. It is, he concludes, "a magnificent conception, full of comfort. This is how the promise 'God seeks what has been driven away' is fulfilled."[31]

Irenaeus appropriated a term from Greek rhetoric to develop this crucial theological concept. The word was *anakephalaiosis*, which is the summary or recapitulation to be delivered near the end of a story or an argument. (Its only use in the New Testament occurs in Eph. 1:10.) As it was employed in speeches, the process involved giving a synopsis of everything important that had transpired to that point in the account. By rehearsing the details of the argument at the close, the speaker sought to give the details a richer texture and to cast them in the light of the argument's conclusion.

To Irenaeus, Christ is the "summary" of the "argument" that God has been developing in his covenantal relationship with the human race since the fall of Adam and Eve. Working with a theme outlined by Paul in Romans 5, Irenaeus says that just as sin and death entered the world through the disobedience of one man (Adam), so too through the obedience of one man (Christ) did justice and life become established as the destiny for the fallen race of humans. As the first Adam was formed from the virgin soil of the earth, so too was the second Adam born of Mary:

> Therefore the Lord acknowledged himself as Son of man, recapitulating in himself that primal man from whom the formation of the woman was made, so that as through the defeated many our race went down to death, so again through man the victor we might ascend into life, and as death won the prize over us by a man, so again by a man we might win the prize over death.[32]

As it was first outlined by Irenaeus and then incorporated in Christian doctrine over the course of several centuries, the doctrine of recapitulation revolutionized the view of history the early church inherited from classical culture and the ancient world. In the form that Homer established and Greek and Roman culture later elaborated on, the epic tradition had bequeathed a cyclical view of history to late antiquity. The gods of Greek mythology are legion, but in the welter of their competing and conflicting actions, it is impossible to detect anything like a single, overarching divine purpose or promise. In Homer's epic, all that matters to Odysseus, and all that he can hope to accomplish, is to return home, to go back to where he started, after twenty years of suffering, strife, and survival. "The world of Homer is unbearably sad," says W. H. Auden, "because it never transcends the immediate present.

One is happy, one is unhappy, one wins, one loses, finally ones dies. That is all." Blessings and sufferings come and go, but they never point beyond themselves or hint of a meaning, or glory, yet to be revealed. Homer's world is "a tragic world but a world without guilt for its tragic flaw is not a flaw in human nature, still less a flaw in an individual character, but a flaw in the nature of existence."[33]

The early church sought to counter such fatalism vigorously, and according to Hans Urs von Balthasar, Irenaeus offered the earliest comprehensive challenge to the classical vision. "Irenaeus's work marks the birth of Christian theology," he argues. Before Irenaeus, little more than an "amorphous" form of paganism had challenged the Christian mission on intellectual grounds. But then "Gnosis, which, largely with the tools and materials of the Bible, had erected a totally un-Christian structure of the highest intellectual and religious quality and won over many Christians."[34]

Gnosticism created a chasm between creation and redemption, and more forcefully than any other early church theologian, Irenaeus set out to bridge the gap. With its emphasis upon the unity of God's activity throughout history, the doctrine of recapitulation provided him with a means of reaffirming the ties between the first Adam and the second Adam, Jesus Christ, and it also connected the lost Eden with the promised New Jerusalem. As Father, as Son, and as Holy Spirit, the same God has been at work within and throughout the history of the created order. Having created all things through the Word, he overcame the fall, not by returning us to the perfection of the past, but by transforming us through his love and his promises for the future; in the Son, he became flesh and suffered a shameful death on the cross, and through the Spirit, he raised that same Jesus from the dead; through the work of the Spirit, God will complete the redemption of all things and reconcile us to himself.

The story of God's recapitulating power places a strong emphasis on the diversity of divine actions in the drama of creation, fall, redemption, and reconciliation. Through the concept of the *economic* Trinity, early church fathers such as Ignatius, Clement, and Origen were able to stress the unity that underlay that diversity. "By means of his trinitarian conception of the divine economy, Irenaeus was able to allow history to be itself, by virtue of its very relation to God," writes Gunton. "Time and space are given their distinctive dynamic of interrelatedness by God's creating, upholding, redeeming and perfecting activity."[35]

In giving meaning to the sweep of human history even as it grants that history the right "to be itself," Irenaeus's trinitarian vision balances the providence of God with the freedom of human action and upholds both the primacy of eternity and the integrity of time. In Gunton, we come again upon an image

Beginning with the Word

that has become familiar to us, and that is of God as an author or play-wright. God writes the story of history, leaving latitude to human freedom, while promising deliverance from humanity's self-imposed bondage. God accomplishes this task by becoming a character—a suffering character—in the drama he is writing and directing. Thus, as he responds to a rebellious human race and undertakes the work of reconciliation, God does so "in such a way as to allow the characters to develop according to its [the world's] and their intrinsic logic."[36]

History is the theater of God's glory in which the possibilities of that logic unfold, and the drama that develops proves to be a mysterious mix of purpose-ful providence and improvisational freedom. To be certain, it can be difficult at any particular time to gain a clear sense of the direction in which the drama is headed, and frustration can readily set in, as we wait and wonder when, and whether, God will "restore it all." The Wisdom literature of the Bible bears ample witness to the suffering tenacity of God's servants, as they struggle to divine his will and detect his mercy. "How long, O LORD?" the psalmist asks:

> Will you forget me forever?
> How long will you hide your face from me?
> How long must I bear pain in my soul,
> and have sorrow in my heart all day long?
> How long shall my enemy be exalted over me? (13:1–2)

At this point, it may be wise to remind ourselves of what Hans-Georg Gadamer says about the relationship between suffering and wisdom. We re-member that he spoke of a "fundamental negativity" that each of us encounters in life. This negativity always involves the thwarting of expectations, and it points to the intimate relationship between experience and insight. Through our sufferings, we learn "not this or that particular thing," but we acquire instead "insight into the limitations of humanity, into the absoluteness of the barrier that separates man from the divine."[37] Through suffering and reversal, we learn how little we can predict or control in the course of our own lives, let alone in the collective wonder and misery of history. For as MacIntyre reminds us, it is "only in fantasy" that "we live what story we please." Each of our lives is "always under certain constraints," as we play our parts "upon a stage . . . we did not design" in a drama "that was not of our making."[38]

This brings me to a final word about my own experience of learning those limits. In the opening chapters of this book, the death of my brother figured significantly in my discussion of modern theories of language and their com-plex relationship to historic Christianity. Although I clearly had no idea of this at the time of Gordy's death, the loss of my brother set me on a path that would lead to a lifetime of thinking about the relationship of the word and the thing. My efforts to summon my brother came to naught, no matter how often I sounded his name. I was beginning to acquire wisdom and to understand the sometimes dizzying complexity of the connections between language and my life. As the logic of that life unfolded through a series of twists, turns, and meanderings, it took a great deal of time for me to grasp what it meant that the Word had become flesh and dwelt among us. Through my belief in the mercy of the cross and the power of the empty tomb, I found myself drawn into a story vastly larger and incredibly longer than my own journey of three score and ten or so years promised to be. To trust in the crucified and risen Christ meant to believe that the longing to see the word and the thing made one again is not an idle fantasy but a grounded hope. For even though now we may "know only in part," then we will come to know fully, even as we "have been fully known" (1 Cor. 13:12).

7

Defending a Great Hope

The Word and the Thing Become One

so much depends
upon

a red wheel
barrow

glazed with rain
water

beside the white
chickens.
—William Carlos Williams,
"so much depends"

If one day our words
Come so close to the bark of trees in the forest,
And to orange blossoms, that they become one with them,
It will mean that we have always defended a great hope.
—Czeslaw Milosz, "An Appeal"

For several generations, English students have regaled themselves by writing parodies or spinning overblown analyses of an unusually brief and deceptively simple poem by William Carlos Williams, one of the foremost American poets of the modernist era. I remember joining in the fun decades ago on a car ride with two fellow graduate students, as we constructed a series of intricate, arcane, and absurd interpretations of the bare assertion that "so much depends" upon a wheelbarrow, some rain water, and a few chickens (46). We had a great time poking fun at the pretensions of poetry and the gassy garrulity that we, as fledgling critics, were learning to use. Williams seemed to be an easy target, for in another poem we had read that semester, he had announced:

> It is difficult
> to get the news from poems
>   yet men die miserably every day
>   for lack
> of what is found there. ("Asphodel," 146)

Such a claim may sound like a case of special pleading on behalf of an activity most of us would have little to say about. Noting that the poem was written shortly after the end of the Second World War, critic David Bromwich says its "mood of hope qualified by anxiety" can be found in other poems written at that time. As an example, he cites lines written by Wallace Stevens in the middle of the war—"How simply the fictive hero becomes the real; / How gladly with proper words the soldier dies, / If he must, or lives on the bread of faithful speech"—and takes the metaphor to imply somewhat defensively that the poet's wartime task was as crucial as that of the soldier. "Both Stevens and Williams were too old then to serve as actual soldiers," he concludes, "and their hopes for poetry were uneasily linked to a distant pride in those who risked their lives."[1]

If Bromwich is right about this, and I suspect he is, there may be something to Williams's boasts on behalf of poetry. After all, in referring earlier to Alasdair MacIntyre, I made a related point, which was that in our understanding of language and our reading of life's meaning, so much depends, not upon a red wheelbarrow, but upon the context that envelops and embeds each of our actions, memories, and hopes. We can only tell what to make of any fact of our lives or any event in our experience, by asking a prior question, in MacIntyre's words: "Of what story or stories do I find myself a part?"

In this chapter and the next, I will be arguing that when it comes to stories, so much also depends on what we make of the fiction-myth distinction that Frank Kermode, Wallace Stevens, and many others in our day appear to take as a given. That distinction matters because it registers dramatic changes in the way that the question of religious belief has been framed over the past

Beginning with the Word

two centuries. This shift is hinted at in a tantalizing passage from a letter Emily Dickinson wrote late in life. "On subjects of which we know nothing, or should I say *Beings*—," the poet says, "we both believe, and disbelieve a hundred times an Hour, which keeps Believing nimble."[2]

With this piquant observation, Dickinson captures the feel of a new dynamic of religious belief that emerged suddenly in the cultures of the North Atlantic in the middle of the nineteenth century. In a matter of decades, open unbelief became a widespread, socially acceptable, and intellectually respectable phenomenon. We can feel the consequences of this unbelief at work in such great writers as Dickinson, Herman Melville, and Fyodor Dostoevsky. Their stories, novels, poems, and self-descriptions convey an intimate awareness of how readily the modern mind can shuttle back and forth between the poles of belief and affirmation on one side and unbelief and negation on the other.

These writers and others from the late modern period bear witness to a revolutionary shift in the struggle over religious creeds and theological systems. Through all of Christian history, from the first century to the nineteenth, orthodoxy had considered itself to be in competition with other systems of belief, from the paganism of the late Roman Empire to Islam in the late Middle Ages. There were also, of course, pitched battles within the Christian tradition, first between the Roman Church and the Eastern Church leading to the schism of the eleventh century, and then in the explosive proliferation of denominations brought about during and after the Reformation of the sixteenth century.

Yet as long as the conflict proved to be one between Christianity and other religious systems or among factions of the Christian church itself, the pattern of the struggle remained clear. Battles took place between warring church bodies, and the opponents knew each other as distinct social, political, and ecclesiastical entities, and as advocates of specific theological systems or creeds.

The ground began to shift, however, with the internalization of belief that began in the Reformation and progressed with ever-greater speed during the Enlightenment and with the rise of religious toleration. By the time romanticism emerged at the end of the eighteenth century, the move inward had become all but complete, as universal characteristics of the human mind and spirit were called on to sustain the faith, now that its historical sources seemed weakened and suspect.

The romantic citadel of the self, however, was not able to provide stability or security for long. The Darwinian theory of natural selection had no need of a conscious, divine power to explain the origin, intricacy, or destiny of life. Instead, it offered an alternative narrative for the whole of natural history and human development, replete with a comprehensive material explanation of human origins and destiny.

One crucial consequence of this material narrative has been to establish and secure a comprehensive alternative to all providential accounts of life's meaning, so that even when we stand in the heart of belief, we sense there is nearby another vantage point from which nature and our experience might look entirely different. Consider, for instance, the implications of the narrative of material explanation for a person who has come to a point of belief after a long period of unbelief. Even the most fervent convert will realize that he or she is free to choose to return to unbelief and find within its precincts a sweeping account of the origin, growth, decline, and destiny of humans. Thus, to be a modern believer is to recognize that in the deepest personal sense, belief is optional; whatever an individual can accept and affirm, he or she is also free to reject and deny—and to do so in the twinkling of an eye.

"The Giant in the Human Heart was never met outside," Dickinson once wrote to a friend, describing brilliantly what belief and its struggles have felt like to many men and women of the past two centuries.[3] For one who is modern in this sense, the distinction between myth and fiction is neither fixed nor final because the desiring and reflective self finds itself torn between the security of belief and the plausible viability of unbelief. And this is not a struggle with powers and principalities outside the self and across the world. Instead, it is a battle with the "Giant in the Human Heart," who has no plans to let that heart rest in the comforting assurances of myth or delight in the ironic complacencies of fiction.

In the Steps of Jack Gladney

Near the end of Don DeLillo's bitingly ironic yet heartbreakingly moving 1985 novel *White Noise*, we come upon a conversation between a wounded man and a nun delegated to care for him. The man is Jack Gladney, the chair of Hitler Studies at College-on-the-Hill, and the nun is a blunt woman with the hefty Germanic name of Sister Hermann Marie.

Although Jack Gladney professes no religious beliefs, he is an erstwhile seeker. On the wall of the trauma room in which Sister Hermann dresses his wounds hangs a picture of John F. Kennedy and Pope John XXIII holding hands in heaven, which is depicted as "a partly cloudy place." The picture makes Jack feel "sentimentally refreshed," and he fishes for a word of assurance from his caregiving nun: "What does the Church say about heaven today? Is it still the old heaven, like that, in the sky?" (302).

"Do you think we are stupid?" is her surprising reply. Baffled by this response, Jack asks what heaven is, "if it isn't the abode of God and the angels and the souls of those who are saved?" Sister Hermann rounds on him again, even more brusquely than before: "Saved? What is saved? This is a dumb head, who would come in here to talk about angels. Show me an angel. Please. I want to see" (302–3).

This is not what Jack wants to hear, so he pushes back, telling Sister Hermann Marie that nuns are supposed to "believe these things," for when he sees a nun, it cheers him up to be "reminded that someone stills believes in angels, in saints, all the traditional things." She gets the point: "This is true. The nonbelievers need the believers." Even though they themselves may be bankrupt on the belief front, it nevertheless reassures the masses to believe that someone else still invests a great deal in belief. "Frustrated and puzzled," Jack comes "close to shouting" at Sister Hermann and demands to know why the picture of the pope and the president is on the wall, if none of the nuns believe in heaven, hell, or anything in between. "It is for others. Not for us," she replies. When Jack asks, "What others?" she replies:

> All the others. The others who spend their lives believing that *we* still believe. It is our task in the world to believe things no one else takes seriously. To abandon such beliefs completely, the human race would die. This is why we are here. A tiny minority. To embody old things, old beliefs. The devil, the angels, heaven, hell. If we did not pretend to believe these things, the world would collapse. (303)

Jack remains incredulous, calling her seeming "dedication" a case of "pretense." On the contrary, she replies, the pretense of the nuns is actually a form of dedication. Someone has to seem to believe, and the lives of the nuns are no less serious than they would be if they actually believed what they profess. The more that "belief shrinks from the world," the greater the need for pretense. She says:

> Wild-eyed men in caves. Nuns in black. Monks who do not speak. We are left to believe. Fools, children. Those who have abandoned belief must still believe in us. They are sure that they are right not to believe but they know belief must not fade completely. Hell is when no one believes. There must always be believers. Fools, idiots, those who hear voices, those who speak in tongues. We are your lunatics. We surrender our lives to make your nonbelief possible. You are sure that you are right but you don't want everyone to think as you do. There is no truth without fools. (304)

Jack tries to keep the conversation going, but the nun wants nothing more to do with him, and like so many other ideas, exchanges, and events in *White Noise*, the scene shifts, attention drifts, and life goes on in all its inexplicably bizarre splendor.

In this conversation, it is Jack Gladney's desperate need to believe in belief that makes Sister Hermann Marie's cynical dismissal so biting. The college professor takes it for granted that the spirit and reality of unbelief permeate the life of his disjointed, divorce-riddled family. Yet surely there must exist somewhere a select group of paid professionals who do believe and who thereby make it possible for all the rest of us to feel "sentimentally refreshed" by the thought that someone clings to the myth, even though we know it to be a ludicrous fiction.

Jack Gladney is one in a long line of romantic figures who seek to live by out-sourcing their adult commitments and responsibilities. In a curious way, they have inherited a rebellious streak that we can trace back to Martin Luther—"Here I stand, I can do no other"—to Milton's Satan in *Paradise Lost*, and to a host of figures in nineteenth-century literature: Shelley's Prometheus, Melville's Ahab, Henry James's Daisy Miller, and Dostoevsky's Ivan Karamazov. This is, to be sure, a widely varied group whose individual lives were embedded within distinctly particular narratives, and my point is not to assert that they are theologically or morally equivalent. Rather, the point is that, like Jack Gladney, all of them assume toward the world the stance of children who labor within parental frameworks, even as they rebel against them.

We can find, for example, a classic instance of the Gladney phenomenon in Ralph Waldo Emerson's "Self-Reliance." In this great American hymn to individualism—which claims that "a foolish consistency is the hobgoblin of little minds"—Emerson declares at one point that "the nonchalance of boys who are sure of a dinner, and would disdain as much as a lord to do or say aught to conciliate one, is the healthy attitude of human nature." The boy is "independent, irresponsible," and looks out upon "such people and facts as pass by," judging and using them as he wishes and wills (261). He does so with little sense of obligation to those who have gone before him and with no sense of responsibility to those who presently sustain him. This is the case, even though he could not survive without the benefit of their past efforts or without the blessing of the present commitments of others. Someone must have grown the crops, just as someone must be preparing the meal, and although the nonchalant boy knows these things, he is loath to concern himself with them.

The Gladney phenomenon is a widespread reality in contemporary culture, rife as it is with a spirit of irony and parody. It is operative within contemporary literature and criticism as well, as the recent rise of interest in the phenomenon of the *postsecular* attests.[4] The postsecular critics are united in their belief that humanists of the past two centuries have persistently misinterpreted the religious situation of what they, the humanists, take to be a post-Christian

Beginning with the Word

world. Like Gladney, the postsecular critics often seem to have a yearning for belief that is satisfied mainly by their comforting admiration of others who do believe, even if those others live out their beliefs in ways the critics would never countenance for themselves.

As a case in point, Pericles Lewis asks why modern critics have consistently used secularization theory to explain why novelists moved away from religious forms of narrative (epics, spiritual autobiographies), in which gods, demons, and sprites dabble in human affairs, and toward naturalistic techniques and stories about an "empirically observable world." Lewis believes the critics have misread the novels because they have uncritically embraced "the secularization thesis [which] characterizes the emergence of modernity as the result of increasingly rational modes of thought and a rejection of belief in the supernatural. Alluding to Friedrich Schiller, Max Weber called this process 'the disenchantment of the world.'"[5]

Through their postsecular lenses, John McClure and Tracy Fessenden spy troubling figures and religious reactionary forces rumbling in the background, while to Lewis and Amy Hungerford, developments on the postsecular front appear on the whole to be more promising.[6] Either tacitly or explicitly, however, all four critics agree that the return to religion in literary studies must maintain a sharp distinction between religion as a system of doctrine and source of values—often labeled *fundamentalism* by them—and religion as a source of intriguing imagery and assorted insights.

Fessenden expresses a genuine sense of alarm over the slyly pervasive power of Christianity, which has seeped into every corner of contemporary political and intellectual discourse and even into the domain of the "secularization-as-progress" narrative. Writing in the latter years of the presidency of George W. Bush, she pleads for "a newly energized and contestatory pluralism" that will be able to ferret out fundamentalism wherever it tries to hide. In the final words of her book, Fessenden longs for the emergence of a new world "where appeals to freedom, values, even faith mean more and otherwise than what the loyalty oaths of our present climate would make of them."[7]

"By now the worldwide resurgence of religious fundamentalism is painfully evident to everyone," echoes John McClure in his introduction to *Partial Faiths*. Are we bound to fall into the fundamentalist trap, he asks, as soon as we acknowledge the presence of religious voices and struggles in modern fiction? McClure seeks to solve this problem and meet this danger through the promotion of what philosopher Gianni Vattimo has called "weak religion." In using this term Vattimo has something quite specific in mind, namely the *kenotic* self-emptying that marks the story of the God who became a man and accepted suffering and death on a cross.[8]

In its orthodox form, this self-emptying has always had its place as one episode set within the greater story of redemption and resurrection. The weakness and passivity of Jesus Christ entail a temporary and reversible relinquishment of divine power. Christ suffers on the cross and remains dead from Friday noon to Sunday morning. The death of Jesus and his descent into hell on Holy Saturday involve, in the words of Balthasar scholar Edward T. Oakes, "nothing less than a change in the relationship between God and the world *that affects the relations within the Godhead.*" Through the sufferings of God the Son, the intimate knowledge of human pain and longing are brought into the experience of God the Father, while through the power of the Father, the Spirit raises Christ Jesus from the dead, thus confirming that "the bonds of love in the Trinity are ultimately stronger than the godforsakenness that God in his triune counsels freely assumed into the Godhead."[9]

Or to put the same point in more dramatic and direct language, we can turn to an assurance offered by Godric, the medieval saint in Frederick Buechner's acclaimed novel: "The secret that we share I cannot tell in full. But this much I will tell. What's lost is nothing to what's found, and all the death that ever was, set next to life, would scarcely fill a cup" (96).

For Vattimo, however, the cup has been drained dry, and the *kenotic* self-emptying of Christ serves not as an episode within the drama of redemption but as the principle that determines God's very being, or what Vattimo might call God's "fate." He defines salvation as "an event in which kenosis, the abasement of God" is being realized ever more fully in modernity. In turn, this emptying of God "undermines the wisdom of the world" and our dreams of reason that construe "God as absolute, omnipotent and transcendent." So it is, Vattimo concludes, that "secularization—the progressive dissolution of the natural sacred—is the very essence of Christianity."[10]

The championing of secularization—"the progressive dissolution of the natural sacred"—might seem a curious activity for a putatively *postsecular* critic such as McClure to engage in. Yet he is willing to cast his lot with the kenotic because in a secular world overseen by a kenotic God, "weak religion" and "belief in belief" at least offer a modicum of tepid inspiration and diffident consolation. McClure takes figures as varied as Vattimo, Mircea Eliade, and Richard Rorty to be promoting a kind of "demystification in reverse" that creates a space in which "spiritually inflected alternatives" may be allowed to challenge "relentlessly secular modes" of interpretation as well as the "fiercer enclosures of fundamentalism." After all, the "extraordinary does not employ the totalizing language of dogmatic theology." On the contrary, its hues are mottled and its tones are muted, for "its promptings are partial, or plural, or only imperfectly decipherable to human ears."[11]

In the end, what does the postsecularity praised by McClure amount to? He says that both the fiction and criticism written under its aegis represent a turn of "secular-minded" folk "back toward the religious." The movement has an "ontological signature" marked by a "religiously inflected disruption of secular constructions" of reality. Perhaps most importantly, the postsecular embodies an "ideological" commitment to rearticulate the relationship of "a dramatically 'weakened' religiosity with secular, progressive values and projects."[12]

McClure's frequent use of the word *inflected* is telling, for it takes us to the heart of his project and of much of the recent championing of the "religious turn" in literary criticism. For this project, the grammar and syntax that shape our everyday beliefs and inform our actions are given to us by a "secular" and progressive political tradition. What religion does is to add a particular tone or pitch to the sentences we write and the worlds we build on the foundation established by that grammar. Postsecular religion, in other words, adds to the secular political agenda the "oversound" that Eve imparts to the birds of Eden in Robert Frost's sonnet, "Never Again Would Birds' Song Be the Same." Adam, who was in Eden before Eve appeared, thinks it likely that under her influence the birds in the garden have added "an oversound" to their own songs; as they have listened to her, they have caught "her tone of meaning," even if they have had to do so "without the words." Frost's play on the theme of sounds and inflections comes out of a robust romantic tradition that sought to invest the disenchanted modern world with the solemn grandeur of a Christian understanding of nature and history. And what he offers is a secularized and aestheticized version of the fortunate fall: "Never again would birds' song be the same. / And to do that to birds was why she came" (308).

McClure's concept of the *postsecular* flows from a far different source—the millennial apocalypticism of nineteenth-century socialism and Marxism—but it shares Frost's interest in the romantic quest for a spiritually rich but theologically equivocal religiosity. In their own way, the postsecular theoretical efforts along these lines mirror the endeavors of the modernist artists of a century ago. Like McClure and his cohort, James Joyce, T. S. Eliot, William Faulkner, and others sought to tap the power of allusion as they siphoned off the imagery from religious and cultural traditions they considered to be spent. (In the ironies and allusions of *Walden*, Henry David Thoreau had proved himself an early master of this genre.) The wholesale borrowing of titles, phrases, verses, and images from the Christian and classical added *inflected* resonance to such works as *Ulysses*, *The Waste Land*, and *Absalom, Absalom!*

Eliot and others came to realize, however, such religious allusions have no sustaining power of their own, for like Emerson's nonchalant boys, they depend on a dynamic world of adult action and care for its sustenance. In a work written during the Second World War, the Quaker philosopher of religion Elton Trueblood argued that "the terrible danger of our time consists in the fact that ours is a *cut-flower* civilization." As beautiful as such flowers may be, they will soon die "because they are severed from their sustaining roots."[13]

Trueblood's point is that ethical systems cannot flourish indefinitely once they have been cut off from their roots in specific religious beliefs and practices. The same might be said of the effort to mount a religious challenge to secularity through a mere change in the tone of one's voice and the range of one's allusions. When the melody fades, the counterpoint and undertones sound cacophonous, and when the sentences trail off and the grammar of assent finds nothing it can affirm, religiously inflected discourse sounds more like a feeble form of whistling in the dark than anything else.

Although Lewis and Hungerford appear to make a deliberate choice not to link their postsecular critiques to a specific political position such as McClure's "progressive values and projects," they nevertheless strive, as he does, to articulate a view of literature as a source of religiously inflected meaning. For Hungerford in particular, the religious power of literature draws on our longing to discover the meaning and mystery that seem to hover about our experience every day.

As she tries to account for the irruptions of religious experience that continue to mark contemporary life, Hungerford champions the virtues of "belief without content." For she is convinced that "belief in meaninglessness . . . has become deeply embedded in American religious practice since the fifties." She terms this "a various thing"; it may involve a sense of belief for its own sake or the idea of belief as a state of mind or form of profession without content. In this form, belief may involve engaging in practices the origin and meaning of which we neither understand nor explain.

Hungerford reasons that in an age saturated in the critique of religion, "belief without meaning" enables us to "maintain religious belief rather than critique its institutions." At the same time, this reconfigured understanding of belief serves "to buttress the authority of the literature that seeks to imagine such belief." For her, the goal is to explore the way literature and religion work in tandem in late modernity to build bridges that can span the gap "between conviction and relativism" and "between doctrine and pluralism."[14]

Hungerford's proposal is elegant and forthright. She writes persuasively of the efforts that some modern fiction writers—from J. D. Salinger to Toni Morrison to Cormac McCarthy—have made to retain the "idea of belief" without the substance of it. She speaks of "messages" and "revelation(s)" that "bias" life as we know it, even though we cannot know what such messages mean or what such revelations point to. For Hungerford, this holds true for

Beginning with the Word

explicitly Christian authors, including Marilynne Robinson, and Tim LaHaye and Jerry Jenkins of *Left Behind* fame, as well as for more skeptical writers of fiction. Whether they affirm orthodox doctrine or reject all forms of creedal belief, for these contemporary religious writers, Hungerford believes, it is not belief in God but a belief in "form as such" that matters and has its place "at the center of their religious imaginations."[15]

To press her argument, Hungerford draws on the work of Clifford Geertz and Robert Orsi, both of whom explain the religious impulses animating those contemporary fiction writers who "imagine belief . . . as itself a practice, something as much like a set of rituals as it is like a set of doctrines." Geertz's work in the 1970s blazed the trail for all who wish to shift the focus from religious doctrines and institutions to the powers of "the meaning-making subject." This subject "constructs" the world of religion "through action and word in everyday life" and through the rituals that we have woven into the fabric of that life. Building on Orsi's study of "lived religion," Hungerford says that to think of belief in the conventional manner—to consider it as a set of propositions to which one assents—is to ask "the wrong question," and those who do ask such questions are largely "the naïve, the old-fashioned, the child, the student, the Fundamentalist, (and also, one might add, the atheist)."[16]

Following Orsi's lead, Hungerford claims that the question of belief is "an unwitting masquerade" for the evangelical Protestant effort to turn the whole of the religious life into a matter of individual conversion: "Do you believe in Jesus? Have you been saved?" She prefers "the better question," which she calls the "Catholic, Jewish, or agnostic question." It has to do with what you do rather than what you affirm: "Have you been to mass? Have you ever prayed to St. Jude? Are you observant? Do you talk 'Jewish'?" These questions blunt the force of evangelical Protestant inwardness and bring our focus back to the way "historically situated persons" in fact live out their religion. Hungerford is willing to grant that for some people, practicing religion socially includes wrestling with the question of belief. Yet her concession on this point leads her to assent to Paul Tillich's notion of "meaninglessness," as he develops the theme in his exploration of "the God who appears when God has disappeared in the anxiety of doubt."[17]

This brings us back to the conversation between Jack Gladney and Sister Hermann Marie. Like Jack Gladney, contemporary American literature, as Hungerford defines it, relies on others to believe things it cannot assent to. As Sister Hermann says, "Those who have abandoned belief must still believe in us." Jack Gladney is comforted by the thought that someone somewhere believes in popes and presidents holding hands in heaven. For his emotional well-being, and for the good of contemporary American literature, "there must always be believers. Fools, idiots, those who hear voices, those who speak in tongues."

Although she sets her argument—as Lewis, McClure, and Fessenden do—in a postmodern context, Hungerford's treatment of religion and literature has roots reaching back to the Enlightenment. We can see an earlier version of her argument in a short story by Isak Dinesen, one of modern fiction's savviest interpreters of our enlightened and romantic past. In "The Poet," which is set in 1836, two Dinesen characters are having a conversation about art and belief, with one of them, Count Augustus von Schimmelmann, doing almost all of the talking.

As they sit in the forest, Count Augustus reminds his friend, Councilor Mathiesen, that all of us are, "in the spiritual world, dependent upon people stupider than ourselves." To explain what he means by this, he offers the case of an artist painting a simple rose. It is not possible to paint this or any other object, he observes, so that "I, or any other intelligent critic, shall not be able to decide, within twenty years, at what period it was painted, or, more or less, at what place on the earth." The painter would never have thought for a moment that he was creating a picture of a rose as it looked in Persia in the early 1600s or as it appeared to an observer in late nineteenth-century Holland. My insights about the historicity of art, says Schimmelmann, mean that "I am thus so far superior to the artist, that I can mete him with a measure of which he himself knows nothing." Yet such superiority comes at a cost, for while the critic can admire a painting, he cannot produce one: "I should never have the courage to paint a rose as it looks. For how does a rose look?" (382–83).

The same holds true for the larger, general questions "of virtue, justice, or, if you will, of God." Schimmelmann says that if someone were to ask what the truth about God might be, "I should answer: 'My friend, your question is without meaning.'" The Hebrews conceived of their God "like this," the Aztecs "like that," and the Jansenites "again, like that." Schimmelmann claims his own is an "enlightened" view of religion, which sees religious truth-claims for what they are, each distinct set of claims being but a patchwork quilt of aspirations and assumptions (383).

Still, Schimmelmann admits that "for this superior view of mine," he nevertheless stands "in debt to the naïve people who have believed" it possible to hold a "direct and absolutely truthful idea of God." If they had set out "only to create a special Hebrew, Aztec, or Christian idea of God, where would the presuppositions of the observer have been found?" That observer would have been in the same predicament as the Israelites, when the pharaoh decreed that they must "make bricks without straw. Indeed, my friend, while the fools

Beginning with the Word

could have done without us, we are dependent upon the fools for our better knowledge" (383–84).

To conclude his argument, Schimmelmann asks Mathiesen to imagine the two of them taking a morning walk during which they pass a pawnbroker's window. There they see a painted board, and on it are printed the words "Clothes mangled here." Schimmelmann then imagines his friend announcing: "Look, clothes are mangled here—I shall go and bring my washing." At which point Schimmelmann says he would inform his friend, "that you will find neither mangle nor mangler here, that the painted board is for sale" (384).

"Most religions are like that board, and we smile at them," he ruefully concludes:

> But I should have no opportunity of smiling, or of feeling or showing my superiority, and, in fact, the painted board would not be there at all, if, at some time or other, some people had not believed firmly in the possibility, in the wisdom, of mangling clothes, had not even been firmly convinced of the existence of their own mangle, with which clothes were indeed mangled. (384)[18]

The critical observer smiles at the foolishness of the believer, but if that believer did not believe, the critical observer would have no chance to feel or show the superiority of skeptical wisdom.

What Schimmelmann says about religion and the "clothes mangled here" sign—that they are things we both smile at and are dependent on—seems true of postsecular criticism's relationship to religious belief. As long as religion remains a meaning-enhancing concept or a nostalgic marker of a world we have lost, we can remain bemused by the spectacle and heartened by the gestures. But if religion stakes a claim to anything more than therapeutic goals and wistful moods, postsecular theory is ready to sound the alarm.

Even as these works by McClure, Lewis, Hungerford, and Fessenden open many windows, they close just as many doors for a Christian engagement with modern literature. Without question, they give us fresh perspectives on modern religious experience and its vital links to literature and theory, and they are undeniably right to insist that ours is anything but a glib and uniform secular age. In addition, these and other works of postsecular criticism generously welcome others, including religiously committed individuals, into their conversations about literature.

This openness represents a gain, but it is a limited one, for an unquestioned commitment to what I have called the structuralist paradigm remains securely in place for theory, even in its postsecular phase.[19] Gilbert Ryle once described Descartes's mind-body dualism as "the ghost in the machine." The same might be said of postsecular criticism, for which religion seems at best a wraithlike presence wafting its way through the immanent cosmos. The postsecularists realize, as Sister Hermann Marie tells Jack Gladney, that "there is no truth without fools," and they encourage us to take heart from those modern fictional characters who hint to us, in the words of Shakespeare's Ariel, of a "sea-change into something rich and strange." But although, like the nuns of whom Sister Hermann Marie speaks, fiction and poetry may need to "surrender their lives" to make the nonbelief of others possible, the critics themselves would not wish to be mistaken for believers. After all, one can imagine them asking, along with Sister Hermann, "Do you think we are stupid?"

The Broken Symbol and the Building Story

A common theme weaves its way through many of the works of literature and theory we have discussed in these last several chapters. It is that although knowledge makes belief impossible, desire makes the quest for belief endure. From Kermode's distinction between myth and fiction, to Sister Hermann Marie's brusque replies about the stupidity of belief, to the postsecular critics' efforts to separate the seed of faith from the husk of belief—characters and critics alike appear eager to distinguish themselves from those foolish enough to believe they can know the truth about God. Yet at the same time, these skeptical observers find themselves having to agree with Augustus von Schimmelmann, that "for this superior view" of theirs, they stand "in debt to the naïve people who have believed" it possible to know and trust in God.

Although the default position of modern criticism may be to side with the "superior view," for more than a century, many poets and novelists have not been so quick to choose sides. They have embraced neither the glossy narrative of secular progress nor the sobering story of material explanation. As they witnessed the emergence of unbelief in the nineteenth century and tracked its progress through the next century, these writers saw unbelief as something more than a decisive turning point in the history of personal and cultural liberation. Instead, in their creative works and personal lives, they often treated unbelief as a facet of belief rather than a successor to it. That is why, more often than not in the literature of the past 150 years, the conflict between belief and unbelief has played itself out more readily within the private struggles of individuals than in public battles between the forces of progress and reaction.

For a sense of how this dynamic of belief and unbelief manifests itself in a contemporary work of fiction, we can turn to a superb contemporary novel,

The Assault by the Dutch writer Harry Mulisch. This brooding work delves deeply into questions having to do with stories and truth, faith and reason, fiction and myth. In a compelling story, Mulisch puzzles over the mixture of freedom and fate that marks human experience, and the novel shuttles incessantly between belief and unbelief as it focuses on history and human destiny.

The Assault explores these matters in a manner that suggests but by no means promotes a Christian interpretation of narrative as one of several possibilities for an understanding of human experience. "Mulisch is identified, in reference works, as an 'absurdist,'" John Updike has written, "but there is nothing absurd about this economically and thoughtfully worked-out novel except, perhaps, the wartime reality that serves as its premise." The events in *The Assault* are harrowing, and as they persistently resurface in the memory and experience of its protagonist, Anton Steenwijk, they provide "the crucial clues to the shape imposed, in one white-hot night of forging, upon [Anton's] own life."[20]

The opening scene in *The Assault* takes place in January 1945 in Haarlem, a Dutch city nestled within a slivered salient of territory that remained under Nazi rule only months before the fall of the Third Reich. Under the conditions of a blackout, the Steenwijk family is spending yet another night huddled against the cold in the living room of their small home. While Anton reads a book and his mother salvages yarn from an unraveling sweater, his father and his brother Peter discuss the latter's translation of a passage from Homer.

As he points out a mistake in the translation, Mr. Steenwijk gives a brief etymological history of "symballeton," the word his son has translated incorrectly. "Remember the word 'symbol,' which comes from *symballo*, 'to bring together,' 'to meet,'" he explains. "Do you know what a *symbolon* was?" Peter doesn't care about the answer, but Anton does: "What was it, Papa?" "It was a stone that they broke in two," his father replies. Imagine that I am a guest of someone in a faraway land, he says. When I ask my host whether he would be willing to receive my son as a guest on a later visit, the question becomes one of identity. "How can he be sure that you really are my son? We make a *symbolon*," Mr. Steenwijk says. "He keeps one half, and at home I give you the other. So then when you get there, they fit together exactly" (14–15).

Just minutes after this conversation ends, six shots ring out in the darkness. The Steenwijks peer through a crack in the curtains and see a dead man lying in the street in front of their neighbors' home. The victim is Fake Ploeg, the Chief Inspector of Police and a brutal Nazi collaborator. As the Steenwijks look on in bewilderment, they see their neighbors, Mr. Korteweg and his daughter Karin, come out and drag Ploeg's body from the gutter in front of their own home to a point directly in front of the Steenwijk's dwelling.

Events then unfold at a breathtaking pace. Against his parents' wishes, Peter rushes out to remove Ploeg's body, but before he can do so, scores of German troops descend upon the neighborhood, and he vanishes in the darkness. A few minutes later, helmeted soldiers crash through the Steenwijks' door and herd Anton and his parents out into the freezing night air. Anton's parents are led away, and he watches helplessly as soldiers set fire to his home, which collapses "under a fountain of sparks as high as a tower" (29). Anton is driven away, and although he does not know it, by that time, his brother, mother, and father have all been shot to death. Over the course of a few terrifying minutes, Anton's life itself has become a *symbolon,* and it will take almost four decades for the broken pieces to come together and yield a provisional meaning at last.

If the pieces of this *symbolon* are to be put together again, that will be due either to an accident or an act of providence because Anton himself will never try to track down the pieces and solve the puzzle. Instead, he deliberately seeks to cut himself off from the past by sealing the borders of his mind against any invasive memories of the event. He trains to be a doctor and chooses anesthesiology as his specialty, for reasons tangled up with his painful past. He held to a "more or less mystical notion that the narcotics did not make the patient insensitive to pain so much as unable to express that pain, and that although drugs erased the memory of pain, the patient was nevertheless changed by it" (80).

Anton is just such a patient. His life has been transformed, and he continues to be driven and directed by the shocking events of a single night, but he stubbornly refuses to admit that is the case. To emphasize the disjointed nature of Anton's approach to his own past, Mulisch organizes *The Assault* as a series of episodes instead of chapters. Chapters serve as parts of a narrative whole, while episodes may be random occurrences without structure or meaning.

As the events in the novel unfold and the episodes accumulate, it seems as though young Anton is deliberately pursuing an Emersonian and Nietzschean approach to the past. In refusing to think of either the past or the future, Anton lines up almost perfectly with the Emerson of "Experience":

> Life is a series of surprises, and would not be worth taking or keeping, if it were not. God delights to isolate us every day, and hide from us the past and the future. We would look about us, but with grand politeness he draws down before us an impenetrable screen of purest sky, and another behind us of purest sky. "You will not remember," he seems to say, "and you will not expect." (483)

Nietzsche prized Emerson highly, and his lament in "On the Uses and Disadvantages of History for Life" speaks of a powerful longing to be free of "the pressure of what is past." Nietzsche writes:

Consider the cattle, grazing as they pass you by: they do not know what is meant by yesterday or today, they leap about, eat, rest, digest, leap about again, and so from morn till night and from day to day, neither melancholy nor bored. . . .

A leaf flutters from the scroll of time, floats away—and suddenly floats back again and falls into the man's lap. Then the man says "I remember" and envies the animal, who at once forgets and for whom every moment really dies, sinks back into night and fog and is extinguished for ever. Thus the animal lives *unhistorically*: for it is contained in the present, like a number without any awkward fraction left over; it does not know how to dissimulate, it conceals nothing and at every instant appears wholly as what it is; it can therefore never be anything but honest. Man, on the other hand, braces himself against the great and ever greater pressure of what is past: it pushes him down or bends him sideways, it encumbers his steps as a dark, invisible burden which he would like to disown.[21]

Yet no matter how hard Anton tries to live unhistorically, the events of that January 1945 night repeatedly slip past his defenses and overwhelm his resistance. More than two decades later, for example, on a stifling summer's day in 1966, a chance encounter brings back the banished memories. As Anton sits in a crowded café, listlessly following the conversational banter of friends and relatives, he overhears a snippet of a private conversation taking place only a few feet away: "I shot him first in the back, then in the shoulder, and then in the stomach as I bicycled past him" (108).

Hearing this, Anton blurts out, "Are you talking about Ploeg, Fake Ploeg in Haarlem?" The man he asks turns out to be Cor Takes, one of Ploeg's assassins. Having stumbled upon a witness to the events, Takes is eager to learn what he can. But Anton resists. "There's nothing to discuss, really," he stammers. "What happened, happened. It doesn't bother me, believe me. It happened over twenty years ago. I have a wife and child and a good job" (109–10).

Not to be denied, Takes presses ahead, forcing Anton to travel down paths of memory to destinations he does not want to reach. Takes admits the other collaborators knew that the murder of Ploeg would prompt a brutal Nazi response. Yes, innocent people would be murdered in retaliation. But "is that a reason for not doing it?" he asks. When Anton refuses to answer, Takes does so for him. "The answer is no," he says. "If you believe we shouldn't have done it, then you also believe that, in the light of history, the human race shouldn't have existed. Because then all the love and happiness and goodness in this world can't outweigh the life of a single child" (112–13).

The problem Cor Takes sets is a variation on a theme explored to devastating effect in Fyodor Dostoevsky's *The Brothers Karamazov*. It brings together themes having to do with the narrative shape of human experience and unsettling questions about the problem of evil and the goodness of God.

In Dostoevsky's novel, it is Ivan Karamazov who raises these issues and asks the very question that Takes appears to answer in his response.

As the action of *The Brothers Karamazov* unfolds, Ivan teeters on the brink of madness, consumed by his loathing of his father and by an inner torment that divides his soul. One evening, he recites to his brother Alyosha a story he has written about Jesus Christ. As a preface to this fable, Ivan explains why he has come to reject both God and his creation. His objections to God are rooted in the problem of evil, in general, and the suffering of children, in particular. Adults know good and evil and possess freedom of a kind, but children have not eaten from the tree of knowledge. "If everyone must suffer, in order to buy eternal harmony with their suffering, pray tell me what have children got to do with it?" Ivan wants to know. "Why do they get thrown on the pile, to manure someone's future harmony with themselves?" To acquiesce in the suffering of children is too great a price to pay for eternal "harmony; we can't afford to pay so much for admission. And therefore I hasten to return my ticket," he concludes (244–45).[22]

At this point, Ivan senses he has cornered Alyosha, so to clinch the argument he poses a devastating question. He asks his brother to imagine he has been given the power to grant eternal peace and happiness to the entire human race. But there is a catch. To make the system run smoothly for eternity, Alyosha must agree to "torture one tiny creature." Imagine a desperate young girl "beating her chest with her little fist," as she suffers unspeakable torments and endures God's unbroken silence. Ivan asks, "[Could] you raise your edifice on the foundation of her unrequited tears—would you agree to be the architect on such conditions? Tell me the truth." Alyosha's answer is simple: "No, I would not agree" (245).

Ivan claims he is not rejecting God but only the world he has created and governs.[23] Paraphrasing the opening of John's Gospel ironically, he assures Alyosha, "I believe in order, in the meaning of life, I believe in eternal harmony, in which we are all supposed to merge, I believe in the Word for whom the universe is yearning, and who himself was 'with God,' who is himself God, and so on, and so on and so forth, to infinity" (235).

Diane Oenning Thompson sees Ivan's rejection of Christ and creation as a denial of figural interpretation. Ivan reduces Christ's life and death to a common "historical event, stupendous and miraculous in its uniqueness, but now past and done with like all others." For this Karamazov brother, the Incarnation, crucifixion, and resurrection of Christ serve no larger purpose and possess no special power.[24] They do not fulfill God's past promises nor do they give reason to trust his pledges for the future. In rejecting Christ, Ivan seeks to sever the links between the redemptive events of Scripture and the subsequent history of the world. His rejection of figural understanding strands us in the eerie world of Quentin Compson: "Father was teaching us that all men are just accumulations dolls stuffed with sawdust swept up from the trash heaps where all previous dolls had been thrown away the sawdust flowing from what wound in what side that not for me died not" (175–76).

What Ivan and Quentin claim—that life is a series of discontinuous episodes—represents what Anton Steenwijk also desperately wishes to believe. He cannot bear the implications of Cor Takes's question—"Is that a reason for not doing it?"—concerning the killing of Ploeg and its bloody aftermath. But try as he might, he cannot deny the logic of Takes's reasoning. "If you believe we shouldn't have done it," the latter argues, "then you also believe that . . . the human race shouldn't have existed." Instead of refuting the claims Takes makes, Anton simply resolves not to think about the matter. "In love," as in all things, "he simply let things happen to him" (97).

Or so Anton thinks. But things do not just "happen" to him. Instead, the past seems to pursue him intentionally with a power he cannot resist. As a case in point, not long after Anton has spoken with Takes, he comes to realize that Fake Ploeg's assassination had in fact determined his choice of a wife. For a brief period after the killing of his family and the destruction of his home, Anton had been placed in a Haarlem jail cell. He shared that darkened space with another person, a woman with whom he spoke only briefly. When he meets Takes two decades later, Anton learns that the woman in the cell (Truus Coster) was Takes's lover and his accomplice in the murder of Ploeg. Anton had never seen her face but did remember her voice. Now, years after the fact, he is stunned to realize that he chose his own wife, Saskia, because her voice resembled that of the mystery woman in the darkened cell and because her face was the image of what he had imagined his cellmate's face to be. Saskia "was the embodiment of an image he must have been carrying about in his head, without knowing it, since he was twelve." If this was true, and if Saskia "was not allowed to be herself but represented someone else, then wasn't he in the process of breaking up his marriage?" She could not be another person— i.e., herself—for Anton unconsciously demanded that she stand in for Truus Coster, and so, "in a sense, he was involved in murdering her" (130).

Thus it was, that over the years, one chance encounter after another has dropped a new piece of the *symbolon* into Anton's hands. And the final fragment falls into place in late 1981, when he finds himself swept up into a massive antinuclear demonstration on the streets of Amsterdam. In the crush of people, Anton collides with Karin Korteweg, the neighbor who had planted Ploeg's body in front of the Steenwijk home. Anton has not seen Karin since that night, but as the press of the crowd drives them along, he learns from her the missing details that complete the puzzle at last and bring the *symbolon* together.

Karin tells him that his brother Peter, armed with Ploeg's gun, had broken into their home that night. As he waved the gun at Karin and her father and vilified them as "monsters," several German soldiers rushed into the home and shot Peter. Having learned that fact, Anton continues to press ahead. He wants to know why Karin and her father had dumped Ploeg's body in front of the Steenwijk home. She explains ruefully that as the Nazi collaborator lay dying in front of their home, all her father could think of were his own pet lizards. "My God, the lizards!" he cried. According to his daughter, these reptiles represented something magical and inscrutable to Mr. Korteweg, "something about eternity and immortality, some secret he saw in them." He could not let them die, even if the Steenwijk family had to be sacrificed in order to save them. Dumbfounded, Anton asks Karin, "Do you mean that without those lizards, none of this would have happened?" (181).

That rhetorical question leads to a more serious one, which Anton feels compelled to ask, thirty-six years after the murder of his family. "Why did you put him [Ploeg] in front of our door," he questions Karin, "and not at the Aartses' on the other side?" This secluded and childless couple had kept to themselves throughout the war. Why would Karin and her father spare them but doom the Steenwijks and their young sons? She tells Anton, "I had already taken a step toward their house, but then Father said, 'No, not there. They're hiding Jews.'" Karin says she had had no idea that a Jewish couple and their small child had been hiding in the Aartses' home for almost two years (183).

Having labored for so long to repress his memories of that night and having refused to believe there could be any pattern embedded within those events and the subsequent episodes in his own life, Anton is overwhelmed by Karin's disclosures. Nobody on his block had known or liked the Arises, who shunned their neighbors and seemed to care for no one. Yet by sheltering a Jewish family, they managed to save several persecuted innocent lives. And then there was crazy Mr. Korteweg, worshiping his lizards and saving the lives of the Jews. Unwittingly and unwillingly, Anton has stumbled on the last remaining secrets involving those now ancient events:

> So this was why Ploeg's body had landed on the other side, at their own door, so that . . . Anton couldn't take any more.
> "Goodbye, Karin," he said. "Please excuse me, I . . . Good luck to you."
> Without waiting for an answer, leaving her standing there, he turned away and forged through the crowd, going this way and that, as if to make sure that she could never find him again. (183)

Beginning with the Word

As the final scene of *The Assault* draws to a close, the long-scattered pieces at last "fit together exactly," just as Mr. Steenwijk had said they would when he spoke of the *symbolon* on that dark night so many years before. As a character, Anton Steenwijk is anxious about what these events might mean for his life, while as an author, Harry Mulisch seems strikingly ambivalent about the point of it all. Consider the two options Anton has for interpreting these events: either his family was killed that night because of a neighbor's passion for lizards, or they died so that several hounded and helpless Jews might be saved from the Holocaust.

It may be that for Mulisch the meaning of these events brings together elements of both ways of interpreting them. Anton's family died for an absurd reason as well as for a noble end, and so do all human lives involve a mix of the sublime and the ridiculous, the heroic and the farcical. Whatever we are to make of this crazy human drama, it's we who do the making, Mulisch seems to conclude, for there is nothing to discover in the midst of life and nothing to await at its end.

"Was everyone both guilty and not guilty? Was guilt innocent, and innocence guilty?" Anton asks himself, after parting with Karin. Six million Jews had died at the hands of the Nazis, but these three had "unknowingly saved themselves and the lives of two others, and instead of them, his own father and mother and Peter had died, all because of some lizards." It's too much to think about, too much to bear. "But what does it matter?" the last paragraph of *The Assault* asks. "Everything is forgotten in the end. The shouting dies down, the waves subside, the streets empty, and all is silent once more" (184–85). In silence, the word and the thing become one at last because language has nothing left to say.

In the world as Harry Mulisch envisions it, this may be the final secret the *symbolon* has to tell, but the ending of *The Assault* leaves open another possibility. It is that speech, rather than silence, fills the void and that life is a meaningful story rather than a parade of aimless episodes. This is not to say that Mulisch reaches this conclusion but only to note that, unlike Stevens, Kermode, and company, he acknowledges this to be a possibility.[25]

One way to consider this possibility would be for us to return briefly to our earlier and extensive discussion of sign theory. The Greek word for "sign"— *semeion*—gave its name to semiotics, the science of signs that developed in tandem with structuralism at the beginning of the twentieth century. For semiotics and structuralism alike, the individual word stood in isolation and received its meaning from the differences that distinguished it from other signs in the vast web of *langue*, the language system. As a sign, the word marks the absence of the reality to which it points.

This understanding of *semeia* differs radically from the use of the same term in the New Testament. There signs are events that proclaim the mercy and judgment of God and herald the coming of his kingdom. The "child wrapped in bands of cloth and lying in a manger" is to be the sign for the shepherds (Luke 2:12); Jesus applies to himself "the sign of the prophet Jonah" (Matt. 12:39); and in Acts, Luke quotes from the prophet Joel in order to emphasize the eschatological work of the Spirit: "And I will show portents in the heavens above / and signs on the earth below" (2:19).

Common to these and the other usages of *semeia* in the New Testament is the clear sense that a sign can never be understood on its own in isolation from what it serves, which is the larger account of God's power and glory especially as they are embodied in the person and work of Jesus Christ. When the event—be it a miracle, a proclamation, or an act of obedience—is taken up into the story of which it is a part, it becomes, in effect, a piece of that stone which, as Anton Steenwijk's father patiently explained on that January night in 1945, becomes at last a part of the *symbolon* that reveals our identity and discloses the meaning hidden deep within our experiences past, present, and future.

Defending a Great Hope

They differ in countless ways, but Quentin Compson, Ivan Karamazov, and Anton Steenwijk do share a lack of faith in "the assurance of things hoped for, the conviction of things not seen" (Heb. 11:1). None of them could imagine sharing Dilsey's faith in a personal God who has the power to forgive sins and raise the dead. That is to say, that unlike Dilsey, they lack the narrative confidence that derives from being able to see "the first and the last." They reject the ideal of eternal harmony, which involves the hope that words and things will someday become one.

Unable to imagine the future with hope, these characters dwell in a nether region located somewhere between a barren present and a bountiful past. For Quentin and Benjy Compson, the ideal of the past is bound up with their childhood memories of Caddy and of an idyllic time prior to their loss of her; for Ivan, the ideal is the innocence of children too young to know of death, too thoughtless to know of sex, and too innocent to choose the evil that adults wantonly embrace; and for Anton, the lost past became that time before when his family was intact, alive, and as secure as they could be within the Nazi's world.

For Quentin, Ivan, and Anton, words call to mind things they have lost and point to desires whose satisfaction they will never enjoy. Like many other individuals, real and imagined, who play their parts in the dramas of late modernity, these fictional characters are torn between a spirit of lamentation and a sense of resignation. As such, they have been powerfully shaped by a modern version of the ancient heresy of gnosticism and what Colin Gunton calls its "eschatology of return."

Early gnosticism took issue with the doctrine of providence as the church defined it. If God was, as the orthodox claimed him to be, a creative and mighty God, how were we to explain the frightfully unequal distribution of happiness and suffering to be found throughout the world? To solve this problem, the gnostics "held the material world, rather than human fault, to be the cause of evil." A lesser god, a demiurge, must have created the physical realm, and the spiritual God, "who had nothing to do with the material world . . . led those who were spiritual into a higher, non-material redemption."[26]

As Gunton outlines the second-century situation, the early church had two different strategies to counter this teaching. Origen of Alexandria put forward one of them when he challenged gnosticism, but he did so only after acknowledging what he considered to be the rightness of its central complaint. Granted, he said, there is in this life an unevenness to the fate of humans, but there is a reason for it, and it has to do with the choices that souls have made in another world *before* they take bodily form in this one.

To Gunton, the central flaw in Origen's theory has to do with its idea of the fall as an event that took place before the creation of time and the universe. If this were true, then the "creation of this material world . . . [would have been] essentially a repair job, contingent on there having been a fall," and redemption would entail a return to a perfect order outside of time and to a perfect state prior to the fall. As a result, having concluded that the creation was marred and compromised before it even came to be, Origen was all but compelled to define redemption as "a movement back to the beginning rather than forward to perfection. Accordingly, the destiny of human souls is to return to the timeless perfection of the beginning."[27]

We witness a longing for a pure beginning in several of the works of fiction we have discussed. It is there in the desperate confusion of Benjy Compson, as he futilely struggles to articulate his sense of emptiness and loss, in the wake of Caddy's departure. We come face-to-face with this longing in Quentin Compson, whose fantasies return compulsively to dreams of a world before the sexes were divided and the ticking and grinding of time began. We also meet this nostalgia for a lost past in Anton's anguished quest to suppress all memories of the events that led to the loss of his family, home, and world.

By default and without conscious choice, Benjy, Quentin, and Anton adopt a gnostic slant on their lives in particular and the human condition in general.

There is nothing they need to do consciously to appropriate gnostic categories, which are pervasive and readily accessible in our late modern world. Gnosticism is consonant, after all, with the naturalistic materialism that undergirds the structuralist paradigm. For the materialist and gnostic alike, the world is an imprisoning closed system from which the spirit longs and strains to be freed. In the cosmology of its original, ancient origins, gnosticism set this struggle within a metaphysical framework of dualism. The modern gnostic merely relocates the struggle, shifting it from its heavenly and earthly plane to its new location in the struggle of the will against the body.[28]

The theme of a resurgent gnosticism figures explicitly in the theological work of Gunton and Hans Urs von Balthasar, and it takes on implicit importance for Karl Barth, when he describes our engagement with the immanent cosmos. As Barth understood better than any other theologian of the twentieth century, in an immanent universe, all conceptions that humans devise to describe God become myths created and projected out of a profound sense of need.

Like Barth, Balthasar took the Christian faith to be a staunch opponent of myth rather than a propagator of it, as naturalism would have it. To Balthasar, it is materialism—materialism of the kind that structuralism takes as a given—that forever prompts the profusion of myth. Only through the mastery of matter, including the body, can the imprisoned human will find deliverance for the spirit. In his introduction to a selection of Irenaeus's second-century writings on gnosticism, Balthasar presses this point:

> Modern materialism . . . is opposed to the Christian principle of Incarnation. At least in practice, it regards matter as something to be dominated, and in man himself as the way to power. Myth and Christianity are opposed on every point. Myth seeks the ascent of man to spirit; the Word of God seeks descent into flesh and blood. Myth wants power; revelation reveals the true power of God in the most extreme powerlessness. Myth wants knowledge; the Word of God asks for constant faith and, only within that faith, a growing, reverent understanding. Myth is the lightning that flashes when contradictory things collide—absolute knowledge, eternal quest; the revelation of God's Word is gentle patience amidst the intractable tensions of life.[29]

This modern inability—or refusal—to regard matter as the good gift of God raises a host of problems, argues Gunton. As one example, he offers a critique of the same passage from Steven Weinberg that we discussed in an earlier chapter. Gunton quotes the last sentences in Weinberg's *The First Three Minutes*, and he is particularly interested in the assertive final sentence of the book: "The more the universe seems comprehensible, the more it seems

Beginning with the Word

pointless." To this the theologian replies with a question: "What assumption underlies the pessimistic denial of the point of it all?"[30]

The answer, Gunton says, is that Weinberg must believe "that because the universe is temporally limited, it is pointless." It may appear to have rational structures and to manifest a remarkable architecture of beauty, but the universe can only be "fundamentally meaningless, because it is destined to disappear." Yet must the universe itself be eternal if it is to possess a meaning? In Judaism and Christianity alike, only God is eternal by nature. If we and the creation are to endure forever, that can only come about as a result of the gift of God's transforming, life-giving power.

According to Gunton, the modern age has come to equate temporality with meaninglessness, precisely because it has lost confidence that there is a "logic of temporality: a meaning to be found within the structures of created temporality." Having lost its faith in what I have called the *storied order* of creation and human history, late modernity takes finitude to be the source of its emptiness and despair. If there is no point—no finite beginning, no pivotal crisis, no promised end—to the course of nature and the array of experience, then only the possibility of endlessness can endow life with meaning. "But is a piece of music pointless because it has a last note, a life because it is bracketed by birth and death?" Gunton asks. "Not necessarily. It depends upon what is understood of the possibility of salvation, of a final meaning, of recapitulation, indeed, of resurrection."[31]

We recall that for Irenaeus, it is Jesus Christ who undoes the damage of the fall through his recapitulation of the whole of human history. This is a forward-looking doctrine, not a backward one, for redemption comes at the end of a transforming journey through death and resurrection rather than through some restorative retreat to a state of innocence before time. "God's providence," writes Gunton, therefore has "a direct concern with the destiny of this world, whose structures" are bound up with those who bear God's image. "God provides, that is to say, not for a *spatial* ascent out of the material world, but for a *temporal* movement in and with it, in eschatological perspective."[32]

To make transformation a central category of redemption is to cast the question of word and thing, and of story and reality—myth and fiction— into a new framework. *Presence* and *absence* are spatial categories, as are *signifier* and *signified*. If you are present, you are *here* adjacent to me or in my vicinity, while if you are absent, you are *somewhere* else out of sight. A spatial orientation informs Plato's view of words as proxies standing in for the wordless idea. The space they occupy is empty, for they point to a truth whose home is elsewhere.

Irenaeus and Gunton offer a different way to conceive of signs and the realities of presence and absence.[33] For our view of language, the doctrine of recapitulation shifts the emphasis from space to time, and it exchanges the certainty of presence for the hopefulness of promise. This doctrine and the hope it sustains are driven by promises of the kind proclaimed by Reverend Shegog on Easter and hinted at in the *symbolon* that is at last pieced together for Anton Steenwijk. Our dilemma is not that our spirits are imprisoned by our bodies but that our rebellion has bound our wills and estranged us from God. It is that rebellion that drives the dynamics of word and thing for us.

Seen in this light, presence and absence have to do with time more than space, and the primary tension is between present and future, not body and spirit. In the Incarnation, God reverses the order established by myth. In myth, redemption always comes by way of flight from the embodied state or escape from the tyranny of time. In the gospel of the incarnate Word, the exact opposite holds true. In the memorable formulation offered by Dietrich Bonhoeffer in a 1944 prison letter, "the difference between the Christian hope of resurrection and the mythological hope" is that the former sends a person back into "life on earth in a wholly new way." Unlike believers in the redemption myths, Christians have "no last line of escape available from earthly tasks and difficulties into the eternal, but, like Christ himself," we must "drink the earthly cup to the dregs," and only in our doing so are we "crucified and risen with Christ. . . . Redemption myths arise from human boundary-experiences, but Christ takes hold of a man at the center of his life."[34]

In the Incarnation, what Balthasar calls a "stupendous exchange" takes place: "God becomes 'nothing', so that the 'nothings' might become God," and through this event, which Irenaeus called "recapitulation," Christ, the second Adam, "repeats the whole natural development of man at the higher level of divine reality. Sinful, lost, and wandering man is not just put back on course by the companionship of love; more profoundly, he is taken up into that love."[35]

And so is the entire created universe taken up into the story of that love as well: "The creation itself will be set free from its bondage to decay and will obtain the freedom of the glory of the children of God. We know that the whole creation has been groaning in labor pains until now" (Rom. 8:21–22). The end toward which nature and history are moving "is life and not death." Further, the "final word on the creation as a whole, human and nonhuman alike, is that which will be spoken by the crucified Lord on his return."[36] In his first letter to the Corinthians, Paul puts the matter this way: "For as all die in Adam, so all will be made alive in Christ." The crucified and risen Christ represents "the first fruits" of the promise of life eternal made to "those who

Beginning with the Word

belong to Christ. Then comes the end, when he hands over the kingdom to God the Father, after he has destroyed every ruler and every authority and power" (1 Cor. 15:22–24).

We began this chapter with the poetry of William Carlos Williams, and we will close with a word of hope delivered by Czeslaw Milosz, a poet of incomparable power. A number of his poems focus on the relationship between language and reality—between word and thing—and an especially pertinent one dates from 1954, just a few years after Milosz had begun a self-imposed exile from his native Poland, then occupied by the Soviet Union. The poem is titled "An Appeal," and Milosz addresses it to

> You, my friends, wherever you are,
> Whether you are grieving just now, or full of joy,
> To you I lift this cup of pungent wine.

To these friends he poses a question. "Tell me," he implores them, "Whether you really think that this world / Is your home?" Do you believe

> That your internal planet
> That revolves, red-hot, propelled by the current
> Of your warm blood, is really in harmony
> With what surrounds you? Probably you know very well
> The bitter protest, every day, every hour,
> The scream that wells up, stifled by a smile,
> The feeling of a prisoner who touches a wall
> And knows that beyond it valleys spread,
> Oaks stand in summer splendor, a jay flies
> And a kingfisher changes a river to a marvel. (268)

Like much of Milosz's work, "An Appeal" balances on the knife's edge between gnostic deliverance and Christian promise. The poem's imagery of a spirit imprisoned within a body dovetails with that to be found in any number of postromantic poems and novels. Its hope lies in some capacity of the spirit to endure eternally, and its confidence rests upon "a hidden certainty" rather than on any outward revelation:

> In you, as in me, there is a hidden certainty
> That soon you will rise, in undiminished light,
> And be real, strong, free from what restrained you.
> That . . . above everything,
> It will be given to you to run as celestial fire,

To set sails ablaze with your flame at dawn
When ships trail smoke and archipelagoes
Wake up, shaking copper from their hair.

"From the ashes of winter," Milosz calls out to his friends, patiently and "in the simplest words," to assure them that "the heart is still beating" and "nothing is lost." Meanwhile, the challenge and the promise remain:

Nothing is lost, if one day our words
Come so close to the bark of trees in the forest,
And to orange blossoms, that they become one with them,
It will mean that we have always defended a great hope. (268–69)

To have our words "become one" with the trees and the blossoms—this is our "great hope." To my students, such images seem at times oblique or obscure, until we begin to discuss the rich, intricate history of Christian thought about the word and the thing. In that context, the idea of a "great hope" begins to resonate, for it reaches into the fathomless sources of their own longings for reconciliation and renewal.

About this "great hope," Milosz asks, "How should I defend it?" He determines to do so "by naming things," yet the task "isn't easy" because of the sheer weight of the mythological past and the linguistic record. "I say the word 'dawn' / And the tongue by itself affixes 'rosy-fingered' / As in the childhood of Greece." The sun and moon themselves "have the face of Gods," and isn't that Poseidon who is pulling the water-skiers, "Ploughing the waves with his motor, towing a retinue of nymphs"? Yet the task of naming remains, as does the hope that the word and the thing will someday be one:

And yet, I affirm, this is the earth of wonder.
It gives us the gift of eternal youth.

To you I lift this cup, here, on the stage,
I, one voice, no more, in the vast theater.
Against closed eyes, bitter lips,
Against silence, which is slavery. (270)

8

Dwelling in Possibility

Visions of Justice, Dreams of Deliverance

> I dwell in Possibility—
> A fairer House than Prose—
> More numerous of Windows
> Superior—for Doors—
>
> Of Chambers as the Cedars
> Impregnable of eye—
> And for an everlasting Roof
> The Gambrels of the Sky—
>
> Of Visitors—the fairest
> For Occupation—This—
> The spreading wide my narrow Hands
> To gather Paradise—
> —Emily Dickinson, #466

The story of Israel's exodus from Egypt helped make it possible for the slaves to project a future radically different from their present. From other parts of the Bible, especially the prophetic and apocalyptic books, the slaves drew descriptions which gave form and, thus, assurance to their anticipation of deliverance. The troublesome question, according to Aunt Ellen, a freedwoman in North Carolina, had not been *if* the slaves would be free, but *when*: "When we used to think about it, it 'peared like de Judgement, sure to come, but a powerful step off." As that 'powerful step' loomed closer, ... slaves turned, as had generations of Christians before them in time of crisis, to the biblical promises of God for reassurance.

—Albert Raboteau, Slave Religion: The "Invisible
Institution" in the Antebellum South

With its vision of our words becoming "one with orange blossoms" and "the bark of trees in the forest," Czeslaw Milosz's "An Appeal" brings us back to the beginning of our reflections on language and reality, word and thing. And by calling this a matter of "great hope," the poet places the question of the word within the framework of narrative. He and we live in a fractured time, the period stretching between a lost wholeness and a longed-for reunion. Our lives and our language are out of kilter, and if we were to be stripped of memory and hope, we would be of "all people most to be pitied."

It is precisely this situation of displacement and brokenness that the doctrine of reconciliation addresses, when it speaks of us as living between the fall of the first Adam and the return of the second Adam, Christ. In the apostle's words, God "chose us in Christ before the foundation of the world . . . [and] destined us for adoption as his children through Jesus Christ" (Eph. 1:3–5). Here, as we stand between the fall of Adam and Eve and the final "gathering up of all things" in Christ, we dwell within a divine storied order.

To speak of a storied order and a worded reality may appear to be an effort to rationalize a static hierarchy of some kind, and this is indeed one way natural law theory has been put to use over the centuries. Yet this need not be the case, for the doctrine of recapitulation provides us with a flexible means of conceiving of the divine order of creation. Colin Gunton makes this point by contrasting different interpretations of the opening chapter of Genesis. Some influential early readings of Genesis 1 claimed it taught that God created a limited number of fixed forms that were then used as models for all of creation, "rather as an architect draws a plan and then puts it into reality." Yet Genesis need not be read in this manner, Gunton claims, and in any case "evolutionary theory's positing of an open multitude of developing forms" did irreparable harm to models of fixity. "Genesis teaches an open world, full of the kind of rich possibilities for development that evolutionary theory teaches," although, as Gunton points out, that is not to say Genesis lines up with the various "Darwinist dogmas" that are "in competition with one another."[1]

For our understanding of time, history, and narrative, he argues, the crucial point is that creation itself "has a destiny, a purpose." In and of itself,

Beginning with the Word

creation is perfect, "but perfect here is not a static concept." Take the case of a newborn child. In its beauty, complexity, and innocence, we might call it "perfect," but with the understanding that it is "there to become something else." It is destined to grow into "a mature human being who is to be made perfect through time." For all things made by God, there is "no creation 'in the beginning' without an eschatological orientation." To assert that God created the world *ex nihilo* is to say he made it to become perfect, something capable of praising and glorifying God "for what it has been enabled by him to become." It is therefore established and secured by God, "not as a timeless mechanism or cosmos, but to form the basis for a history whose meaning, through time, takes shape in relation to its creator."[2]

If history is a narrative whose meaning unfolds over the course of time and in relationship to the purposes of God, that means a revolutionary spark burns at the core of human experience. God's kingdom is yet to come, and through the work of Christ and the agency of the Spirit, God is seeking to transform his people and their world. It was no accident that the modern world's first two political revolutions—in 1640s England and late eighteenth-century America—flourished in soil nourished by a Calvinist vision of cultural transformation. H. Richard Niebuhr observes that from the beginning, the Calvinist tradition was marked by a powerful tension between the fixity of a predestined order and the fluidity embodied in the "thought that what the gospel promises and makes possible, as divine (not human) possibility, is the transformation of mankind in all its nature and culture into a kingdom of God in which the laws of the kingdom have been written upon the inward parts."[3]

From the visionary radicalism of John Milton's politics and poetics in the seventeenth century to the celebration of possible worlds in the work of Paul Ricoeur, the twentieth-century French philosopher, the Reformed tradition's eschatological openness has exercised a deep influence on modern conceptions of literature and its power. For Emily Dickinson, that power is housed in the dwelling place of "Possibility— / A fairer House than Prose—." *Prose* traces the contours of the world as we find and know it, while *possibility* opens onto the world of what might be.

Dickinson's concept of possibility derives from the great theme of the promises of God, which runs from the first chapters of Genesis to the final verses of Revelation. Possibility and promise—they are the linchpins of hope in the Scriptures. Without them, and without the resurrection of Christ that secures and establishes their power, we would be trapped within the confines of a "strictly immanent cosmos" in which the word and the thing could never become one. As Paul tells the Corinthians, "if Christ has not been raised, your faith is futile, and you are still in your sins." It follows, that "if for this life only we have hoped in Christ, we are of all people most to be pitied" (1 Cor. 15:17, 19).

To Paul Ricoeur, language itself becomes an instrument of power because of its ability to open upon a world governed by Easter Sunday's possibilities rather than by Good Friday's cruelties. "Why should we draw new meanings from our language," he asks, "if we have nothing new to say, no new world to project?" What we create with language would make no sense, if it did not serve, in part, as a way of "letting new worlds emerge by means" of metaphor and story. In turn, Ricoeur observes, those "new worlds" have the power to shape profoundly "our understanding of ourselves."[4]

A New World Emerges

To envision what this play of possibilities might mean, I need to return briefly to the hard but formative experiences that opened the world of literature to me. When my brother died, I was a sophomore in high school. My father was a bricklayer, and we lived in a modest home nestled within a tightly packed neighborhood of factory workers, shopkeepers, and laborers. My parents had roots in the Swedish immigrant church, but they were not deep and they received little nourishment during the early years of their marriage. As a result, by the time I came along, our family rarely went to church, and my only formal religious training came by way of the Sunday school classes my parents had my brother and me attend sporadically.

Yet whatever I picked up during that one hour on Sunday morning proved to be a feeble counter to what I was learning in my everyday experience of living in the neighborhood, attending a public school, and watching television. Those adolescent experiences and my subsequent conversion to the Christian faith came into clearer focus for me more than two decades later, when I first read and then began to teach "Either-Or," a poem by Czeslaw Milosz. The title alludes to the treatise in which Søren Kierkegaard speaks of our need to choose between an aesthetic and an ethical approach to human values.

Milosz's poem plays with the possibilities Kierkegaard's stark alternatives present. It opens with a conditional, dependent clause—"If God incarnated himself in man, died and rose from the dead"—and moves on to argue that if this is true, then all of our endeavors matter to the degree that they acquire their meaning from this event. If Jesus Christ was indeed the Word made flesh, we should think of this fact by day and by night, "every day, for years."

Beginning with the Word

We should consider "human history [to be] holy," and we ought to "testify" publicly "to the divine glory. / With words, music, dance, and every sign." But if the Christian doctrine of the Incarnation

> is a fiction
> And what we are taught in schools,
> In newspapers and TV is true:
> That the evolution of life is an accident,
> As is an accident the existence of man,
> And that his history goes from nowhere to nowhere,

we must draw conclusions about the "innumerable generations" who deluded themselves and denied their natural instincts for no other reason than to avoid going to hell for a sin—that is, an indiscretion—as silly as "licking clean a pot of jam." If the Christian message of hope and reconciliation is a fiction, the only things left for us to do are to confess our limitless capacity for self-delusion and to "complain of our transience."

The poem fascinated me in part because it seemed to summarize perfectly the two competing narratives at the center of modern experience. One of them is the story that I had learned as a child from "schools, / In newspapers and TV." It is that tale full of sound and fury, signifying nothing, a story of matter in motion and organisms locked in an endless cycle of birth, growth, decay, and death. This is the master narrative of naturalism, from which the creed of the immanent cosmos is derived.

The other narrative is the story into which I was taken up, when I came to believe in the crucified and risen Christ. It proclaims the creative and re-demptive love of a trinitarian God whose authority and personality ground and govern the created universe in which the drama of human freedom and divine redemption plays itself out. In this open world of promise and pos-sibility, we should consider history to be "holy" and our time should be filled with "words, music, dance, and every sign" that testify "to the divine glory."

Or do they require such a choice? "Not at all! Why either-or?" Milosz answers, as his poem heads toward its conclusion. In the final two stanzas, he explains that in the contemporary world, we inevitably find ourselves shift-ing back and forth between the poles of belief and unbelief depicted in the *either-or* dichotomy. We may pay homage to the "Mystery" of God "every Sunday," but "it is better that not everyone is called to the priesthood. / Some are for prayers, others for their sins" (540–41).

When I first read and taught the poem, I was particularly intrigued by Milosz's mention of "what we are taught in schools, / In newspapers and

TV" because during my childhood years, it was there I acquired many of my values. On the screen, in the streets, and at the schoolyard, I developed a hazy image of a God who was nothing more than a Great Force living in silence somewhere beyond the stars. As far as I could tell, this God took no interest in the needs of my heart, had no concern for the direction of my life, and could not have cared less about the course of history. As Milosz says, in the world overseen—and overlooked— by such a deity, "the evolution of life" seems to be "an accident, / As is an accident the existence of man."

This is what I was learning, but I didn't like it, for it unnerved me to think of life in this manner. I remember feeling particularly unsettled when I read in my eighth grade earth science textbook that the elements of a human body were worth—in 1960s dollars—roughly $2.10. (A United States government agency calculated the value at $4.50, a decade or so ago.) As Hamlet asks, what is the point of human life, if each of us is an ensemble of elements accidentally gathered together for no discernible purpose:

> What is a man,
> If his chief good and market of his time
> Be but to sleep and feed? A beast, no more. (IV.4.34–36)

To be "no more" than a beast—that thought was distressing to me, especially after my brother died. I thought my fears of meaninglessness and death were unusual, and I was sure I was doomed. I was convinced, for example, that I would not live to be as old as Gordy had been—eighteen years, eleven months—when he had died. A numbing fear sometimes gripped me in the night, and a sense of blankness could just as easily cast a pall over my spirit at midday. Life's emptiness weighed upon me, and I experienced a loneliness of the kind that theologian Helmut Thielicke describes well: "If I believe only in nothingness, if there is no Creator and Father, then I am not only left in dreadful loneliness, but I must also despairingly take charge of my own life."[5]

I had no clue as to where I might turn for help. Numbed by their own grief, my parents found it hard to offer comfort, and I did not dare to speak of my anxieties to my high school friends. Only in that realm Emily Dickinson calls the dwelling place of possibility—in the poems and novels I was reading in high school English—did I find a space in which I could hear and speak with others about the things that mattered most to me. In that place of possibility, voices from across the centuries—those of William Shakespeare and Robert Frost, Nathaniel Hawthorne and Emily Dickinson, and John Keats and Thomas Hardy—rang out and broke what had become a deafening silence.

Beginning with the Word

It may seem counterintuitive, but Hardy's novels in particular exercised what I might call a redemptive influence. *The Return of the Native* was on my senior English syllabus, and I found it so compelling I went on to read *The Mayor of Casterbridge*, *Tess of the D'Urbervilles*, and *Jude the Obscure* on my own. In those books, I came upon a sense of irony that had to do with something greater than the simple matter of characters failing to understand themselves or their experience fully. What I encountered in Hardy was a tragic irony that had wormed its way deep into the core of life, where the desires of the heart faced the heartlessness of the world.

Nothing epitomizes Hardy's irony more pungently than an incident that takes place days before Tess Durbeyfield's marriage to Angel Clare. Troubled over a traumatic sexual experience in her past, Tess writes a letter to Angel that explains how she had been violated and pleads with him to have compassion upon her. She slides the note under his door and waits for a response that never comes. On the morning of their wedding day, she slips into Angel's room to search for the letter, only to find it tucked under the carpet near the doorsill. The letter had never reached him, and from that missed opportunity, all the tragic events of the novel then unfold.

When I read *Tess of the D'Urbervilles*, that incident summed up the lessons of the schooling I had received in my home and on the street. It was a message that declared that our intentions never jibe with our actions, our goals never match our accomplishments, and our longings—for the healing of spirits and the binding up of wounds—never line up with our lives. The narrator of Herman Melville's *Bartleby, the Scrivener* memorably frames the question of irony, when he hears that Bartleby may have worked at the Dead Letter Office in Washington:

> Conceive a man by nature and misfortune prone to a pallid hopelessness, can any business seem more fitted to heighten it than that of continually handling these dead letters and assorting them for the flames? For by the cartload they are annually burned. Sometimes from out the folded paper the pale clerk takes a ring:—the finger it was meant for, perhaps, molders in the grave; a bank-note sent in swiftest charity:—he whom it would relieve, nor eats nor hungers any more; pardon for those who died despairing; hope for those who died unhoping; good tidings for those who died stifled by unrelieved calamities. On errands of life, these letters speed to death.
>
> Ah Bartleby! Ah humanity! (34)

I wondered, is there ever an end to irony? Or does it endure forever, as it stretches from the silence of the atom to the empty sanctuaries of intergalactic space? I looked everywhere for any evidence of irony's end, but I always came up empty-handed, thwarted by the power of the grave and disenchanted by the emptiness of words.

This was how matters stayed, until God led me to the cross of Christ and brought me to the empty tomb. There are ironies and reversals aplenty in the story of Jesus Christ, but they have to do with the overturning of the order in which death and brokenness reign, as they tell of a weakness that has unfathomable power, of a folly that is divinely wise, and of a death that opens to life. Here in the story of the cross and the tomb, I found a deep, inexhaustible source of all hopes for my life and for the lives of others, living and dead. Yet even as I eagerly laid claim to this gift of a newfound hope, I remained grateful for the powerful play of possibilities that literature had put before me.

"Saying the Thing Which Is Not": Literature and the Powers of Possibility

There are times when the question of possibilities moves out of the pages of books and onto the stage of public affairs. One such occasion came in 1968, the most tumultuous year in modern American history. In late spring of that year, the theme of possible worlds came to the fore during a tragic time of loss, and it did so in a eulogy offered by Edward Kennedy at the funeral Mass for his brother, Robert, in New York's St. Patrick's Cathedral. Before a congregation packed with dignitaries and grieving family members and a television audience numbering in the tens of millions, Ted paid tribute to Bobby by quoting remarks his brother had uttered "many times, in many parts of this nation" during the 1968 presidential campaign: "Some men see things as they are and say, 'Why?'; I dream things that never were and say, 'Why not?'"

In sounding a note of grief-stricken hope, these words comforted the nation at a desperate time. Bobby Kennedy had made the quote a central element of his insurgent campaign against Lyndon Johnson, and in doing so, he was borrowing from his brother John, who had used almost identical words in a 1963 speech to the Irish Parliament. On that occasion, the president had said that others may see "things and . . . say 'Why?' . . . But I dream things that never were—and I say: 'Why not?'" John Kennedy followed those words with a tribute to the inventive virtues of the Irish people:

> It is that quality of the Irish, the remarkable combination of hope, confidence and imagination, that is needed more than ever today. The problems of the world cannot possibly be solved by skeptics or cynics, whose horizons are limited by the obvious realities. We need men who can dream of things that never were, and ask, "Why not?" It matters not how small a nation is that seeks world peace

and freedom, for, to paraphrase a citizen of my country, "The humblest nation of all the world, when clad in the armor of a righteous cause, is stronger than all the hosts of Error."[6]

In his 1963 speech, John F. Kennedy correctly attributed this quote to the Irish playwright George Bernard Shaw, and his brother Bobby often did so as well in his campaign for the presidency five years later. But Ted Kennedy did not mention Shaw in his eulogy, and it was through his speech that the phrase entered the mainstream of American culture, with its Irish provenance lost to all but the few who read the footnotes.

Even at that, however, the attribution to Shaw tells only a part of the story, for none of the Kennedys ever explained the context in which the stirring words were embedded in Shaw's work. And that makes all the difference, for the "dream of things that never were"—used to inspire the Irish people, to galvanize American voters on the stump, and to comfort a grieving nation—came not from the heart of a dreamer but from the tongue of a schemer.

The words that the Kennedys used to great effect are in fact spoken by the serpent to Eve in *Back to Methuselah*, a series of Shavian plays that are prefaced by a long essay. In this brilliant but befuddling work, Shaw did his best to weave a tapestry of enchantment out of the dull threads of Darwinian theory. In the first play of the sequence, Adam and Eve have just finished a conversation about the burdens of life and the reality of death, when the serpent appears and offers them a way to avoid the mortality they dread. "The serpent never dies," he explains. "Some day you shall see me come out of this beautiful skin, a new snake with a new and lovelier skin. That is birth." When Eve says she has "seen that," and that it is a "wonderful" thing, the serpent replies: "If I can do that, what can I not do? . . . When you and Adam talk, I hear you say 'Why?' Always 'Why?' You see things; and you say 'Why?' But I dream things that never were; and I say 'Why not?'" He tells Eve that he "made the word dead to describe" his old skin that had been cast off when he was renewed and then created the word "born" to name that renewal of life. To clinch his argument, he asks Eve a question that mockingly echoes the evangelical language of conversion: "Why not be born again and again as I am, new and beautiful every time?" (6).

A rich history of ideas lies behind this passage, and Shaw outlines that history in the witty but wearying preface to *Back to Methuselah*. Darwinism lurks at the heart of this discussion but is not its only focus, as Shaw ranges widely over the terrain of modern religion, literature, and science to demonstrate how it came to be that his twentieth-century serpent is able to claim that the power to name has become the power to remake the world. At times, the serpent's dialogue with Eve reads like a prospectus for language theory of the late twentieth century. "Instead of saying that the discovery of vocabularies could bring hidden secrets to light, they [Friedrich Nietzsche and William James] said that new ways of speaking could help get us what we want," wrote Richard Rorty in 1980.[7] The serpent couldn't have said it better.

In a fundamental sense, Rorty and the serpent have a point. It has to do with what Ricoeur memorably termed the "symbolic dimensions of our being in the world." Discourse is always about something, Ricoeur notes, and only a "few sophisticated texts" meet the ideal of "a text without reference," in which "the play of the signifier" breaks entirely free from any reality of the signified. Written works always speak in one way or another about the world, and only human beings "[have] a world and not just a situation."

"For me," writes Ricoeur, "the referent of all literature" is the world (Welt) that language creates out of the environment (Umwelt) of human experience. In Ricoeur's words, the works of literature that "we have read, understood, and loved" manage to "light up our own situation" by taking the episodes of our experience of the world and casting them within a narrative framework. The references of literature "open up the world" for us, by pointing not only to what we are, but to what and whom we might become. "In this sense," Ricoeur concludes, "Heidegger rightly says . . . that what we understand first in a discourse is not another person, but a project, that is, the outline of a new being-in-the-world." Writing reveals "the destination of discourse as projecting a world."[8]

For Ricoeur, metaphor provides the key to literature's capacity to open possible worlds before us. Through metaphor, the imagination provides a concrete dimension to that moment in our encounters with new thoughts, perceptions, or realities, when we realize that what we already know must be suspended, so that we might learn something new—about ourselves, the world, or God. Through their capacity to say that "one thing is another"—to say, "a mighty fortress is our God" or "the Lord is my shepherd"—metaphors serve as models "for changing our way of looking at things, of perceiving the world."[9]

Poetic language has as much to do with reality as any other use of language does, but it deals with it "by the means of a complex strategy" involving the temporary suspension of ordinary categories of thought and reasoning. In this process the established meaning of a word is set aside, and a second-order function of language is brought to the fore. This function engages the "Why not?" of Bobby Kennedy's persistent campaign-trail question. With the literal sense of what is having been suspended, the metaphor's strangeness opens before us a vision of what might be. "To imagine," writes Ricoeur, "is to address oneself to what is not."[10]

Beginning with the Word

Ricoeur's vision of poetic language involves a greater sense of mystery than does Rorty's pragmatic plan to use words to "get what we want." As it suspends and displaces the ordinary meaning and reference of a word, metaphor arrives at a deeper truth. "It constitutes," Ricoeur says, "the primordial reference [to reality] to the extent that it suggests, reveals, unconceals—or whatever you say—the deep structures of reality to which we are related as mortals who are born into this world and who *dwell* in it for a while." To describe what occurs in metaphor, Ricoeur quotes from an essay by Douglas Berggren, who argues that the capacity to understand a metaphor requires "a peculiar and rather sophisticated intellectual ability which W. Bedell Stanford metaphorically labels 'stereoscopic vision': the ability to entertain two different points of view at the same time." This is, of course, a familiar argument to us by this point. It echoes closely Fitzgerald's definition of what it means to have a first-rate intelligence—"the ability to hold two opposed ideas in the mind at the same time"—and it also speaks of the to-and-fro quality of the mind that Milosz captures in "Either-Or." The power to bring new worlds into being highlights the imagination's unique ability to provide "*models for* reading reality in a new way. This split structure"—this tension between the need for language both to describe reality and to envision its transformation—"is the structure of imagination as fiction."[11] These models for "reading reality" in new ways have the potential to transform us because they shape our understanding of ourselves, our world, and our possibilities.[12]

It is easy to celebrate metaphor's ability to open new worlds of possibility, as long as we think of those worlds as being attractive and plausible. But what happens to the question "Why not?" if our capacity to imagine turns into a power to lie? It was this question that Jonathan Swift posed almost three centuries ago in *Gulliver's Travels*. In a letter to Alexander Pope in 1725, Swift explained that he had been at work on "a treatise proving the falsity of that definition *animal rationale*; and to show it should be only *rationis capax*." That is, humans are not "rational animals" but simply "animals capable" of reason. "Upon this great foundation of misanthropy," Swift told Pope, "the whole building of my Travels is erected; and I never will have peace of mind till all honest men are of my opinion."[13]

Gulliver's Travels addresses the "Why not?" question in its final section, which deals with Gulliver's adventures in the land of the Houyhnhnms, a species of rational horses who rule their domain and have turned the Yahoos, who look and act like humans, into virtual slaves who do their bidding. Gulliver's own Houyhnhnm master is appalled by the stories he relates of life in England, where humans have perfected the arts of deception. As Gulliver tells of the chicanery, greed, and conflict that mark English political life and social behavior, he paints a picture of a desolate land ruled by hypocrisy and lies. His account of his homeland, along with his penchant for shading the truth and hiding key facts, prompt his Houyhnhnm master to note that Gulliver "often *said the Thing which was not*" (241).

This makes no sense to the Houyhnhnms, who cannot understand the practice of lying. "For he argued thus," Gulliver says of his master, "that the Use of Speech was to make us understand one another, and to receive Information of Facts; now if any one *said the Thing which was not*, these Ends were defeated; because I cannot properly be said to understand him." According to Gulliver's master, the person who uses language in such a manner makes it impossible for me to understand him, and "he leaves me worse than in Ignorance; for I am led to believe a Thing *Black* when it is *White*, and *Short* when it is *Long*" (223).[14]

So what exactly is it that we do, when we "dream things that never were and say, 'why not?'" Are we using metaphor to expose an unjust order and envision a transformed one? Or in "saying the thing which is not," are we deceiving ourselves and others through the abuse of language? What are we to make of the fact that the same capacity that equips us to dream also enables us to lie?

Anguish and Freedom: The Limits and Powers of Literature

These complex issues involving literature, language, and human possibilities stand out with particular clarity in the African American experience. Black voters provided substantial backing for Robert Kennedy in the presidential race of 1968, and when he addressed black audiences, the quote from Shaw struck a sensitive nerve. More than a century after the end of the Civil War, it spoke, to paraphrase Langston Hughes, of a dream still deferred.[15]

That dream—of African American freedom and equality—found eloquent and powerful expression in a book written a full fifteen years before the Civil War, the *Narrative of the Life of Frederick Douglass, an American Slave.* Published only several years after he had escaped from slavery, Douglass's narrative sold briskly—thirty thousand copies in the first five years—and became a galvanizing force in the abolitionist movement.

Douglass's narrative begins with a series of straightforward assertions that cast the brutal realities of slavery in stark relief. "I was born in Tuckahoe, [Maryland]," he explains, but "I have no accurate knowledge of my age." The "whispered opinion" was that "my master was my father," but as to the "correctness of this opinion, I know nothing; the means of knowing was withheld from me." In keeping with slaveholding custom, Douglass was

Beginning with the Word

separated from his mother as an infant, so "I never saw my mother, to know her as such, more than four or five times in my life; and each of these times was very short in duration, and at night." She died on a neighboring farm when he was seven or so, and her son was "not allowed to be present during her illness, at her death, or burial." Never having known her to any real extent as a tender, living presence, Douglass reports, "I received the tidings of her death with much the same emotions I should have probably felt at the death of a stranger" (*Narrative*, 15–16).

Douglass's description of his early experiences provides a chilling and revelatory account of slavery's power over the mind and heart. The slaves on his plantation called the home of their master, Colonel Lloyd, the *Great House Farm*. For all the slaves, to be given the privilege to run an errand to that home was considered the greatest of honors. Douglass reports that on their way to the master's house, slaves would "make the dense old woods, for miles around, reverberate with their wild songs, revealing at once the highest joy and the deepest sadness." While their songs might be "jargon" to others, they were "full of meaning to themselves." Douglass says, "I have sometimes thought" that the mere hearing of those songs could do more than "the reading of volumes of philosophy" could do to impress upon their hearers "the horrible character of slavery."

Douglass then confesses that when he had been a slave, he too did not "understand the deep meaning of these rude and apparently incoherent songs. I was myself within the circle; so that I neither saw nor heard as those without might see or hear." The analysis here is astute, and it relates directly to what Emily Dickinson and Paul Ricoeur say about dwelling in possibility and opening to the play of possible worlds. Among other things, the institution of chattel slavery was meant to keep its victims from acquiring any sense that their terrible lot could ever change. For the system and the slaveholders who operated within it, there was no place for the play of possibilities—for imagining the "thing that is not"—in the experience of the subjects who were meant to remain in bondage (*Narrative*, 23–24).

During his childhood, Frederick was shuttled from one household to another within his owner's extended family. At the age of nine, when he was sent to live with one branch of the family in Baltimore, he was befriended by the mistress of the house, Sophia Auld, who took pity on him and set out to teach him to read. Her efforts angered her husband, however, and he brought them to a halt immediately. "It was unlawful, as well as unsafe, to teach a slave to read," Hugh Auld told his wife. "[Teach him] how to read, [and] there would be no keeping him. It would forever unfit him to be a slave." If you taught a slave to read, he'd "become unmanageable, and of no value to his master. As to himself, it could do him no good, but a great deal of harm. It would make him discontented and unhappy" (*Narrative*, 37).

The slave revolts of 1822 (planned by Denmark Vesey in Charleston) and 1829 (led by Nat Turner in Virginia) had alarmed the slaveholders. In the case of both Vesey and Turner, religious training had led to literacy, which in turn had opened to them and others the visionary imagery and power of the Bible, particularly the prophetic books of the Old Testament and the book of Revelation in the New. In a "confession" made just before his execution, Nat Turner "reminded his interviewer that Jesus brought 'not peace but a sword' (Matt. 10:34)." He claimed that the Holy Spirit had inspired him to read the words of Jesus aright, and soon, everywhere he looked, he saw signs of the crucified warrior, Jesus Christ, calling him to battle.[16]

In reacting to the revolts, both plantation owners and political leaders rushed to limit religious freedom and to put an end to black literacy. Punishment for violating this law was often swift and severe. As the grandson of a former slave recalled decades later, if a slave began to learn to read and write, and that fact became known to his overseer or master, it was not uncommon for that slave's fingers to be cut off, as an immediate penalty and a lasting warning.[17]

For many slaves in general and for Frederick Douglass in particular, their masters' fears only spurred them on in their quest to learn to read and write. Douglass says Hugh Auld's words "sank deep into my heart, stirred up sentiments within that lay slumbering and called into existence an entirely new train of thought." His admonitions served as a "special revelation" that cleared up for young Frederick many "dark and mysterious" elements of his experience as a slave. He understood at last, for example, what "had been to me a most perplexing difficulty—to wit, the white man's power to enslave the black man." From that moment, he said—from the moment in which he learned both the rudiments of reading and heard hints of its power—"I understood the pathway from slavery to freedom." Hugh Auld had done him a great favor by speaking so bluntly of the power of reading, so, Douglass reports, "I set out with high hope, and a fixed purpose, at whatever cost of trouble, to learn how to read" (*Narrative*, 37–38). Young Frederick compensated for the loss of Mrs. Auld by turning the white children on the streets of Baltimore into his teachers. When he headed out on errands for the Aulds, he carried two items with him—a handful of bread to pay those children for teaching him the words he needed to know and a book to write those words down in.

For Frederick, reading broke open a hole high in the wall of slavery's prison and shed light over the institution's darkened corners and dreadful processes. It also enabled him to develop an inner vision of a world in which he might one day be free. "Without knowing exactly what she was doing," Douglass's

Beginning with the Word

biographer observes, "Sophia Auld began the end of slavery for this particular slave. Perhaps not entirely unwittingly . . . , she was a dangerous subversive" for having taught a slave to read.[18]

In light of what Hugh Auld had said, Frederick sensed that reading had the power to carry him "outside the circle." One of his prized possessions was a copy of *The Columbian Orator*, a collection of political speeches and classical orations meant to train American youth, especially boys, in the traditions of great oratory and the virtues of the American way. In particular, Douglass was captivated by a speech on Catholic emancipation by the Irish playwright Richard Brinsley Sheridan. Along with other speeches and essays in the *Orator*, this work "enabled me to utter my thoughts, and to meet the arguments brought forward to sustain slavery." Yet at the same time, Douglass notes, "while they relieved me of one difficulty, they brought on another even more painful than the one of which I was relieved." The more he read, the more he came to look at white slaveholders as nothing but robbers who traveled around the globe to search for men, women, and children to steal (*Narrative*, 42).

So it was "that very discontentment which Master Hugh had predicted" came to "torment and sting [his] soul to unutterable anguish." Douglass moved out of the circle only to stumble into the pit of despair:

> [Reading] had given me a view of my wretched condition, without the remedy. It opened my eyes to the horrible pit, but to no ladder upon which to get out. In moments of agony, I envied my fellow-slaves for their stupidity. I have often wished myself a beast. I preferred the condition of the meanest reptile to my own. Any thing, no matter what, to get rid of thinking! It was this everlasting thinking of my condition that tormented me. There was no getting rid of it. (*Narrative*, 42)

"Whenever my condition was improved," Douglass wrote, "instead of its increasing my contentment, it only increased my desire to be free." He became convinced that "to make a contented slave, it is necessary to make a thoughtless one." As long as the slave stayed "within the circle" and knew nothing of an "outside" that could be imagined or desired, resignation remained an option. But once the person in bondage learned of "things that never were"—such as freedom—and began to "say 'Why not?'" the contrast between bondage and freedom proved all but unbearable. "I often found myself regretting my own existence, and wishing myself dead; and but for the hope of being free, I have no doubt but that I should have killed myself" (*Narrative*, 83, 43).

With his account of suffering and injustice, disillusionment and hope, Douglass taps into a vein of what Perry Miller called "the Augustinian strain of piety" that ran deep in the Puritan theology of New England and, later, in the broad stream of American evangelical religion.[19] Grounded in the theology of the Pauline Epistles, this vision places a strong emphasis on the bondage of the human will, the power of God's deliverance, *and* the gulf that stretches between us in our sin and God in his mercy. As a convert to evangelical Christianity Douglass was trained in this piety, and as a slave he learned firsthand about the powers of bondage.

Biographer Peter Brown tells us that in the years immediately after Augustine's conversion, the new Christian read the Letters of Paul and largely interpreted them as a pagan would. He took Paul, that is, to be preaching a gospel of "spiritual ascent" in which the "inner" man (the soul) lived and grew in a state of constant renewal, while the "man" (the body) continued its long, slow process of decay. Yet as he dug deeper into the Scriptures and analyzed his own spiritual practices, Augustine found this dualism wanting, and he began to trade vertical metaphors of life as an ascent to God for horizontal figures of the Christian life as a long journey down a road. The "moments of clear vision of truth" had once been for Augustine rungs on the ladder to heaven, each a step higher on the ascent to truth. Now he saw them as "points of light 'along the darkening highway.'" Augustine never enjoyed travel because he associated it with "a sense of protracted labor and of the infinite postponement of his dearest wishes," but he came to endure it reluctantly because for him the journey had replaced the ascent as the way to God. For Augustine the Christian, the hope for "the things that never were" was a hope deferred, and the question "Why not?" would be answered only at the end of time. In the words of Brown:

> A new tone has come to suffuse Augustine's life. He is a man who has realized that he was doomed to remain incomplete in his present existence, that what he wished for most ardently would never be more than a hope, postponed to a final resolution of all tensions, far beyond this life. Anyone who thought otherwise, he felt, was either morally obtuse or a doctrinaire. All a man could do was to "yearn" for this absent perfection, to feel its loss intensely, to pine for it. *"Desiderium sinus cordis"*: "It is yearning that makes the heart deep." This marks the end of a long-established classical ideal of perfection: Augustine would never achieve the concentrated tranquility of the supermen that still gaze out at us from some mosaics in Christian churches and from the statues of pagan sages. If to be a "Romantic," means to be a man acutely aware of being caught in an existence that denies him the fullness for which he craves, to feel that he is defined by his tension towards something else, by his capacity for faith, for hope, for longing, to think of himself as a wanderer seeking a country that is always distant, but made ever-present to him by the quality of the love that "groans" for it, then Augustine has imperceptibly become a "Romantic."[20]

Augustine may have been a romantic in this sense, but one would be hesitant to say the same of Douglass, for there is a profound difference between wounds of self-laceration and scars from a bondsman's lash. The fifth-century North African theologian may accept responsibility for his own suffering and inner division, but the nineteenth-century American slave can hardly take the blame for the pain he endures. One has to do with sins centered in the self, the other with injustices woven into the fabric of the language and social reality of antebellum America.

For Augustine, it took an internal revolution, sparked by the grace of God working on his heart, to free him from the "horrible pit" of his condition. Douglass needed something qualitatively different from that to free him from his bondage. He had undergone a conversion to evangelical Christianity at the age of thirteen in 1831, the same year in which he bought his copy of *The Columbian Orator*. It was also at this time that he first began to hear his master, Hugh Auld, and his associates speaking animatedly of "abolitionists." Douglass did not know what the term meant, until he read a Baltimore newspaper account of petitions "presented to congress praying for the abolition . . . of the slave trade between the states of the Union." From that point on, the words "abolition" and "abolition movement" possessed for Douglass a talismanic power: "There was HOPE in those words" (*Bondage*, 229–30).

Douglass later wrote of this experience that his own conversion had intensified his hatred of slavery. He reports he "saw the world in a new light" and found himself "animated by new hopes and desires." His "great concern was, now, to have the world converted," for he thought such a mass conversion might lead to the abolition of slavery. Still, in the meantime, he anguished over the thought of being a "slave for life." Devastated by the thought of everlasting bondage, Douglass sought the counsel of Charles Lawson, a black layman who lived not far from him in Baltimore. Douglass tells the story of their relationship in a brief set of exchanges that reads like a dramatic tableaux. With a small amount of explanatory and transitional material removed, their conversation went as follows, with Frederick posing the initial question:

"How can these things be—and what can *I* do?"
"*Trust in the Lord*."
"I [am] a slave, and a slave FOR LIFE."
"The Lord can make you free, my dear. All things are possible with him, only *have faith in God*. Ask, and it shall be given. If you want liberty, ask the Lord for it, *in faith*, AND HE WILL GIVE IT TO YOU." (*Bondage*, 231–32)

Douglass took this advice and waited for God and the abolitionists to bring an end to his suffering and to the whole of the abominable system of slavery. Yet his patience wore thin, and when his defiance became obvious to the Auld family, they decided to solve the problem by renting him for a year to Edward Covey, a farmer known as a breaker of slaves.

In Douglass's case, Covey took to the task with relish, and each week he subjected his new charge to a severe beating with sticks and cowskins, and he forced his new, prized possession to work in the field from dawn until dark each day. At the end of six months, matters came to a head, when Frederick collapsed in the stifling heat of an August afternoon. Covey beat him ferociously and might have killed him, if Frederick had not escaped into the woods for several days.

When Douglass returned, Covey set out to teach him a final lesson. Yet the master's resolve was more than matched by the subject's determination. As he recuperated Douglass had resolved to give up his religious reservations against resisting a master, "and my hands were no longer tied by my religion." Having "backslidden" from the religious creed of the slave, he vowed "to make my fallen state known to my Sunday-pious brother, Covey" (*Bondage*, 282).

He did so when the slaveholder attacked him the morning after his return. When Douglass refused to submit, Covey was startled and cried out, "*Are you going to resist*, you scoundrel?" When the slave responded, "Yes, sir," the battle was joined. Covey was no match for Douglass, and having failed to draw "a single drop of blood" in two hours of fighting, he slinked away, "puffing and blowing at a great rate" (*Bondage*, 283, 285).

Douglass lived another six months on Covey's farm, but the breaker of slaves never laid a hand on him again. To recount these events, Douglass employed scriptural imagery but did so in a manner as to highlight how far he had traveled from the passivity put on him by the Christian quietism that had been preached to him as a slave. The language of conversion shifts from a sinner and savior framework to a model of self-assertion and survival: "I was a changed being after that fight. I was *nothing* before; I WAS A MAN NOW." The feeling of elation he felt in the wake of his victory was to Douglass "a resurrection from the dark and pestiferous tomb of slavery, to the heaven of comparative freedom." No longer "*afraid to die*," Douglass became "a freeman in *fact*, while I remained a slave in form" (*Bondage*, 286).

Reformation and Revolution

As our exploration of Frederick's resistance and renewal makes clear, there are limits to the analogies we might draw between the experiences of Augustine

Beginning with the Word

and those of Douglass. There are many ways we could speak of these limits, but the most direct might be to begin with a sharp distinction between the fifth-century bishop and the nineteenth-century abolitionist on the question of sin and slavery.

To Augustine, the primary bondage of human life was that of our will to our sin. God in his mercy can deliver us from this personal bonadage, although our struggles will not cease until we die. From the institutional bondage of slavery, however, it never would have occured to Augustine to call for deliverance. He considered the institution a consequence of sin and an inevitable reality. As bold as he was, Augustine never believed humans could or must transform the material and social conditions of their lives.

For Frederick Douglass, on the other hand, the thought of enduring slavery became unbearable when he learned, through reading, of the freedom that might be his, if he could somehow get "outside the circle" and take his place in the open space of freedom. He was reluctant to revolt openly, largely as a result of the religious training he received in a slaveholding culture. But that reluctance began to fade when he imagined a future of freedom and contrasted it to the unbearable thought of being a slave for life. Fueled by his vision of freedom, and equipped with a vocabulary of resistance, revolt, and self-determination, Douglass could never again submit to the idea of a fixed social order. Unlike Augustine, who had remained a citizen of a static classical order, Douglass was the product of liberal, democratic ideals that stressed the possibilities of transformation and the inevitability of progress.

At the same time, for all the differences between the understandings they have of the human condition, there remains a powerful point of connection between Augustine's longing for deliverance and Douglass's dream of freedom. It has to do with their shared sense of the dependence of human hope on the category of possibility.

This connection may seem clearer to us if we look at a few developments that contributed to the early modern transformation of the Augustinian vision. We can pick up the trail at the point at which the Protestant Reformers appropriated key strands of the Augustinian argument about the longing for the kingdom of God and the call for the transformation of the human will. Like Paul and Augustine before them, Martin Luther, John Calvin, and Jonathan Edwards spoke openly of the tie between the waywardness of the human will and the suffering of a sin-darkened world.

Calvin framed this matter starkly in the *Institutes of the Christian Religion*. "Not only has punishment fallen upon us from Adam, but a contagion imparted by him resides in us," he argued, and our deepest problem is "that this perversity never ceases in us, but continually bears new fruits—the works of the flesh that we have already described—just as a burning furnace gives forth flame and sparks, or water ceaselessly bubbles up from a spring."[21]

Nevertheless, no matter how deeply the stain of sin has seeped into creation, to Calvin the world remained "a dazzling theater" in which the light of God's glory floods the stage. In like manner, to Jonathan Edwards the world around us speaks, as biographer George Marsden explains, "the language of God; 'the heavens declare the glory of God,' as it says in the Psalms." Sin has corrupted the universe, but only partially, and those who have had their spiritual sight restored through the love of Christ and the work of the Holy Spirit "can see all of reality not as essentially impersonal but as, in its essence, a beautiful expression of God's love."[22]

Over the course of the seventeenth and eighteenth centuries, this bracing Augustinian vision slowly gave way to a more sanguine view of the self. Under the influence of Enlightenment rationalism, a growing number of men and women gave up their concerns over the wickedly "bad will"—Edwards's term—and undertook instead what Reinhold Niebuhr has called an "effort to derive evil from specific historical sources." This view of evil grew out of a "one-dimensional" view of history, according to which the sources of evil lie not in the universal wickedness of the heart but in particular agencies of corruption. We might trace that evil to "the corrupting influence of religion" or find its source in "tyrannical governments and ignorant legislators who had disturbed the harmony of nature." But wherever that source may lie, the moral and spiritual imperative was clear: track down the source and root it out.[23]

The quest to eliminate the "historical sources" of evil fueled the revolutionary fervor of late eighteenth-century France, and it drove many of the reform movements of the nineteenth century. In a number of cases, like that of slavery, the efforts to abolish an evil practice were necessary and just. Plantation-based slavery had grown as a result of the specific practices of traders, shippers, and landowners in the early modern West, and it flourished because governments in the old and the new world alike either tolerated or actively promoted the practice. Yet the most vital fact about the practice of chattel slavery on Southern plantations was that it had a discernible beginning and a documented history. As such, it might also have a conceivable end. This is what Douglass realized when he heard Hugh Auld rebuke his wife for teaching a slave to read; and, indeed, to this boy in bondage, reading opened a host of new possibilities that grew out of his "deep conviction that slavery would not always be able to hold me within its foul embrace" (*Narrative*, 16).

For the adolescent Douglass, nothing had hinted at a "new world" of freedom as compellingly as the speeches he read in the *Columbian Orator*. For him, the possibility of a life beyond slavery honed his vision even more sharply than did the reality of his bondage. His initial despair over the contrast between slavery and freedom eventually gave way to a determination to escape and to carry on the fight for abolition as a free man.

Learning to read and write had carried Douglass "outside the circle" and enabled him to assert his own dignity and to imagine the possibility of liberty. In other words, through his stealthy and determined efforts in the mid-nineteenth century, Frederick Douglass managed to seize for himself privileges that had been available to the peoples of northwest Europe and their American descendants for the better part of three centuries. Beginning with Descartes and broadening rapidly in the Enlightenment, reason was taken to be supreme among human capacities, and with the widespread availability of the printing press, the ability to write "was taken to be the *visible* sign of reason."[24]

That being the case, it is hardly surprising that slaveholding states enacted laws that prohibited teaching slaves to read and write. Henry Louis Gates argues that when they are considered in the aggregate, the many slave narratives of the nineteenth century represent "the attempt of blacks to *write themselves into being.*" The premise was that, through the mastery of Western languages, a black man or woman would be able "to posit a full and sufficient self" through an act of self-imagining and self-inscription. Faulted by Hegel for lacking any collective history, "blacks effectively responded by publishing hundreds of individual histories" that functioned as parts standing in for the whole. In the twentieth century, novelist Ralph Ellison explained, "We tell ourselves our individual stories so as to become aware of our *general* story."[25]

In describing the work of Douglass, and of Harriet Jacobs and others, as efforts to "write themselves into being," Gates provides a bridge that connects nineteenth-century African American narratives and twentieth-century theories that speak of the power of language to imagine possible worlds. We have heard Paul Ricoeur argue that our use of language would make no sense if it did not serve the purpose of "letting new worlds emerge" to shape the way we understand and govern ourselves in the world. Frederick Douglass would have understood this point fully.

Precisely because with words we can say "the thing which is not," poetry and fiction may support and sustain our efforts to envision a transformed world. By showing us "possible modes of being," stories may point the way to profound changes in what we believe and how we act. One pleasure we derive from reading a novel, for example, comes from the freedom we have to don the emotional, spiritual, or intellectual garb of a character. What would I do, if I were Arthur Dimmesdale or Hester Prynne living in a seventeenth-century Puritan village? How would I respond to loss and disappointment, if I were Dorothea Brooke in George Eliot's Victorian England? How would

I act, if I faced the odds that Bigger Thomas had to face growing up in Chicago's depression-era South Side? And in a more general sense, what might we learn—and how might we be changed—if a poem or a story were to place before our mind's eye the contours of a world healed, transformed, and reconciled to God?

So it was, that in exercising its potent influence over the mind and heart of Frederick Douglass, literature played to one of its greatest strengths, which is that of providing a narrative context for our understanding of the past, the present, and the possible future. That is, it can open to us the story of the future as well as that of the past.

Robert Jenson suggests that we know of God's identity only through what he has revealed of himself in his acts of deliverance and through the Scripture's narrative account of his creative, sacrificial, and redemptive care for the world he has made. "God is whoever raised Jesus from the dead, having before raised Israel from Egypt," writes Jenson. The God of the Bible "can truly be identified by narrative," and as a result, his self-identity "is constituted in *dramatic coherence*." Aristotle provides the classic definition of such coherence when he describes an effective story as one in which events unfold "unexpectedly but on account of each other." In a compelling drama, before an event occurs, we cannot predict precisely what is to happen, but after the events have played themselves out, we "see it was just what had to happen."[26]

Jenson observes that because Aristotle "regarded liability to historical contingency" to be a flaw, he "drew no metaphysical profit from his observation" concerning the contingent nature of dramatic narratives that work. The God of the Bible, however, defines himself by the contingencies of the creative and redemptive commitments he has chosen to make and communicate. As Jenson explains, the Bible presents the divine "commitment in a history" to be a sign of "ontological *perfection*." God binds his own story to the story of the creatures he created, and in the deepest sense, he "can have no identity except as he meets the temporal end toward which creatures live."[27]

It is notable that the Bible establishes God's identity "not from the beginning but from the end, not at birth but at death, not in *persistence* but in *anticipation*." The God of Israel and of Jesus Christ is not "eternally himself" in that he forever maintains a "beginning in which he already is all he ever will be." Instead, he is eternally himself in that he "unrestrictedly anticipates an end in which he will be all he ever could be." The outcome of events constitutes a story, and within the sequence of events, the openness of the future frees each present moment from a sense of fated inevitability. Because the future will be that time when God "will be all that he ever could be," the present is free to live within the play of contingent possibilities. God's future, that is,

Beginning with the Word

"liberates each successive specious present from mere predictability" and in doing so, God opens the present to the transforming power of possibilities.[28]

To illustrate God's view of the future, Jenson examines the story of the Exodus, whose meaning "was not mere escape from the Egyptian past but the future the escape opened." The gods of Egypt possessed identities that were grounded "in the persistence of a beginning," he writes. By their very nature, "they *are* Continuity and Return. The Lord's meaning for Israel is the opposite." Just as the system of plantation slavery was an abomination to Douglass and his fellow slaves, so was "the archetypically established order of Egypt . . . the very damnation from which the Lord released [Israel] into being." The God of Abraham, Isaac, and Jacob "is not salvific because he defends against the future but because he poses it." In *posing* the future, God links the fulfillment of the deepest of human dreams—for a world ruled by "righteousness and justice and love"—to his character as a promise-making and promise-keeping God.[29]

9

A Good Man Is Hard to Find

Christen and the Poets

Christ and the Poets

Mother has now been gone five Weeks. We should have thought it a long Visit, were she coming back—Now the "Forever" thought almost shortens it, as we are nearer rejoining her than her own return—We were never intimate Mother and Children while she was our Mother—but Mines in the same Ground meet by tunneling and when she became our Child, the Affection came—

—Emily Dickinson, letter, December 1882

Several years after the fact, Flannery O'Connor wrote to a friend to describe a sharp exchange she had had with the novelist Mary McCarthy at a dinner party. It turned out to be a dispute, albeit a brief one, about the relationship of word and thing, language and truth, religion and literature. "She departed the Church at the age of 15 and is a Big Intellectual," O'Connor wrote of McCarthy, and it was clear that the vaunted public intellectual intimidated her younger, fiction-writing guest.

The dinner began at eight, and by one in the morning, O'Connor reported, "I hadn't opened my mouth once, there being nothing for me in such company to say." She felt like a dog "who had been trained to say a few words but overcome with anxiety had forgotten them." Then, at some point "toward morning," the conversation turned to the subject of "the Eucharist, which I, being the Catholic, was obviously supposed to defend." McCarthy said that whenever she received the Host in her childhood, she had liked to imagine "it as the Holy Ghost," that "most portable" person of the Trinity. But now, she explained, she took it to be nothing but "a symbol and implied that it was a pretty good one. I then said, in a very shaky voice, 'Well, if it's a symbol, to hell with it.'" That was the only defense that a weary O'Connor could mount in the middle of the night, but in her words, "I realize now that this is all I will ever be able to say about it, outside of a story, except that it is the center of existence for me; all the rest of life is expendable."

O'Connor relates this account with relish in a letter to Betty Hester, the correspondent known as "A" in *The Habit of Being*, the first edition of the short-story writer's letters. She employs the story to illustrate a point she has already made in that letter about her fictional use of Christian imagery. After describing a scene in "A Temple of the Holy Ghost," O'Connor cautions Hester to "understand though, that, like the child [in the story], I believe the Host is actually the body and blood of Christ, not a symbol. If the story grows for you it is because of the mystery of the Eucharist in it" (976–77).

During the writing of this book, I have thought often of Flannery O'Connor's account of this incident and of both her stalwart defense of Christian doctrine and her stubborn refusal to allow the language of Christian belief—the cadences and assertions of the creeds, the poetic images and rhythms of the liturgy, and the resonant doctrines of the faith—to be ground down into a pile of allusive fragments or polished off as a set of portable symbols. O'Connor spent much of her time writing about Southern Baptist fundamentalists in her stories, but she never succumbed to the temptation Sister Hermann Marie describes so bluntly to Jack Gladney in *White Noise*. Unlike "all the others" who forsake belief and rely on the wild-eyed men in caves and nuns in black "to believe things no one else takes seriously," O'Connor did not foist the responsibility for belief on the characters in her fiction or the people in the Southern Baptist world all around her.

Instead, she gladly assumed those responsibilities as her own. At the age of thirty she wrote to an admirer that she was glad he could "see the belief" in her fiction "because it is there. The truth is my stories have been watered and fed by Dogma." Belief mattered to her, for she called herself "a Catholic not like someone else would be a Baptist or a Methodist but like someone else would be an atheist." And whatever success she already had enjoyed as a writer, she attributed the clarity of her strong beliefs to her vision of things. "If my stories are complete," she wrote, "it is because I see everything as beginning with original sin, taking in the Redemption, and reckoning on a final judgment" (930).

Beginning with the Word

Finding a Good Man

"A good man is hard to find," Red Sammy Butts declares to no one in particular one day in the early 1950s, as he waits on a family that has stopped for
lunch at his roadside diner in rural Georgia. "Everything is getting terrible,"
he says in O'Connor's story. "I remember the day you could go off and leave
your screen door unlatched. Not no more."

That last comment catches the attention of Grandmother Bailey, the ma-
triarch of the family party. In response, she launches into a speech about how
"Europe was entirely to blame for the way things were now," and she and Red
Sammy then speak about "better times," as her family washes down dinner
with "Co'-colas" before heading back down the road to Florida (142).

They never reach their destination, however, for between them and their
goal stands the Misfit. He is a convict who has escaped from the state peni-
tentiary along with two accomplices. They have begun a crime spree, and they
too have Florida in mind as their final destination. The convicts come upon
the Baileys shortly after the family has had an accident that has left them and
their car stranded in a ditch.

Grandmother Bailey recognizes the Misfit from the photos of him in the
papers, and he tells her it would have been better for all "if you hadn't of
reckernized me" (147). What follows that chilling statement is an extended
discussion between the Misfit and the Grandmother, which is punctuated by
the sounds of gunfire, as the Misfit's accomplices take the Grandmother's son,
daughter-in-law, and grandchildren into the woods and shoot them one by one.

As that drama unfolds, the Grandmother presses her own case, three times
telling the Misfit, "I just know you're a good man." To which he replies, "Nome,
I ain't a good man." He describes how his mother and father had been just
fine in their own way, but he was different from the start. He led a checkered
life that led to prison, where, in his words, "I set there and set there, trying
to remember what it was I done and I ain't recalled it to this day." But that's
the way life is, he concluded, so it didn't matter what you did, for "sooner
or later you're going to forget what it was you done and just be punished for
it" (148, 150).

When the Grandmother keeps repeating the name of Jesus, uttered more
in desperation than supplication, the Misfit warms to the subject. "Jesus was
the only One that ever raised the dead," he says, "and He shouldn't have done
it. He thown everything off balance." If he did rise from the dead, then we
ought to "thow away everything" and follow him. And if he didn't, "then it's
nothing for you to do but enjoy the few minutes you got left the best way you
can—by killing somebody or burning down his house or doing some other

meanness to him. No pleasure but meanness," he said, as his voice became a snarl. "I wisht I had of been there"—in Jerusalem when Christ was crucified and rose again from the dead on the third day—the Misfit says, because "if I had of been there I would of known and I wouldn't be like I am now" (152).

When he says this, the Grandmother reaches out to touch him, and calls him "one of my children!" Startled, he leaps back, shoots her three times in the chest, and is done with it. As he stands over her lifeless body, the Misfit offers a valedictory judgment: "She would have been a good woman, if it had been somebody there to shoot her every minute of her life." This is followed by a confession, which are the final words of the story: "It's no real pleasure in life" (152–53).

"A Good Man Is Hard to Find" is an alternatingly humorous and harrowing story that ties together many different threads of the argument that has unfolded throughout this book. The Misfit's description of prison reads like a schematic of the immanent and ironclad cosmos of modern naturalism and its linguist derivative, the structuralist paradigm: "Turn to the right, it was a wall. Turn to the left, it was a wall. Look up it was a ceiling, look down it was a floor" (150). To the Misfit, the cosmos is a prison, all the way from the icy heights in which the galaxies make their way, to the cells whose walls recently bound him in, down to the "prison-house of language" with which he tries to justify his actions and puzzle out the meaning of his seemingly senseless life.

With its title and theme, O'Connor's story of the Grandmother and the Misfit provides us with a final opportunity to examine language and belief, and words and the Word. In this chapter our exploration will take the form of a story of nineteenth-century longings and twentieth-century discoveries. It will be the story of how many powerful writers in the nineteenth century came to long and search for a personal God who could heal their wounds and break their bondage to death. Whether they wrote fiction, poetry, or memoirs, these writers serve as the hungry, visionary poets of this chapter's title. Like Frederick Douglass and Emily Dickinson, these nineteenth-century writers "dwelt in possibility" and sought the face of a gracious God. As private and idiosyncratic as these searches may often have seemed to be, they were in fact harbingers of the powerful renewal of trinitarian thought—and the doctrine of Christ—in twentieth-century theology.

The Possibility of Christ

We have seen how Paul Ricoeur describes fiction and poetry as means by which "new possibilities of being-in-the-world are opened up within everyday reality."[1] Works of literature allow us to dwell in possibilities and encourage us to imagine what the world and our lives might be like *if*... Consider, for instance, the Misfit. He is a poet of sorts, for he imagines what it means for Paul to tell the Corinthians, "If Christ has not been raised, your faith is futile, and you are still in your sins" (1 Cor. 15:17). The Misfit concludes, along with Paul, that "if the dead are not raised, 'Let us eat and drink, for tomorrow we die'" (1 Cor. 15:32). ("Enjoy the few minutes you got left the best way you can" is the way the Misfit paraphrases it.)

In this chapter, we will see that in the nineteenth century certain writers reached similarly blunt conclusions about the nature and personality of God the Father. It is not that Jesus Christ was absent from their thoughts or that he was portrayed unattractively in their art, for he could be found seemingly anywhere one looked in the imagination of the day. In some places, he could be met as the Spirit of God in human form; in others he could be encountered as the brother of the human race; and in still others, he could be worshiped as the paragon of human virtue and potential.

Christ *the good man* seemed to show up everywhere in the nineteenth century. What was harder to find in the literature and dominant theologies of the day, was Christ *the Son of God*, who was conceived by the Holy Ghost and born of the Virgin Mary, who suffered under Pontius Pilate and was crucified, dead, and buried, and who rose on the third day, who ascended into heaven, and who sits at the right hand of God the Father almighty. The questions on the lips of Emily Dickinson, Herman Melville, Fyodor Dostoevsky, and a host of others in the late nineteenth century were, "Where has that Christ gone?" "Does he dwell in the land of the dead?" "Will he ever return?"

"Questions always bring out the undetermined possibilities of a thing," writes Hans-Georg Gadamer. The art of questioning, he claims, lies at the heart of human understanding, for it "opens up possibilities of meaning, and thus what is meaningful passes into one's own thinking on the subject. . . . To understand meaning is to understand it as the answer to a question."[2] This is as true of the act of understanding a historical period as it is of the art of interpreting what another person says in conversation or on the printed page.

For me the idea of a dynamic of cultural questions and theological responses first came to mind several decades ago, when I read *Christianity and Classical Culture* by Charles Norris Cochrane. In painstaking detail and with a breathtaking sweep, Cochrane's study describes how Christian theology, particularly in the work of Augustine, overcame the fatalism at the heart of classical thought. Augustine did so by establishing through the Trinity "a fresh foundation for . . . the values of personality." His thought wedded the power of God to the incarnate, personal Word, and in Cochrane's words, this trinitarian move dissipated "the nightmare involved in the concept of nature as a closed system, determined by its own exclusive laws and, therewith, of the antithesis between human liberty and natural necessity which rendered mankind a stranger in his own household."[3]

In effect, Cochrane argues that Augustine's vast influence on late antiquity stemmed from the powerful questions he put to the Christian Scriptures and the classical tradition alike. And so it has been the case throughout the history of the church that such questions have brought out many "undetermined possibilities" of Christian doctrine. This proved to be the case with a series of questions that were posed by the literature of the nineteenth century and eventually responded to by the theology of the twentieth.

At this point it might be useful to put three such questions before us. The first is to be found in a fable written by a German romantic writer, Jean Paul, who wrote of a brokenhearted Christ and the discovery he has made:

> Then there arose and came into the temple . . . the dead children who had awakened in the churchyard, and they cast themselves before the lofty form upon the altar, and said, "Jesus! have we no Father?" and he answered with streaming eyes, "We are all orphans, I and you; we are without a Father."[4]

The second question is one that we have already come upon in an earlier chapter. It is the one Captain Ahab poses in *Moby Dick*, when he asks, "Where is the foundling's father hidden?" His own answer is that "our souls are like those orphans whose unwedded mothers die in bearing them; the secret of our paternity lies in their grave, and we must there to learn it" (373).

And the final question comes to us in a poem by Emily Dickinson:

> My period had come for Prayer—
> No other Art—would do—
> My Tactics missed a rudiment—
> Creator—Was it you?
>
> God grows above—so those who pray
> Horizons—must ascend—
> And so I stepped opon the North
> To see this Curious Friend—
>
> His House was not—no sign had He—
> By Chimney—nor by Door—
> Could I infer his Residence—
> Vast Prairies of Air

Beginning with the Word

Unbroken by a Settler—
Were all that I could see—
Infinitude—Had'st Thou no Face
That I might look on Thee?

The Silence condescended—
Creation stopped—for me—
But awed beyond my errand—
I worshipped—did not "pray"— (#525)

These passages ask plaintive and pointed questions about a distant God and a powerless or missing Christ. If we are to feel their force and to understand the source of their power, we need a sense of the context in which it became necessary to raise questions of this kind. In this case, the specific context involved the nineteenth-century rise and demise of the romantic vision of the self as a Christlike force.

We can see the scope of that vision in the works of several great American writers from the middle of that century. In "Song of Myself," for example, Walt Whitman dismisses the gods of theism as a group of "old cautious hucksters," and he bestows their "rough deific sketches" on "each man and woman I see." For Whitman, "the mechanic's wife with her babe at her nipple" is Christ, "interceding for every person born," and "the snag-toothed hostler with red hair" takes over the task of "redeeming sins past and to come" (73–74). And in a poem inspired by his viewing of the bodies of slain Union soldiers, Whitman offers a picture of the brotherly Christ who lives, as we do, within the imprisoning limits set by death:

Then to the third – a face nor child nor old, very calm, as of
    beautiful yellow-white ivory;
Young man I think I know you – I think this face is the face
    of the Christ himself,
Dead and divine and brother of all, and here again he lies. (441)

As Whitman jostled with the countless Christs on the streets of Manhattan, to the north, in rural Massachusetts, Henry David Thoreau was conjuring images of Christ in the solitude of his cabin at Walden Pond. "We loiter in winter while it is already spring," the man from Concord complained. "In a pleasant spring morning all men's sins are forgiven. Such a day is a truce to vice. While such a sun holds out to burn, the vilest sinner may return" (573). And if, "through our own recovered innocence we discern the innocence of our neighbors." Thoreau wondered, who needs the crucified and risen Christ?

"For my part I would rather walk toward Rutland than Jerusalem," he wrote to a friend as he worked on *Walden*. That Vermont town is a "modern town," after all, with "no holy sepulchre, but prophane green fields and dusty roads." In such a town, you may "live as holy a life as you can," for "the sacredness . . . is all in yourself and not in the place."[5]

In this cultural milieu, Christ was not the only Son of God but rather the older brother of humanity. His perfections mirrored our own, Ralph Waldo Emerson argued in an address to a group of Harvard divinity students in 1838. Christ was unique but only because "alone in all history, he estimated the greatness of man. One man was true to what is in you and me. He saw that God incarnates himself in man, and evermore goes forth anew to take possession of his world." The problem with "the Church," Emerson told these divinity students, is that it does not preach "the true Christianity,—a faith like Christ's in the infinitude of man. . . . None believeth in the soul of man, but only in some man or person old and departed" (88). Either I am godlike and Christ is my brother, or else I am nothing. In Emerson's words: "That which shows God in me, fortifies me. That which shows God out of me, makes me a wart and a wen" (80–81).

The Christ that Whitman, Thoreau, and Emerson celebrated was our sibling, not God's Son. He gave nothing and demanded nothing beyond the ordinary benefits of a good example. When Thoreau was dying of tuberculosis, and a friend asked him "how he stood affected toward Christ," Henry replied, "A snow-storm was more to him than Christ." In like manner, his Aunt Louisa worried over the state of his soul and wondered whether he had made his peace with God. "I did not know we had ever quarrelled, Aunt," was Henry's reply.[6]

To its critics, such "self-as-Christ" romanticism came to seem "naïvely optimistic" about human nature and human progress. As H. Richard Niebuhr observed long ago, "in its one-sided view of progress," the romantic theology of the nineteenth century "saw the growth of the wheat but not that of the tares, the gathering of the grain but not the burning of the chaff." If Christ is our brother and we are his godlike siblings, then the Christian faith is but a hymn to human glory. And so it was, Niebuhr notes, that in the nineteenth century, "a God without wrath brought men without sin into a kingdom without judgment through the ministrations of a Christ without a cross."[7] Or in the words of church historian Jaroslav Pelikan, "It is sometimes difficult to see in the Jesus of [nineteenth-century] Rationalism and Romanticism just why he was ever crucified, so accommodated had his image become to the spirit of the times."[8]

For a time in the nineteenth century, the confidence that the likes of Emerson and Thoreau placed in human nature seemed well founded and secure. It was grounded in the general philosophical and political optimism of the age and also in what literary historian Jay Fliegelman has described as a particular reconfiguration of family relations that took place in eighteenth- and early nineteenth-century England and America. Long-standing patriarchal patterns of family government were quickly "giving way to a new parental ideal characterized by a more affectionate and equalitarian relationship with children." The goal, says Fliegelman, was to raise children who would be good citizens ready "for a life of rational independence and moral self-sufficiency."⁹

In the aftermath of the American and French revolutions, fathers were out and siblings—with their liberty, fraternity, equality—were in. For many who lived in the flush times of revolution and at the high tide of romantic optimism, the overthrow of parental authority aroused feelings of liberation. Thoreau captures this perfectly in his introduction to *Walden*: "You may say the wisest thing you can, old man,—you who have lived seventy years, not without honor of a kind,—I hear an irresistible voice which invites me away from all that. One generation abandons the enterprises of another like stranded vessels" (331).

This revolution in family relations and political theory developed in tandem with a view of the self that the philosopher Charles Taylor has intriguingly named the "buffered self." Even as new conceptions of authority were securing children and citizens against the whims of arbitrary power, developments in the theory of the self were putting buffers in place to protect that self from threats far and wide. "To be a buffered subject," explains Taylor, is "to have closed the porous boundary" that divides our inner world of thought and feeling from the outer world of nature. In turn, it is to assume one lives in "a disenchanted world," that is, a world taken to be a mechanism driven by indifferent forces rather than a creation ruled by a personal God.¹⁰

Although he never used the term, Emerson frequently sang the praises of the confident, buffered self. We recall the blithe assurance of his claim that "the nonchalance of boys who are sure of a dinner, and would disdain as much as a lord to do or say aught to conciliate one, is the healthy attitude of human nature" (261). In the sibling culture of the nineteenth century, as long as the meals were assured and the home was secure, the children were content to roam on their own with their parents out of sight and out of mind. As long as the theory of human nature and the circumstances of history made perfection seem plausible and progress inevitable, it was fine to be alone in the world with only your brothers (including Jesus) and your sisters by your side.

In the spirit of high romantic optimism that marked the revolutionary era in Europe and spurred the Emersonian generation in America, the innocent, infinite self appeared poised to expand and improve forever, and it was hard to conceive of any possible limits to its powers or potential. This is the point of Emerson's statement that God incarnates himself in every human being and evermore goes forth to take possession of his world. This God is an immanent and irresistible force. In Taylor's terms, we might say that God is a *buffered spirit* working his will upon the world from within, a spirit that drives individuals and propels the progress of nature and history alike.

As the nineteenth century unfolded, however, Dickinson, Melville, and others found the romantic self pressing up against limits and barriers on every side. These limits had to do with everything from the finality of death to the brute otherness of nature and a growing uneasiness about the divided nature and perverse potential of the self. Some at the time, like Friedrich Nietzsche and Fyodor Dostoevsky's Ivan Karamazov, sensed what O'Connor's Misfit feels and articulates so forcefully. If God does not exist and if Christ was not raised from the dead, then we live beyond good and evil (Nietzsche) and all things are permitted (Ivan Karamazov). Or in the words of the Misfit, if Christ was not raised from the dead, then life is simply a case of "no pleasure but meanness." Nietzsche, Ivan Karamazov, and the Misfit tell a story of how over the past two centuries, the joy has often given way to the terror of abandonment. In the world as such writers render it, a good man may be hard to find, but it is even harder to hear a gracious God or to see his providence at work in the world.

We feel that terror of abandonment in the first of the several questions posed for us earlier. It is the question the spirits of the dead children pose to Christ in Jean Paul's fable: "Jesus! have we no Father?" Christ's bleak reply is, "We are all orphans . . . and we are without a Father." It is important to note that this episode occurs in a dream in the mind of a character wrapped within a fable contained within a novel. It is not a declaration of the death of God, but it does hint at the fear that he may have abandoned us. Jean Paul's sorrowful Christ reports that he has "ascended into the suns," "gazed down into the abyss," and "cried aloud—'Father, where art thou?'" But he saw nothing and heard nothing in response and must tell the children that they are orphans stranded on the godforsaken island of the world.[11]

Theologian Helmut Thielicke astutely observes that the Christ who cries out in Jean Paul's fable "is no God. Thus Christ himself is only the highest of finite creatures" and not in any way a "representative of the absent God." He is not the Son of God but the brother of men and women, and as such, he has no more power over death and meaninglessness than any of the rest of us do. It is for that reason that his vision proves to be so terrifying. What Thielicke calls the "decisive theme" of Jean Paul's vision is its picture of the dizzying confusion into which this world is thrown, when it "is deprived if its basis and center by the death of God."[12]

Jean Paul's vision of the orphaned Christ also hints at anxieties that were to grow apace over the nineteenth century. Take a minute and try to imagine nineteenth-century English and American fiction without orphans. Take them away, and little of Dickens and the Brontë sisters would remain. We wouldn't have much from George Eliot, and the pages of Thomas Hardy would be virtually blank. In America, *Moby Dick* and *Billy Budd* would be gone, along with *Huckleberry Finn*. What is *The Scarlet Letter* but a story of a girl's search for the father who has abandoned her? And as Frederick Douglass makes clear, the orphaning of children was built into the system of chattel slavery; like thousands of others born into slavery in antebellum America, Frederick had no idea who his father was.

"Where is the foundling's father hidden?" Melville's Captain Ahab asks in the second of our three questions. This question has to do with the destiny of life as well as its source. "There is no steady unretracing progress in this life," the Captain concludes. We travel the rounds of life again and again, and yet we seem never to move toward any goal. "Where lies the final harbor, whence we unmoor no more?" Ahab is desperate to know. But he knows he never will learn the answer, in this life at least, for his is an orphaned soul, and the secret about the heavenly father will be revealed, if at all, on the far side of the grave.

From Melville to Kafka and beyond, the question of the foundling's father turns many modern narratives into quests for the hidden God. This is the form, for example, taken by the Emily Dickinson poem in which our third question arises. It opens like a nursery rhyme, as the speaker sets out to pray but finds she is missing a "rudiment"—"Creator—Was it you?" Bereft of God, she sets off to search for "this Curious Friend" but comes up empty-handed. God's house is nowhere to be found, and no sign points to his or any other door. All she sees are "Vast Prairies of Air / Unbroken by a Settler—." Staring at the emptiness, the speaker asks: "Infinitude—Had'st Thou no Face / That I might look on Thee?" (#525).

This is a christological question, a query about that face of infinitude that the Gospel of John says dwelt among us in grace and truth as the Word was made flesh. Herman Melville and others were asking similar christological questions at the close of the nineteenth century. For instance, when the tips of his ship's masts seem to burst into flame one night—an instance of St. Elmo's fire—Ahab cries out to the seeming fire: "There is some unsuffusing thing beyond thee to whom all eternity is time." To that force beyond all things, he pleads, "Come in thy lowest form of love, and I will kneel and kiss thee; but at thy highest, come as mere supernal power; and though thou launchest navies of full-freighted worlds, there's that in here that still remains indifferent" (382–83).

Prepare a Body for the Tender Pioneer

To use Gadamer's terms, these powerful nineteenth-century questions brought out countless unrealized possibilities in the Scriptures and the Christian tradition. The response of the church took many different forms, some of which proved fruitless, while others continue to bear a rich yield. One particularly fruitful development came through a renewal and deepening of the doctrine of the person and work of Christ. On this front, Karl Barth led the way, with his stress on the Incarnation as the supreme act of humbling freely chosen by a mighty God.

In an earlier chapter, we examined a small section of Barth's massive *Church Dogmatics* that bears the title, "The Way of the Son of God into the Far Country." We saw how Barth celebrates God's decision to do "something unnecessary and extravagant, binding and limiting and compromising" by choosing from all eternity to "[go] into the far country, into the evil society of this being which is not God and against God. He does not shrink from him . . . [or] leave him to his own devices" (*CD*, IV.1.158). The distance we could never travel, the chasm we could never bridge, Jesus Christ the Son has already made his way across. In the words of Emily Dickinson:

> The Savior must have been
> A docile Gentleman—
> To come so far so cold a Day
> For little Fellow men—
>
> The Road to Bethlehem
> Since He and I were Boys
> Was leveled, but for that 'twould be
> A rugged billion Miles— (#1538)

The God who comes to the far country—our world—must break through the barriers and buffers we have built to keep him out, and he does so in the person of Jesus, "who is qualitatively different from all other men. He is not simply a better man, a more gifted, a more wise or noble or pious, in short a greater man." He is not the brother of humanity but our "Lord and Law-giver and Judge." And as the "Word, [he] did not simply become any 'flesh,' any man humbled and suffering. [He] became Jewish flesh. The Church's whole doctrine of the Incarnation and the atonement becomes abstract and valueless and meaningless to the extent that this comes to be regarded as something accidental and incidental" (*CD*, IV.1.160.166).

To Barth, this fact is crucial because it means that the God of the Old Testament is "already on the way into the far country" to the extent that he reveals and gives himself as a faithful God to an unfaithful people. In his faithfulness, the Son of God stands with the children of Israel under the "wrath and judgment" of God, for "to be flesh is to be in a state of perishing before this God." Christ's history is one of suffering, and his solidarity with men and women takes its form in this guise. His is not the solidarity of godlike power, in the mode of Emerson's or Whitman's self as Christ. Instead, it is a solidarity of sharing—of taking upon himself the rejection and condemnation that are the consequence of human sin. Only in this manner can Jesus Christ break "into that vicious circle of the human plight." (The imagery of the prison and the immanent cosmos seem to be everywhere we look.) In the Old Testament, Barth argues, there is always a tension between "the righteous God and the bitter things which man has to accept from him without murmuring." In the New Testament, this antithesis is done away with, as God "takes the place of the former sufferers" and allows their bitter suffering to "fall upon Himself." Only through the Passion of Jesus Christ do we see suffering and death for what they are, as "God gives Himself to this most dreadful of all foreign spheres" (*CD*, IV.1.171, 174–75). Again, in the words of Emily Dickinson:

> Life—is what we make it—
> Death—We do not know—
> Christ's acquaintance with Him
> Justify Him—though—
>
> He—would trust no stranger—
> Other—could betray—
> Just His own endorsement—
> That—sufficeth Me—
>
> All the other Distance
> He hath traversed first—
> No new mile remaineth—
> Far as Paradise—
>
> His sure foot preceding—
> Tender Pioneer—
> Base must be the Coward
> Dare not venture—now— (#727)

The "Tender Pioneer's" act of mercy is freely chosen, and it means that "God is always God even in His humiliation," and even though he went into a strange land, a far country, God "never became a stranger to Himself." For Barth, this is even the case when in the cry of dereliction from the cross, Jesus asks, "My God, my God, why hast thou forsaken me?" (Mark 15:34 KJV). God takes as his the sinful humans' standing in contradiction to God, but he does "not make common cause with it" (*CD*, IV.1.179–80, 185).

If we believe it to be impossible for God to remain fully in unity with himself even as he takes upon himself the consequences of our sin, the problem has to do with what Barth calls the "small and perverted . . . false idea" we have of God. "We may believe that God can and must only be absolute in contrast to all that is relative, exalted in contrast to all that is lowly, active in contrast to all suffering . . . transcendent in contrast to all immanence, and therefore divine in contrast to everything human, in short that He can and must be only the 'Wholly Other.'" If we think this way, it is because we have "corrupt and pagan" concepts at work in our thought, and it requires the merciful, self-revealing grace of God to show us that he is greater and richer than anything "we had ever imagined" (*CD*, IV.1.186).

In his exploration of this "new mystery" of God's condescending grace manifested in the life, death, and resurrection of Jesus Christ, Barth acknowledges that the great temptation "of every age" has been to resolve the tension "of the deity of Christ by dissolving it, . . . by trying to understand it as the designation of a second divine being of lesser divinity." In the face of such efforts, Barth says we must draw from the New Testament evidence of the "astounding deduction" that "God is, in fact, the One and also Another, that He is indeed a First and a Second, One who rules and commands in majesty and One who obeys in humility" (*CD*, IV.1.196, 202).

We have been considering a number of riddling matters in this book. How is it that "all things came into being" through the workings of the Word that "became flesh and lived among us, full of grace and truth"? What does it mean to say that a word is more like a *picture* than like a *symbol* or a *sign*? How is it possible that God can *commandeer* language and make it the means by which he opens his heart and declares his love and will for us? What grounds do we have to believe with confidence that the world within which we live, as well as the lives we live within that world, have a story-ordered and divinely promised and appointed end?

These are crucial questions, and they deal with difficulties and possibilities a Christian student of contemporary culture cannot help but engage. As we try to understand them, we do best, I believe, when we follow the arc of the very story of redemption that the Christian proclaims. And when we track with

Beginning with the Word

that trajectory, we are always brought back to this world, the one to which that "docile Gentleman" came "so far so cold a Day" for his "little Fellowmen."

As we try to comprehend the staggering concept of the Incarnate Word, I suggest we think for a moment about a universal experience we rarely discuss among ourselves. As we grow up, is it not the case that one of the most awkward, almost unimaginable things we can think of is the fact of our parents having bodily lives? As we become aware of our own bodies and learn to manage their functions, and as we grow into our sexual maturity and find ourselves driven by gusts of wonder, shame, longing, and confusion, we don't really know what to make of the corresponding fullness of our parents' lives. To parents, of course, the fact of a child's bodily life and needs becomes readily apparent in the first minutes of their infant's life. But how is it possible that our parents, in the fullest sense, have bodies that function and flail like our own? Or how could God ever have a body?

I have a deep love for Shakespeare's *King Lear*, in good measure because of the great blend of tenderness and honesty the play shows in its treatment of parents and children. As a consequence of their own helplessness, both the Earl of Gloucester and King Lear become, in effect, their children's children. And that is what both of my parents became to me at the end of their lives. As the sole-surviving child of their marriage, I felt a special sense of responsibility toward my mother and father. When my mother died in 1978, my father was largely incapacitated, and during his own final illness nine years later, I was the only remaining family member. So, in both cases, although I did not give regular physical care to my parents, I did serve as the primary spiritual guide and emotional touchstone for them.

Those extended experiences were filled with moments of unspeakable sadness and sweetness alike. Just as my mother and father had welcomed me into the world in a hospital room decades before, so was I now saying good-bye to them in a similar place. Just as I had been a helpless bundle of needs when I first saw the light, so too were they—once so strong and powerful—now utterly dependent on the care and mercy of others as they entered the darkness. I had always loved my parents and had tried, in my fallen and fitful ways, to honor them and make them proud. But I had never before known the feelings of brokenhearted affection and cherishing care that swept over me as I watched them slip away from me, and from the world, at last.

Several years later, I came across a letter that Emily Dickinson had written to a friend a few weeks after Emily's mother had died. Emily and her sister Vinnie had shared the duties of caring for Mrs. Dickinson, whose body had been ravaged by a stroke. They had fed her, bathed her, and talked with her from morning to night for seven years. And now that she was dead, Emily offered both a confession and a revelation: "We were never intimate Mother and Children while she was our Mother—but Mines in the same Ground meet by tunneling and when she became our Child, the Affection came."[13]

That is another way of saying that when the "high supernal power" (in the words of Melville) of the nineteenth-century God comes to us in that "lowest form of love" that twentieth-century Christology celebrated, our intimacy with God may be restored, and our affection for him may return.

One of the most moving evocations I know of affection for the God who is "our child" can be found in a song cycle assembled, arranged, and sung by the son of former slaves. The artist is Roland Hayes, one of the great tenors of the twentieth century. Hayes established himself as a master of two entirely distinct vocal traditions—the European classical repertoire and the body of what he called "Aframerican religious folk songs." One fruit of his heroic labors in the spirituals tradition is a song cycle called "The Life of Christ," which he first recorded in 1955. Hayes took a series of African American spirituals and wove them into a narrative of the birth, life, and death of Jesus. The songs tell a powerful story of the God who journeyed into the far country to share in the sufferings of his people and to give his life so that they might live.

The cycle opens with "Prepare Me One Body," which Hayes calls a "beautiful Aframerican folk song" and which he takes to have been a dramatization by African American preachers "of such Biblical elements as are to be found in Saint Paul's Epistle to the Philippians (2.5–8): '. . . Christ Jesus: who . . . took upon him the form of a servant . . . was made in the likeness of men . . . humbled himself . . . became obedient unto death, even death on the cross'":

> Prepare me one body, I'll go down,
> I'll go down,
> Prepare me one body like a man.
> The man of sorrows, sinner, see—
> I'll go down, I'll go down—
> He died for you and He died for Me—
> I'll go down and die.
> Prepare me, Lord, one body,
> Prepare me one body like a man.
> I'll go down and die, I'll go down,
> I'll go down, I'll go down and die.

The miracle of the Incarnation is that long before any of us began to grope about in the maze of our confusion and sin, God—as Emily Dickinson and Roland Hayes might put it—prepared a body for the Tender Pioneer to tunnel his way to meet us. While we struggle and stammer with our words that

Beginning with the Word

"strain, crack," "slip, slide, and perish" (*Four Quartets*, 121), the God who lives forever as the Word has come to us in the baby Jesus, and he has become our child, so that our affection might come and we might be his forevermore.

The many emotions and experiences I had felt while caring for my dying parents several decades earlier rushed together one day several years ago, as I held my wife's hand and held my first grandchild in a Minnesota hospital room. Here, in this sweet, smooth face with its dimpled chin, in these ruddy legs and tiny long-fingered hands, in this bundled body so small I could cradle it in my own hands, here I found a gift from God so astonishing that my heart raced, my arms trembled, and glad tears filled the corners of my eyes. I was probably experiencing, as my friends in Applied Health Science might tell me, an adrenaline rush, but I was also sensing the wonder of God's faithfulness, the beauty of his promises, and the mystery of his ways.

That the God of Abraham, that the force that rules the universe, that the power behind and beyond all events and all accidents, took on a body and became a child as fragile and delicate and vulnerable as this little one—this seems to me to be almost beyond imagining. But so it was, for the Word was made flesh and dwelt among us. And so it still is. And so it will forever be, throughout all ages, world without end.

Notes

Introduction

1. Lavinia Dickinson, as quoted in Millicent Todd Bingham, *Emily Dickinson's Home: Letters of Edward Dickinson and His Family* (New York: Harper, 1955), 413–14.

2. David Neff, "You Can't Think Your Way to God," *Christianity Today*, May 24, 2013, www.christianitytoday.com/ct/2013/may/you-cant-think-your-way-to-god.html.

3. David Brooks, "The Age of Darwin," *New York Times*, April 16, 2007, www.nytimes.com/2007/04/16/opinion/16iht-edbrooks.1.5306295.html.

4. T. M. Luhrmann, "Belief Is the Least Part of Faith," *New York Times*, May 29, 2013, www.nytimes.com/2013/05/30/opinion/luhrmann-belief-is-the-least-part-of-faith.html.

5. Karl Barth, *Evangelical Theology: An Introduction*, trans. Grover Foley (Grand Rapids: Eerdmans, 1963), 155–56. For decades, the work of Karl Barth has nourished and deepened my confidence, understanding, and sense of delight as a Christian scholar. In like manner, over the past fifteen years, my acquaintance with John Webster, both in person and in print, has given me a similar sense of courage and clarity about the Christian faith and the life of the mind in the late modern world. What exuberance is on display, for example, in the final passage from a recent essay by this distinguished Barth scholar: "One of the deepest fault lines in the church at the present time runs between those who do their theological reasoning on the basis of a conviction that in Scripture the breath of the divine Word quickens reason to knowledge and love of God, and those who fear (or hope?) that neither Scripture nor reason takes us any further than human poetics. The latter choice generates irony and squabbling, and both of these are sicknesses of the soul. The former is more persuasively present than it has been for some long while, and we should seize the day." "Biblical Reasoning," *Anglican Theological Review* 90, no. 4 (2008): 751.

6. Barth, *Evangelical Theology*, 15.

7. The books are *From Nature to Experience: The American Search for Cultural Authority* (2005; repr., Lanham, MD: Rowman & Littlefield, 2007); and *Believing Again: Doubt and Faith in a Secular Age* (Grand Rapids: Eerdmans, 2009).

8. There are, of course, exceptions to this rule, the remarkable career of Nathan Scott being one of them—see especially *The Broken Center: Studies in the Theological Horizon of Modern Literature* (New Haven: Yale University Press, 1966). Yet these remain exceptions, oases scattered across an otherwise arid terrain.

9. Michael Cromartie, "Dr. Timothy Keller at the March 2013 Faith Angle Forum," Ethics and Public Policy Center website, March 13, 2013, www.eppc.org/publication/dr-timothy-keller-at-the-march-2013-faith-angle-forum/.

10. Amy Hungerford, *Postmodern Belief: American Literature and Religion since 1960* (Princeton: Princeton University Press, 2010), xvi. For a balanced and insightful account of Hungerford's book and other works of postsecular criticism, see Mark Eaton, "American Literary Supernaturalism," *American Literary History* 26, no. 1 (2011): 899–917.

11. St. Augustine, *Confessions*, trans. Henry Chadwick (New York: Oxford University Press, 1991), 3.

12. Alasdair MacIntyre, *God, Philosophy, Universities: A Selective History of the Catholic Philosophical Tradition* (Lanham, MD: Rowman & Littlefield, 2008), 28.

13. Paul Ricoeur, "The Hermeneutics of Testimony," in *Essays on Biblical Interpretation*, ed. Lewis S. Mudge (Philadelphia: Fortress, 1980), 153.

14. George Steiner, *Martin Heidegger* (1978; repr., Chicago: University of Chicago Press, 1987), 15.

Chapter 1 Beginning with the Word

1. F. F. Bruce, *The Gospel of John* (Grand Rapids: Eerdmans, 1983), 31.

2. Brooke Foss Westcott, *An Introduction to the Study of the Gospels* (New York: Macmillan, 1902), 267–68. In the words of historian Mark Noll, the Johannine "affirmation carries the strongest possible implications for intellectual life. Put most simply, for believers to be studying created things is to be studying the works of Christ." Mark A. Noll, *Jesus Christ and the Life of the Mind* (Grand Rapids: Eerdmans, 2011), 25.

3. St. Athanasius, *On the Incarnation*, as quoted in the introduction of *Athanasius*, ed. Khaled Anatolios (London: Routledge, 2004), 41–42.

4. In his defense of the Nicene Creed, Athanasius described the relationship between creation and the Word in the following manner: "In the case of created things, they are said to be from God in that they do not exist randomly and unaccountably; neither do they attain their origination by chance, as those who speak of an origination that comes about from the intertwining of atoms and of like parts; nor, as certain heretics say, is there another creator, nor, as again others say, do all things have their subsistence through some angels. Rather, all things are said to be from God because the existent God, by himself and through the Word, brought all things that formerly did not exist into being. But the Word is said to be and is alone from the Father because he is not a creature; and the Son's being 'from the essence of the Father' is indicative of this sense, which does not pertain to anything that has come into being." *On the Council of Nicaea (De Decretis)*, in Anatolios, *Athanasius*, 196.

The Catholic philosopher Charles Taylor has written insightfully about the role played by what he calls "the ontic logos" in the history of ideas in general and Christian thought in particular. See his *Sources of the Self: The Making of the Modern Identity* (Cambridge, MA: Harvard University Press, 1989), 186–92.

5. Hans Urs von Balthasar, *Love Alone Is Credible*, trans. D. C. Schindler (San Francisco: Ignatius, 2004), 17. "Christianity marched triumphantly to Rome and from Rome to the ends of the earth—what more was needed to prove that this fulfillment was not only ideal but also real? 'Everything that is good and beautiful belongs to us' (Justin Martyr)."

6. Charles Norris Cochrane, *Christianity and Classical Culture: A Study of Thought and Action from Augustus to Augustine* (1940; repr., London: Oxford University Press, 1957), 480.

7. Alfred North Whitehead, *Adventures of Ideas* (1933; repr., New York: Free Press, 1967), 111–12.

8. Francis Oakley, "Christian Theology and the Newtonian Science: The Rise of the Concept of the Laws of Nature," *Church History* 30 (1961), 435.

9. Ibid., 438–39.

10. Michael Allen Gillespie, *The Theological Origins of Modernity* (Chicago: University of Chicago Press, 2008), 14. For a brilliant and impassioned Catholic discussion of the contemporary relevance of nominalism, see Brad S. Gregory, *The Unintended Reformation: How a Religious*

Revolution Secularized Society (Cambridge, MA: Belknap Press of Harvard University Press, 2012). "In Occamist nominalism . . . insofar as God existed, 'God' had to denote some *thing,* some discrete, real entity, an *ens*—however much that entity differs from everything else, a difference Occam highlighted by emphasizing the absolute sovereignty of God's power (*potentia Dei absoluta*) and the inscrutability of God's will within the dependable order of creation and salvation he had in fact established" (38).

11. Richard Rorty, "Nineteenth-Century Idealism and Twentieth-Century Textualism," in *Consequences of Pragmatism* (Minneapolis: University of Minnesota Press, 1982), 139–59.

12. Ibid., 139–40.

13. Ibid., 141.

14. Ibid., 148–49.

15. Ibid., 150.

16. Richard Rorty, *Contingency, Irony, and Solidarity* (Cambridge: Cambridge University Press, 1989), 5.

17. Rorty, *Consequences,* 143; Rorty is quoting Maurice Mandelbaum here.

18. Rorty, *Contingency,* 6.

19. Charles Taylor, "Language and Human Nature," in *Philosophical Papers,* vol. 1 (Cambridge: Cambridge University Press, 1985), 215. As for the range of those "other things," Taylor mentions "kinship systems [Lévi-Strauss], mythologies, fashion (Barthes), the operations of the unconscious (Lacan), with theories drawn in the first place from the study of language. We find terms like 'paradigm,' 'syntagm,' 'metaphor,' 'metonomy' used well beyond their original domain" (215).

20. Alvin Plantinga, *Where the Conflict Really Lies: Science, Religion, and Naturalism* (Oxford: Oxford University Press, 2011), ix–x, 311.

21. Jonathan Culler, *Structuralist Poetics: Structuralism, Linguistics, and the Study of Literature* (Ithaca, NY: Cornell University Press, 1975), 4–5. In the words of theologian Paul D. Janz, structuralism argues that "cultural and social entities are somehow 'intrinsically relational' and [proposes] that their meaning or significance arises solely with reference to the structure they share or presuppose and does not depend on anything intrinsic to them." *God, the Mind's Desire: Reference, Reason and Christian Thinking* (Cambridge: Cambridge University Press, 2004), 27.

22. Robert Scholes, *Structuralism in Literature: An Introduction* (New Haven: Yale University Press, 1974), 10.

23. Frederic Jameson, *The Prison-House of Language: A Critical Account of Structuralism and Russian Formalism* (Princeton: Princeton University Press, 1972).

24. Scholes, *Structuralism in Literature,* 1.

25. Rorty, *Contingency,* 3.

26. William Butler Yeats, as quoted in Richard Ellmann, *Yeats: The Man and the Masks* (New York: Dutton, n.d.), 280.

27. William Wordsworth, *William Wordsworth,* ed. Stephen Gill (Oxford: Oxford University Press, 1984), 134.

28. Hans Frei, *The Eclipse of Biblical Narrative: A Study in Eighteenth and Nineteenth Century Hermeneutics* (New Haven: Yale University Press, 1974).

29. Erich Auerbach, *Mimesis: The Representation of Reality in Western Literature,* trans. Willard R. Trask (Princeton: Princeton University Press, 1953), 15.

30. Paul Ricoeur, *Freud and Philosophy: An Essay on Interpretation,* trans. Denis Savage (New Haven: Yale University Press, 1970), 33–34.

31. Scholes, *Structuralism in Literature,* 2.

32. Frank Lentricchia, *After the New Criticism* (Chicago: University of Chicago Press, 1980), 118. The advocates of structuralism concur: "The relationship between the signifying sound and the signified concept . . . is arbitrary" (Scholes, *Structuralism in Literature,* 13); "In the sign proper as Saussure understood it the relationship between signifier and signified is arbitrary or

conventional: *arbre* means 'tree' not by natural resemblance or causal connection but by virtue of a law" (Culler, *Structuralist Poetics*, 16).

33. Rorty, *Contingency*, 7.

Chapter 2 The Sign in Our Time

1. William Faulkner, *Lion in the Garden: Interviews with William Faulkner*, ed. James B. Meriwether and Michael Millgate (1968; repr., Lincoln: University of Nebraska Press, 1980), 146.

2. Ibid., 147.

3. Of Benjy, Donald Kartiganer writes, "Memory does not serve him as it serves the normal mind, becoming part of the mind and integral to the stream of constantly created perception that makes it up. . . . Benjy does not recall, and therefore cannot interpret, the past from the perspective of the present; nor does the past help to determine that perspective." "The Meaning of Form in *The Sound and the Fury*," in *The Sound and the Fury: A Norton Critical Edition*, 2nd ed., ed. David Minter (New York: Norton, 1994), 330.

4. Hans-Georg Gadamer, *Truth and Method*, 2nd rev. ed., trans. Joel Weinsheimer and Donald G. Marshall (New York: Crossroad, 1989), 356–57.

5. "Locked almost completely into a timeless present," Benjy possesses "not much more freedom than an animal does." Cleanth Brooks cites studies indicating that a sheep can anticipate punishment for perhaps fifteen minutes, a dog for a half hour, whereas a human has an infinite range and unlimited capacity to fear what may come. *William Faulkner: The Yoknapatawpha Country* (New Haven: Yale University Press, 1963), 329.

6. Few realities mark our modernity more clearly than does the shift from sin to finitude as a central category for understanding our human plight. My discussion of Faulkner and Gadamer shows the finitude argument at work. For a countervailing view, one which brings sin and judgment back into the discussion of finitude, see "Ending Time" in Karl Barth, *CD*, III.2.587–640.

7. Jens Zimmermann, "*Ignoramus*: Gadamer's 'Religious Turn,'" *Symposium* 6, no. 2 (2002): 208–9.

8. My own understanding of modernity was powerfully shaped early in my education by the reading of Hans Jonas's work on gnosticism. See his study, *The Gnostic Religion: The Message of the Alien God and the Beginnings of Christianity*, 2nd ed., rev. (Boston: Beacon, 1963).

9. The struggle over these matters has never ended, which is why gnosticism remains the most persistent and perduring of all Christian heresies.

10. St. Augustine, *City of God*, trans. Henry Bettenson (London: Penguin, 1984), 550–51 (bk. 14, ch. 3). Charles Norris Cochrane summarizes the Augustinian view of sin: "It begins with a wrong determination of the will and develops as the result of physical satisfactions derived therefrom, until it is finally confirmed by the bond of habit. Its consequences are thus insidious, far-reaching, and cumulative; the ultimate nemesis being frustration or self-defeat through the loss of genuine freedom and power." *Christianity and Classical Culture: A Study of Thought and Action from Augustus to Augustine* (1940; repr., London: Oxford University Press, 1957), 449.

A classic description of the difference between finitude and sin can be found in Reinhold Niebuhr, *The Nature and Destiny of Man*, vol. 1, *Human Nature* (New York: Scribner, 1943), 167–77: "The Biblical view is that the finiteness, dependence and the insufficiency of man's moral life are facts which belong to God's plan of creation and must be accepted with reverence and humility" (167).

11. Cleanth Brooks, *William Faulkner: First Encounters* (New Haven: Yale University Press, 1983), 48.

12. Gadamer, *Truth and Method*, 405. For the Hebrew conception of names, see O. S. Rankin, "Name," in *A Theological Word Book of the Bible*, ed. Alan Richardson (New York: Collier, 1950), 157–58. For my analysis of Gadamer's theories of name and language, I am indebted to Joel Weinsheimer, *Gadamer's Hermeneutics: A Reading of "Truth and Method"* (New Haven: Yale University Press, 1985), 229–37.

13. Gadamer, *Truth and Method*, 405.

14. Ibid. There are other dimensions to the question of language in the age of Plato that are brilliantly illuminating but beyond the scope of our interests here. Particularly in the study of the shift from orality to literacy—from speech to writing—scholarship of the past half century has opened some illuminating lines of inquiry. Two works in particular stand out: Walter J. Ong, *Orality and Literacy: The Technologizing of the Word* (1982; repr., London: Routledge, 1989), esp. 16–77; and Eric A. Havelock, *The Muse Learns to Write: Reflections on Orality and Literacy from Antiquity to the Present* (New Haven: Yale University Press, 1986), esp. 98–126.

15. Gadamer, *Truth and Method*, 405–6.

16. Ibid., 406.

17. Weinsheimer, *Gadamer's Hermeneutics*, 230.

18. Gadamer, *Truth and Method*, 407.

19. Ibid., 414.

20. For an understanding of how the issues here play out in the thought and life of the early church, see two works by Jaroslav Pelikan. For the positive construal of icons and an iconic view of language, see *The Christian Tradition: A History of the Development of Doctrine*, vol. 1, *The Spirit of Eastern Christendom (600–1700)* (Chicago: University of Chicago Press, 1974), 117–33; and for a countervailing critique of the capacity of language to express and embody the truth, see the discussion of the origins of the apophatic tradition in *Christianity and Classical Culture: The Metamorphosis of Natural Theology in the Christian Encounter with Hellenism* (New Haven: Yale University Press, 1993), 40–56.

21. George Steiner, "The Retreat from the Word," in *George Steiner: A Reader* (New York: Oxford University Press, 1984), 283–304; the essay originally appeared in George Steiner, *Language and Silence: Essays on Language, Literature and the Inhuman* (New York: Atheneum, 1970), 12–35.

22. Steiner, "Retreat from the Word," 283–84.

23. Walter J. Ong, SJ, *Ramus, Method, and the Decay of Dialogue: From the Art of Discourse to the Art of Reason* (1958; repr., Cambridge, MA: Harvard University Press, 1983), 277–78.

24. Ibid., 278–79.

25. Steiner, "Retreat from the Word," 285–86.

26. Paul S. Fiddes says, "The 'Utopian' project of modernity can be portrayed in social terms as the attempt to subjugate the natural world, with all its mysterious and threatening aspects, to the control of human consciousness. The human mind is subject and the world its object, to be investigated and mastered." *The Promised End: Eschatology in Theology and Literature* (Oxford: Blackwell, 2000), 236.

27. Stephen Toulmin, *Cosmopolis: The Hidden Agenda of Modernity* (1990; repr., Chicago: University of Chicago Press, 1992), 106–7.

28. See Charles Taylor, *A Secular Age* (Cambridge, MA: Belknap Press of Harvard University Press, 2007), 25–89.

29. Keith Thomas, *Religion and the Decline of Magic* (New York: Scribner, 1971), 650. "The decline of magic was thus accompanied by the growth of the natural and social sciences, which helped men to understand their environment, and of a variety of technical aids—from insurance to fire-fighting—by which they were able to increase their control of it" (656).

30. Gadamer, *Truth and Method*, 414–15.

31. Paul Ricoeur, *The Symbolism of Evil*, trans. Emerson Buchanan (1967; repr., Boston: Beacon, 1969), 349.

32. Steiner, "Retreat from the Word," 288. Steiner's essay, published in 1961, became both famous and infamous as a consequence of its forceful advocacy of a "two cultures" thesis. In later years, he has moderated his position somewhat: "Undoubtedly, there are innate, perhaps resistant differences between aptitudes to numeracy. But these have been grossly exaggerated. Hence my conviction that even advanced mathematical concepts can be made imaginatively

compelling and demonstrable when they are presented *historically*. . . . It is via these great voyages and adventures of the human mind, so often charged with personal rivalries, passions and frustrations . . . that we nonmathematicians can look into a sovereign and decisive realm." George Steiner, *My Unwritten Books* (New York: New Directions, 2008), 152–53.

33. Thomas Sprat, *The History of the Royal-Society of London, For the Improving of Natural Knowledge* (London: 1667), 111–13.

34. *The Poetry and Prose of William Blake*, ed. David V. Erdman (Garden City, NY: Doubleday, 1970), 95, 693; *The Complete Works of John Keats*, ed. H. Buxton Forman (Glasgow: Gowars & Gray, 1901), 3:232.

35. W. Jackson Bate, *Coleridge* (1968; repr., Cambridge, MA: Harvard University Press, 1987), 163.

36. Samuel Taylor Coleridge, *Samuel Taylor Coleridge: The Major Works*, ed. H. J. Jackson (Oxford: Oxford University Press, 2000), 660.

37. Martin Luther, *The Babylonian Captivity of the Church*, in *Martin Luther's Basic Theological Writings*, ed. Timothy F. Lull (Minneapolis: Fortress, 1989), 291, 288.

38. Coleridge, *The Major Works*, 675.

39. Ibid., 660.

40. Coleridge, as quoted in Bate, *Coleridge*, 163–64.

41. Bate, *Coleridge*, 164–65. Coleridge took allegory to be arbitrary because it was restricted to certain types of human understanding that fell short of the larger imaginative and linguistic ideals a human is capable of realizing. For a good deal of modern literary theory, on the other hand, allegory is arbitrary because language is inherently so. "The transcendental source" of meaning in allegory, writes Paul de Man in a well-known essay from the late 1960s, is "a pure decision of the mind." *Blindness and Insight: Essays in the Rhetoric of Contemporary Criticism*, 2nd ed., rev. (Minneapolis: University of Minnesota Press, 1983), 192.

42. Friedrich Nietzsche, "On Truth and Lie in an Extra-Moral Sense," in *The Portable Nietzsche*, trans. and ed. Walter Kaufmann (New York: Penguin, 1976), 42, 45, 47. Of the influence of Darwin, R. J. Hollingdale writes: "'The total nature of the world,' Nietzsche wrote in *The Gay Science*, 'is . . . to all eternity chaos,' and this thought, basic to his philosophy, arose directly from his interpretation of Darwin. . . . Now God and man, as hitherto understood, no longer existed. The universe and the earth were without meaning. The sense that meaning had evaporated was what seemed to escape those who welcomed Darwin as a benefactor of mankind. Nietzsche considered that evolution presented a correct picture of the world, but that it was a disastrous picture. His philosophy was an attempt to produce a new world-picture which took Darwinism into account but was not nullified by it." *Nietzsche: The Man and His Philosophy*, rev. ed. (Cambridge: Cambridge University Press, 1999), 73.

43. The quest for forgetfulness served as the basis for one of Nietzsche's most brilliantly provocative essays, "On the Uses and Disadvantages of History for Life." From that essay: "When the historical sense reigns *without restraint*, and all its consequences are realized, it uproots the future because it destroys illusions and robs the things that exist of the atmosphere in which alone they can live. . . . Historical verification always brings to light so much that is false, crude, inhuman, absurd, violent that the mood of pious illusion in which alone anything that wants to live can live necessarily crumbles away." Friedrich Nietzsche, *Untimely Meditations*, trans. R. J. Hollingdale (Cambridge: Cambridge University Press, 1983), 95.

44. For Darwin's connection to structuralism in particular and modern theories of language in general, see Gillian Beer, "Darwin and the Growth of Language Theory," in her *Open Fields: Science in Cultural Encounter* (New York: Oxford University Press, 1999), 95–114; Stephen G. Alter, *Darwinism and the Linguistic Image: Language, Race, and Natural Theology in the Nineteenth Century* (Baltimore: Johns Hopkins University Press, 1999); Sarah Winter, "Darwin's Saussure: Biosemiotics and Race in *Expression*," *Representations* 107 (2009): 128–61; and Jonathan Culler, *Ferdinand de Saussure*, rev. ed. (Ithaca, NY: Cornell University Press, 1986), 74–77.

45. See Paul Ricoeur's treatment of this question in *The Conflict of Interpretations*, ed. Don Ihde (Evanston, IL: Northwestern University Press, 1974), 31–34.

46. Ferdinand de Saussure, as quoted in Frederic Jameson, *The Prison-House of Language: A Critical Account of Structuralism and Russian Formalism* (Princeton: Princeton University Press, 1972), 30.

47. John Paul II, *On the Relationship between Faith and Reason* (Washington, DC: United States Conference of Catholic Bishops, 1998), 124–25. For a rich and stimulating examination of the "language and truth" question, see D. Stephen Long, *Speaking of God: Theology, Language, and Truth* (Grand Rapids: Eerdmans, 2009).

48. C. R. Resetarits, "The Genomic Tropes of Dickinson's 'The Veins of Other Flowers,'" *Kenyon Review* 28 (2006): 84.

49. Jameson, *Prison-House of Language*, 6.

50. Ferdinand de Saussure, *Course in General Linguistics*, ed. Charles Bally and Albert Seche-haye, in collaboration with Albert Riedlinger; trans. Wade Baskin (New York: McGraw-Hill, 1966), 18, 20. Of Saussure, Terry Eagleton explains, "He was not interested in investigating what people actually said; he was concerned with the objective structure of signs which made their speech possible in the first place, and this he called *langue*. Neither was Saussure concerned with the real objects which people spoke about: in order to study language effectively, the referents of the signs, the things they actually denoted, had to be placed in brackets." *Literary Theory: An Introduction* (Minneapolis: University of Minnesota Press, 1983), 97.

51. Saussure, *Course in General Linguistics*, 67.

52. The past two decades have witnessed an explosive growth in scholarly studies of changing modern attitudes to the body. They began, not surprisingly, with feminist studies in the 1970s and 1980s but have migrated in recent years to queer studies, disability studies, and various forms of Marxist critique within cultural studies. For this vast literature, the following serve as excellent points of entry into the conversation: David Harley Serlin, *Replaceable You: Engineering the Body in Postwar America* (Chicago: University of Chicago Press, 2004); Elizabeth Haiken, *Venus Envy: A History of Cosmetic Surgery* (Baltimore: Johns Hopkins University Press, 1999); and Sander Gilman, *Making the Body Beautiful: A Cultural History of Aesthetic Surgery* (Princeton: Princeton University Press, 1999).

53. Joel Weinsheimer correctly notes that, however limited this arbitrary view of signs may be in some respects, it does seem "quite plausible that language accrues to things by a societal and impersonal act of institution and convention" (*Gadamer's Hermeneutics*, 230).

54. Richard J. Evans, *The Third Reich in Power* (2005; repr., New York: Penguin, 2006), 549.

55. Peter Berger, *A Rumor of Angels: Modern Society and the Rediscovery of the Supernatural* (Garden City, NY: Anchor, 1970), 54–55.

56. Ibid., 55.

57. Ibid., 55–56.

Chapter 3 Picturing the Truth

1. Hans-Georg Gadamer, *Truth and Method*, 2nd rev. ed., trans. Joel Weinsheimer and Donald G. Marshall (New York: Crossroad, 1989), 416.

2. Joel Weinsheimer, *Philosophical Hermeneutics and Literary Theory* (New Haven: Yale University Press, 1991), 88–90.

3. Gadamer, *Truth and Method*, 416–17.

4. Ibid. "Gadamer sees linguistic accounts as containing within themselves ideal reality in such a way that language is never a mere sign condemned to a secondary instrumental status in the realm of thought, but the very forum of thought and intelligible reality. . . . The real task of thought, according to Gadamer, is to find the structure of intelligible reality in speech itself. Language contains an ideality in such a way that in finding the right words we also find the object of those words. Put negatively, without the right words we would never have a glimpse of the

thing itself." Brice R. Wachterhauser, "Gadamer's Realism: The 'Belongingness' of Word and Reality," in *Hermeneutics and Truth*, ed. Brice R. Wachterhauser (Evanston, IL.: Northwestern University Press, 1994), 162–63.

5. Hans Urs von Balthasar, *Explorations in Theology*, vol. 1, *The Word Made Flesh*, trans. A. V. Littledale and Alexander Dru (San Francisco: Ignatius, 1989), 23.

6. St. Augustine, *Confessions*, trans. Henry Chadwick (Oxford: Oxford University Press, 1992), 3.

7. Mark Twain, as quoted in *The Art of Authorship*, ed. George Bainton (New York: 1891), 87–88.

8. Henry David Thoreau, *Walden*, in *A Week on the Concord and Merrimack Rivers; Walden, or, Life in the Woods; The Maine Woods; Cape Cod*, ed. Robert F. Sayre (New York: Library of America, 1985), 408–9; Ralph Waldo Emerson, *Selected Journals: 1820–1842*, ed. Lawrence Rosenwald (New York: Library of America, 2010), 415–16; *Emerson in His Journals*, ed. Joel Porte (Cambridge, MA: Belknap Press of Harvard University Press, 1982), 78–79. See also Robert D. Richardson, *First We Read, Then We Write: Emerson on the Creative Process* (Iowa City: University of Iowa Press, 2009), 49–63.

9. Emile Benveniste, as quoted in Weinsheimer, *Philosophical Hermeneutics*, 90.

10. Gadamer, *Truth and Method*, 78.

11. Weinsheimer, *Philosophical Hermeneutics*, 91.

12. Hans Urs von Balthasar, *The Glory of the Lord: A Theological Aesthetics*, vol. 1, *Seeing the Form*, trans. Erasmo Leiva-Merikakis, ed. Joseph Fessio, SJ, and John Riches (San Francisco: Ignatius, 1982), 437.

13. Emily Dickinson, *The Letters of Emily Dickinson*, vol. 2, ed. Thomas H. Johnson and Theodora Ward (Cambridge, MA: Belknap Press of Harvard University Press, 1958), 603.

14. Weinsheimer, *Philosophical Hermeneutics*, 91–92. As a function of the mind, meaning points to the fundamental loneliness of the human. "As [man] shares no longer in a meaning of nature, but merely, through his body, in its mechanical determination," argues philosopher Hans Jonas, "so nature no longer shares in his inner concerns." And thus the human mind "marks the unbridgeable gulf between [man] and the rest of existence." *The Gnostic Religion: The Message of the Alien God and the Beginnings of Christianity*, 2nd ed., rev. (Boston: Beacon, 1963), 323.

15. Ptolemy the Gnostic, quoted in Jaroslav Pelikan, *The Christian Tradition: A History of the Development of Doctrine*, vol. 1, *The Emergence of the Catholic Tradition (100–600)* (Chicago: University of Chicago Press, 1971), 90.

16. Pelikan, *Emergence of the Catholic Tradition*, 97. "Above all, Christian Gnosticism was a religion of redemption and of the reconciliation of the human spirit with the ineffable greatness of God. It represented a fundamental distortion of Christian doctrine . . . , and the church had to resist it. But it also represented a serious effort to come to terms with issues of Christian doctrine from which no theologian, be he orthodox or heretical, could escape."

17. Weinsheimer, *Philosophical Hermeneutics*, 100–101.

18. Gadamer, *Truth and Method*, 152.

19. Ibid., 153.

20. Steven Ozment, *The Age of Reform, 1250–1550: An Intellectual and Religious History of Late Medieval and Reformation Europe* (New Haven: Yale University Press, 1980), 60. For my summary of nominalism and for the image of a "desymbolized universe," I am indebted to Amos Funkenstein, *Theology and the Scientific Imagination: From the Middle Ages to the Seventeenth Century* (Princeton: Princeton University Press, 1986), 57–58.

21. For an informative, informal survey of trends in the renaming process, see Sam Roberts, "New Life in U.S. No Longer Means New Name," *New York Times*, August 25, 2010, www .nytimes.com/2010/08/26/nyregion/26names.html.

22. "Canons and Decrees of the Council of Trent," in *Confessions and Catechisms of the Reformation*, ed. Mark A. Noll (Grand Rapids: Baker, 1991), 193.

23. John Paul II, *On the Relationship Between Faith and Reason* (Washington, DC: United States Conference of Catholic Bishops, 1998), 22.

24. Ulrich Zwingli, Johannes Oecolampadius, and Cornelius Hoen quoted in Jaroslav Pelikan, *The Christian Tradition: A History of the Development of Doctrine*, vol. 4, *Reformation of Church and Dogma (1300–1700)* (Chicago: University of Chicago Press, 1984), 193–94.

25. "The Schleitheim Confession (1527)," in Noll, *Confessions and Catechisms*, 52.

26. Robert W. Jenson, *Systematic Theology*, vol. 2, *The Works of God* (New York: Oxford University Press, 1999), 258; the whole of this discussion (250–60) merits close attention. See also Helmut Thielicke, *The Evangelical Faith*, vol. 3, *Theology of the Spirit*, trans. Geoffrey W. Bromiley (Grand Rapids: Eerdmans, 1982), 248–62.

27. Jenson, *Systematic Theology*, 2:6, 216. "The relation between the bread and cup as *signum* and Christ's mystical body as *res* is exceptional in the way called sacramental in that there is a middle reality between what is simply sign and what is simply *res*; this is the body and blood of Christ. The body and blood are at once *signum et res*: they are the thing the bread and cup signify but in turn they are signs, the visible Word of God that promises our communion with God and with one another" (2:251).

28. Pelikan, *Reformation of Church and Dogma*, 189–90.

29. Bruce McCormack, introduction to *Mapping Modern Theology: A Thematic and Historical Introduction*, ed. Kelly M. Kapic and Bruce L. McCormack (Grand Rapids: Baker, 2012), 3.

30. J. Robert Barth, SJ, *The Symbolic Imagination: Coleridge and the Romantic Tradition*, 2nd ed. (New York: Fordham University Press, 2001), 33; the passage on the "reconciling and mediatory power" is from Coleridge, *Lay Sermons*, in *Samuel Taylor Coleridge: The Major Works*, ed. H. J. Jackson (Oxford: Oxford University Press, 2000), 660; and the passage on "servant Nature" is found in *The Complete Works of Samuel Taylor Coleridge*, ed. W. G. T. Shedd (New York: 1884), 1:461. For a thorough survey of romantic theories of the symbol, see Tzvetan Todorov, *Theories of the Symbol*, trans. Catherine Porter (Ithaca, NY: Cornell University Press, 1982), 145–221; and for a helpful discussion of the centrality of symbol for Coleridge's view of the Bible, see Jeffrey W. Barbeau, *Coleridge, the Bible, and Religion* (New York: Palgrave Macmillan, 2008), 41–45.

31. Until he made his break with the liberal tradition—during World War I—Barth "still acted as though his own religious experience stood beyond all doubt. Given the certainty of religious experience, he had the right key in his hand for reading the ways of God off the face of history. He could not really be free of the axiom of religious experience until criticism turned inward; until he realized that the questionability of all things human when seen in the light of the otherness of God and His Kingdom had to apply to him and his friends as well as to their opponents. From now on, knowledge of God—the a priori of all true representations of the Kingdom—would be *the* central question in Karl Barth's new theology. In principle, his break with liberalism was now complete." Bruce L. McCormack, *Karl Barth's Critically Realistic Dialectical Theology: Its Genesis and Development, 1909–1936* (Oxford: Clarendon, 1995), 125.

32. When he addressed God's decision to reveal himself to humanity, Barth customarily spoke in terms usually reserved in the Reformed tradition for the elaboration of the doctrine of double predestination. For Barth, however, God's decision to choose us "in Christ before the foundation of the world" and to "predestine us for adoption" (Eph. 1:4–5) "is not Yes and No, but in its substance, in the origin and scope of its utterance, it is altogether Yes." In brief: "All the joy and the benefit of His whole work as Creator, Reconciler and Redeemer, all the blessings which are divine and therefore real blessings, all the promise of the Gospel which has been declared: all these are grounded and determined in the fact that God is the God of the eternal election of His grace. In the light of this election the whole of the Gospel is light. Yes is said here, and all the promises of God are Yea and Amen (2 Cor. 1:20)" (*CD*, II.2.13–14). The entirety of Barth's discussion of this theme in the *Dogmatics* is titled "The Problem of a Correct Doctrine of the Election of Grace" (*CD*, II.2.3–34).

33. M. H. Abrams, *Natural Supernaturalism: Tradition and Revolution in Romantic Literature* (New York: Norton, 1971).

34. Keith E. Johnson, *Rethinking the Trinity and Religious Pluralism: An Augustinian Assessment* (Downers Grove, IL: InterVarsity, 2011), 152.

35. Eberhard Jüngel offers an excellent discussion of the *vestigia trinitatis* in *God's Being Is in Becoming: The Trinitarian Being of God in the Theology of Karl Barth*, trans. John Webster (Grand Rapids: Eerdmans, 2001), 17–27.

36. Ibid.

37. St. Bonaventure, *The Soul's Journey into God*, in *Bonaventure: The Soul's Journey into God, The Tree of Life, The Life of St. Francis*, ed. Ewert Cousins (Mahwah, NJ: Paulist, 1978), 60. For the contemporary relevance of the *vestigia* tradition, see Johnson, *Rethinking the Trinity*, 141–83; and Trevor Hart, *Regarding Karl Barth: Toward a Reading of His Theology* (Downers Grove, IL: InterVarsity, 1999), 117–38.

38. St. Bonaventure, *Soul's Journey*, 61.

39. As metaphorical likenesses or similarities, the *vestigia* may have an illustrative part to play in Christian thought, but as an apologetic device they have limited usefulness: "If there are *vestigia*, then, for Barth, they could only be recognized by faith from within the framework of understanding and believing determined by the gospel" (Hart, *Regarding Karl Barth*, 134).

40. The issue of the *vestigia trinitatis* is crucial to Barth's doctrine of God and revelation, but it is only one of his many substantial engagements with the theme of the *analogia entis* (analogy of being). His disputes with Roman Catholicism and with many of his fellow Protestant theologians on this score proved pivotal to the development of twentieth-century theology. Of the many critical studies written on this aspect of Barth's career, one of the most recent stands out for its wisdom, clarity, and charity; see Keith L. Johnson, *Karl Barth and the "Analogia Entis"* (London: T&T Clark, 2010).

41. Charles Taylor, *A Secular Age* (Cambridge, MA: Belknap Press of Harvard University Press, 2007), 59–60, 324. The entirety of Taylor's chapter on "The Dark Abyss of Time" (322–51) warrants a close reading.

42. C. S. Lewis, *The Discarded Image: An Introduction to Medieval and Renaissance Literature* (Cambridge: Cambridge University Press, 1964), 99.

43. André Bleikasten, *The Ink of Melancholy: Faulkner's Novels from "The Sound and the Fury" to "Light in August"* (Bloomington: Indiana University Press, 1990), 202.

44. Denis Donoghue, *Words Alone: The Poet T. S. Eliot* (New Haven: Yale University Press, 2000), 284–85.

Chapter 4 From Signs to Stories

1. Ludwig Feuerbach, *The Essence of Christianity*, trans. George Eliot (Amherst, NY: Prometheus, 1989), 40.

2. Karl Barth, *Protestant Theology in the Nineteenth Century*, trans. Brian Cozens and John Bowden (Grand Rapids: Eerdmans, 2002), 521–22.

3. Friedrich Nietzsche, *The Gay Science*, trans. Walter Kaufmann (New York: Vintage, 1974), 181.

4. Stanley Hauerwas, *With the Grain of the Universe: The Church's Witness and Natural Theology* (Grand Rapids: Brazos, 2001), 37–38.

5. Simon During, *Exit Capitalism: Literary Culture, Theory, and Post-Secular Modernity* (New York: Routledge, 2010), ix, emphasis added.

6. David D. Hall, introduction to *Lived Religion in America: Toward a History of Practice*, ed. David D. Hall (Princeton: Princeton University Press, 1997), vii. For lived religion's roots in pragmatism, see Robert D. Richardson, *William James: In the Maelstrom of American Modernism* (Boston: Houghton Mifflin, 2006), 389–416; and Ann Taves, *Fits, Trances, and Visions: Experiencing Religion and Explaining Experience from Wesley to James* (Princeton: Princeton

University Press, 1999), 261–347; for the connection to cultural and symbolic anthropology, see Sherry B. Ortner, "Theory in Anthropology since the Sixties," *Comparative Studies in Society and History* 26, no. 1 (1984): 126–66.

7. For the intellectual origins and theological significance of this shift, see my *From Nature to Experience: The American Search for Cultural Authority* (2005; repr., Lanham, MD: Rowman & Littlefield, 2007).

8. D. G. Hart, *The University Gets Religion: Religious Studies in American Higher Education* (Baltimore: Johns Hopkins University Press, 1999), 250–51.

9. The three critical studies under consideration here are: Tracy Fessenden, *Culture and Redemption: Religion, the Secular, and American Literature* (Princeton: Princeton University Press, 2007); Pericles Lewis, *Religious Experience and the Modernist Novel* (Cambridge: Cambridge University Press, 2010); and Amy Hungerford, *Postmodern Belief: American Literature and Religion Since 1960* (Princeton: Princeton University Press, 2010).

10. Rob Warner, *Secularization and Its Discontents* (London: Continuum, 2010), 2.

11. Charles Taylor, *A Secular Age* (Cambridge, MA: Belknap Press of Harvard University Press, 2007), 22.

12. Mark Eaton, "How 20th-century Novelists Regarded Secularization," *Books and Culture*, August 2010, www.booksandculture.com/articles/webexclusives/2010august/eaton082410.html. A more enthusiastic and comprehensive endorsement of the postsecular project may be found in a section of Graham Ward's *True Religion*, titled "Re-enchantment." It begins: "Ironically, the technology that Weber observed controlling and calibrating the world is the means by which that same world has been re-enchanted. . . . Allied with the glitter of the media and advanced telecommunications, technology has become sexy, seductive and the bearer of messianic possibilities." And this portion of Ward's argument closes with a summative endorsement: "There is a production of the religious, then, in academic conversation that is also re-enchanting our understanding of the world." *True Religion* (Malden, MA: Blackwell, 2003), 129, 131.

13. Fessenden, *Culture and Redemption*, 3.

14. Ibid., 217, 180, 5. In a sympathetic and balanced account of *Culture and Redemption*, Everett Hamner sees Fessenden as one of a growing cadre of "US scholars" whose "textual analyses . . . are growing increasingly conscious of the distinction between the secular and professing secularism—which reacts against religious dogmatism with an equally rigid absolutism." Review of *Culture and Redemption*, *Literature and Theology* 21(2007): 446. In Fessenden's case, at least, this distinction—"between studying the secular and professing secularism"—does not seem to hold up because narratives of human autonomy and material explanation clearly govern her interpretation of American literature and Christian thought.

15. Hungerford, *Postmodern Belief*, xix.

16. Ibid., 139.

17. Ibid., 139–40.

18. Lewis, *Religious Experience*, 51, 192.

19. Garrett Green, introduction to Karl Barth, *On Religion: The Revelation of God as the Sublimation of Religion*, trans. Garrett Green (London: T&T Clark, 2006), 25, 27.

20. For a nuanced treatment of these questions from an explicitly Christian perspective, see Lori Branch, *Rituals of Spontaneity: Sentiment and Secularism from Free Prayer to Wordsworth* (Waco: Baylor University Press, 2006).

21. Bruce L. McCormack, *Karl Barth's Critically Realistic Theology: Its Genesis and Development, 1909–1936* (Oxford: Clarendon, 1995), 77.

22. This passage comes from section 17 of *Church Dogmatics*. The translation is by Garrett Green and is to be found in *On Religion*, 83.

23. George Hunsinger, *How to Read Karl Barth: The Shape of His Theology* (New York: Oxford University Press, 1991), 234.

24. On the question of the testimony of creation, C. Stephen Evans offers a persuasive argument in a recent study of natural theology and the knowledge of God. As Barth does with the secular parables of the kingdom, Evans grants the value of what he calls the "natural signs" that undergird the classical arguments that attempt to prove God's existence. These signs are vital because they point to realities that supposedly help to prove God's existence. Yet as important as they may be, "these signs, like signs in general, do not point in a conclusive or compelling fashion. Signs have to be perceived, and once perceived must be 'read.' . . . The natural signs that point to God's reality are signs that can be interpreted in more than one way and thus are sometimes misread and sometimes not even perceived as signs. They point to God but do not do so in a coercive manner." *Natural Signs and Knowledge of God: A New Look at Theistic Arguments* (New York: Oxford University Press, 2010), 2.

25. John Calvin makes a parallel point in the *Institutes* when he says God "not only sowed in men's minds that seed of religion of which we have spoken but revealed himself and daily discloses himself in the whole workmanship of the universe. As a consequence, men cannot open their eyes without being compelled to see him. Indeed, his essence is incomprehensible; hence, his divineness far escapes all human perception. But upon his individual works he has engraved unmistakable marks of his glory." Just as God has grasped language as a means of revealing himself, so too has he impressed the signs of his power on the objects of his creation. *Institutes of the Christian Religion,* trans. Ford Lewis Battles (Philadelphia: Westminster, 1960), 1.5.1, 51–52.

26. Eberhard Jüngel, *God's Being Is in Becoming: The Trinitarian Being of God in the Theology of Karl Barth,* trans. John Webster (Grand Rapids: Eerdmans, 2001), 19. Jüngel explains, "By 'hermeneutic of signification' is meant an account of understanding oriented to the ontological distinction of *res* [thing] and *signum* [sign]. In Augustine we read: 'All teaching is teaching of either things or signs, but things are learnt through signs'" (19).

27. For a clear and insightful discussion of Barth on the *vestigia,* see Alan J. Torrance, *Persons in Communion: Trinitarian Description and Human Participation* (Edinburgh: T&T Clark, 1996), 194–212.

28. Nicholas Wolterstorff offers an insightful and forceful critique of Barth's view of language in the context of the question of God's speech. The subheading for the final section of Wolterstorff's critique is titled, "Why there's less in Barth on God speaking than first appears," and in it he asks, almost plaintively, "Why does Barth so consistently avoid, and so determinedly resist, saying that human beings sometimes speak in the name of God, and that human speech is sometimes appropriated for divine speech?" *Divine Discourse: Philosophical Reflections on the Claim that God Speaks* (Cambridge: Cambridge University Press, 1995), 72–73; see esp. 63–74 and 301–4.

That strikes one as a fair question, and the best answer to it may well be, "But Barth does accept that human language is indeed appropriated by God for his speech." "The revelation of God," writes Eberhard Jüngel, "thus does not 'commandeer' language as a dumb aggressor but rather gets involved with and in language through speaking" (*God's Being,* 27). In an astute response to Wolterstorff, Brian Hebblethwaite rightly notes that despite the philosopher's reservations about the theologian, "Wolterstorff's own detailed analysis of mediated divine speech is very close to Barth's." *Philosophical Theology and Christian Doctrine* (Malden, MA: Blackwell, 2005), 23.

In the terms I have adopted from Gadamer and Weinsheimer, while there are undeniable differences between Wolterstorff and Barth on the nature of language and the speech of God, both of them align much more closely with the view of words as *pictures* than with words as *symbols* (*analogia entis* and romantic hermeneutics) or words as *signs* (structuralism and poststructuralism).

29. Hungerford, *Postmodern Belief,* xiii.

30. Augustine, *On Christian Doctrine,* trans. D. W. Robertson Jr. (Indianapolis: Bobbs-Merrill, 1958), 14. There is admittedly in Augustine's treatment of both language and Incarnation a

Platonic element of distinction and separation that is entirely absent in the reflections of the philosopher Gadamer and the theologian Barth on the same theme.

31. David Lyle Jeffrey, *People of the Book: Christian Identity and Literary Culture* (Grand Rapids: Eerdmans, 1996), 7.

32. Augustine, *On Christian Doctrine*, 9, 30. The image of creation as a "temporal dispensation" hints at what Calvin would call creation—the "theater of God's glory"—and it anticipates by more than fifteen hundred years Barth's decision to subsume the doctrine of creation within and under the doctrine of election.

33. Jeffrey, *People of the Book*, 83–84.

34. Eberhard Jüngel, *Theological Essays*, trans. J. B. Webster (Edinburgh: T&T Clark, 1989), 65, 70–71. Paul Ricoeur has written with great perspicacity about the complex manner in which the actual use of language—the making of sentences which speak of the world in which we live and of our experience—takes place as an *event* which modifies the *system* of language from which the individual words of that language have been taken. He notes that structuralism is by nature interested in the synchronic, systematic study of the science of signs; it has no place for change and does not seek to account for development. The closed world of structuralism is to the opening world of event as the closed system of human life assumed by Tracy Fessenden, Amy Hungerford, and Pericles Lewis is to the revealing world and will of God, which comes into the "far country of human" experience in order to redeem, renew, and transform the system. For Ricoeur, see especially "Structure, Word, Event," in *The Conflict of Interpretations: Essays in Hermeneutics*, trans. Don Ihde (Evanston, IL: Northwestern University Press, 1974), 79–96.

35. Hans-Georg Gadamer, *Truth and Method*, 2nd rev. ed., trans. Joel Weinsheimer and Donald G. Marshall (New York: Crossroad, 1989), 418.

36. Ibid., 418–19.

37. This translation of *Truth and Method* is given by John Arthos in his recent study, *The Inner Word in Gadamer's Hermeneutics* (Notre Dame, IN: University of Notre Dame Press, 2009), 225; for the standard, widely available translation (2nd rev. ed., trans. Weinsheimer and Marshall) of this passage, see Gadamer, *Truth and Method*, 418–19.

38. On the contrast between Greek and Christian views of embodiment, see Oscar Cullmann's provocative "Immortality of the Soul of Resurrection of the Dead: The Witness of the New Testament," in *Death in the Western World: Two Conflicting Currents of Thought*, ed. Krister Stendahl (New York: Macmillan, 1965), 9–53.

39. Arthos, *Inner Word*, 227.

40. Ibid., 228.

41. Ricoeur, *Conflict of Interpretations*, 79.

42. Ibid., 82–84. William Dowling summarizes nicely Ricoeur's appreciative yet critical approach to Saussure and the larger structural project. "Much of what semiotics discovered in decentering the subject was and is, in Ricoeur's opinion, true and important. For him, its limitations lie in a certain sterility or empty formalism arising from the further claim that consciousness itself is a mere epiphenomenon of underlying systems." *Ricoeur on Time and Narrative: An Introduction to "Temps et Récit"* (Notre Dame, IN: University of Notre Dame Press, 2011), 38.

43. Ricoeur, *Conflict of Interpretations*, 90.

44. Luigi Pirandello, preface to *Six Characters in Search of an Author*, as quoted in Hans Urs von Balthasar, *Theo-Drama: Theological Dramatic Theory*, vol. 1, *Prolegomena*, trans. Graham Harrison (San Francisco: Ignatius, 1988), 245.

45. See also Kevin Vanhoozer, *The Drama of Doctrine: A Canonical-Linguistical Approach to Christian Theology* (Louisville: Westminster John Knox, 2005). "The present work insists that God and humanity are alternately actor and audience. Better: life is divine-human interactive theater, and theology involves both what God has said and done for the world and what we must say and do in grateful response" (37–38).

46. Balthasar, *Theo-Drama*, 1:130–31.

47. Gadamer, *Truth and Method,* 419–21.
48. Ibid., 424.
49. Jüngel, *God's Being,* 138–39.

Chapter 5 Modern Times

1. M. H. Abrams, *Natural Supernaturalism: Tradition and Revolution in Romantic Literature* (New York: Norton, 1971), 13. Abrams's thesis has been contested and challenged on a number of fronts from the 1970s to the present. Yet while he may overstate the secularity of English culture in the romantic era and may overestimate the unity of the major romantic writers on the subject of religion, Abrams's central point about the drive to internalize Christian metaphor and narrative remains a sound judgment. For a balanced understanding of the current status of "romanticism and religion," see Kevin Gilmartin, "Romanticism and Religious Modernity: From Natural Supernaturalism to Literary Sectarianism," in *The Cambridge History of English Romantic Literature,* ed. James Chandler (Cambridge: Cambridge University Press, 2009), 621–47.

2. Hans Frei, *The Eclipse of Biblical Narrative: A Study in Eighteenth and Nineteenth Century Hermeneutics* (New Haven: Yale University Press, 1974), 127–30.

3. The lines are from Book XII: 208–18 and 221–23 of the 1850 edition of *The Prelude.*

4. See Abrams, *Natural Supernaturalism,* 77–79, 385–90, 419–27. "Many Romantic writers testified to a deeply significant experience in which an instant of consciousness, or else an ordinary object or event, suddenly blazes into revelation; the unsustainable moment seems to arrest what is passing, and is often described as an intersection of eternity with time" (385).

5. Samuel Taylor Coleridge, as quoted in Jeffrey W. Barbeau, *Coleridge, the Bible, and Religion* (New York: Palgrave Macmillan, 2008), 155.

6. Karl Barth, *Protestant Theology in the Nineteenth Century,* trans. Brian Cozens and John Bowden (Grand Rapids: Eerdmans, 2002), 404–5.

7. Charles Taylor, *Hegel* (Cambridge: Cambridge University Press, 1975), 546.

8. Karl Marx, *Theses on Feuerbach,* in Frederick Engels, *Ludwig Feuerbach and the Outcome of Classical German Philosophy,* ed. C. P. Dutt (New York: International, 1941), 84. The hymn to history and freedom is offered in the famous passage from *Das Kapital*: "Just as the savage man must wrestle with nature to satisfy his wants, to maintain and reproduce life, so must civilized man, and he must do so in all social formations and under all possible modes of production. With his development this realm of physical necessity expands as a result of his wants; but, at the same time, the forces of production which satisfy these wants also increase. Freedom in this field can only consist in socialized man, the associated producers, rationally regulating their interchange with nature, bringing it under their common control, instead of being ruled by it as a blind power; and achieving this with the least expenditure of energy and under conditions most favourable to, and worthy of, their human nature. But it nonetheless still remains a realm of necessity. Beyond it begins that development of human energy which is an end in itself, the true realm of freedom, which, however, can blossom forth only with this realm of necessity as its basis." Quoted in G. A. Cohen, *Karl Marx's Theory of History: A Defence* (Princeton: Princeton University Press, 2001), 324.

9. Charles Taylor, *Hegel and Modern Society* (Cambridge: Cambridge University Press, 1979), 146.

10. Both the philosophical background and the theoretical significance of the argument I am tracing here are treated fully in an influential book from the early twentieth century; see Hans Vaihinger, *The Philosophy of 'As if ': A System of the Theoretical, Practical and Religious Fictions of Mankind,* trans. C. K. Ogden (New York: Harcourt, 1925).

11. In her recent commentary on 150 Dickinson poems, Helen Vendler provides explications of both of these poems (1551 and 1474) that I have discussed here. Vendler reads the poems pretty much as I do, that is, as meditations on what it means to search for God in a world in which belief has renounced its position of authority. But where Vendler sees Dickinson advocating

the heroic certainty and virtue of unbelief, I see the poet as being decidedly more ambivalent and uncertain. For Vendler's interpretations, see *Dickinson: Selected Poems and Commentaries* (Cambridge, MA: Belknap Press of Harvard University Press, 2010), 475–78, 496–97.

12. Dickinson famously called immortality her "Flood subject," and there are two important things to keep in mind about the topic. The first is that when using the term, either in her poetry or letters, she was inclined to affirm a classical conception that humans possess an immortal soul housed within a mortal body; such a view contrasts sharply with the Christian doctrine of the resurrection of the body. And a second thing to keep in mind is that she remained internally divided on the question of immortality to the end of her life; in certain moods and on some days, she asserted her belief confidently, while at other times she wavered, sometimes dramatically, in her feelings about the subject.

13. Alasdair MacIntyre, *After Virtue*, rev. ed. (Notre Dame, IN: University of Notre Dame Press, 1984), 27.

14. Ibid., 27–28.

15. Ibid., 23–35.

16. F. Scott Fitzgerald, "The Crack-Up," in *The Crack-Up*, ed. Edmund Wilson (New York: New Directions, 1956), 69.

17. Steven Weinberg, *The First Three Minutes: A Modern View of the Origin of the Universe*, updated ed. (New York: Basic, 1993), 154. In a different context, I discuss the Weinberg passage in *From Nature to Experience: The American Search for Cultural Authority* (2005; repr., Lanham, MD: Rowman & Littlefield, 2007), 131–33; I discuss "The Weight of Glory" in *The Culture of Interpretation: Christian Faith and the Postmodern World* (Grand Rapids: Eerdmans, 1993), 216–17.

18. For this reading of the exchange between Quentin and his father, I am indebted to Stephen M. Ross and Noel Polk, *The Sound and the Fury: Glossary and Commentary* (Jackson: University of Mississippi Press, 1996), 102.

19. Cleanth Brooks, *William Faulkner: First Encounters* (New Haven: Yale University Press, 1983), 59.

20. Ibid., 69.

21. Jean-François Lyotard, *The Postmodern Condition: A Report on Knowledge*, trans. Geoff Bennington and Brian Massumi (Minneapolis: University of Minnesota Press, 1984), xxiii.

22. Ibid.

23. Ibid., xxiii–xxiv.

24. Ibid., xxiv. The meaning of Lyotard's definition of postmodernity as "incredulity toward metanarratives" has been debated vigorously for more than a decade in what has become a cottage industry in the intellectual life of evangelicalism and Reformed Christians. For the highlights of the complicated exchanges in this debate, see James K. A. Smith, "A Little Story about Metanarratives: Lyotard, Religion and Postmodernism Revisited," in *Christianity and the Postmodern Turn: Six Views*, ed. Myron B. Penner (Grand Rapids: Brazos, 2005), 123–40; for a rejoinder to Smith, see Ron Kubsch, "Why Christianity Is an Emancipation Narrative for François Lyotard," trans. Richard McClary, *MBS Texte* 93 (2008):3–10. Although Smith is correct to say that for Lyotard metanarratives were specifically those modern master narratives that science and pure reason claimed to legitimate, Kubsch is also right to point out, contra Smith, that the French philosopher did not believe Christianity to be a plausible or viable narrative in any meaningful way.

25. Lyotard, *Postmodern Condition*, xxiv–xxv.

26. Stephen Spender, *The Struggle of the Modern* (Berkeley: University of California Press, 1963), 17, emphasis added.

27. Charles Taylor, *A Secular Age* (Cambridge, MA: Belknap Press of Harvard University Press, 2007), 55.

28. Erich Auerbach, *Mimesis: The Representation of Reality in Western Literature*, trans. Willard R. Trask (Princeton: Princeton University Press, 1953), 73–74.

29. Erich Auerbach, "Figura," in *Scenes from the Drama of European Literature* (Minneapolis: University of Minnesota Press, 1984), 72.

30. Benedict Anderson, *Imagined Communities: Reflections on the Origin and Spread of Nationalism*, rev. ed. (London: Verso, 2006), 24–25.

31. Flora Tristan, as quoted in Patricia Meyer Spacks, *Boredom: The Literary History of a State of Mind* (Chicago: University of Chicago Press, 1995), 164. Spacks makes a clear distinction between boredom and ennui, while I do not do so. "Ennui involves a judgment on the universe; boredom, a response to the immediate. Ennui belongs to those with a sense of sublime potential, those who feel themselves superior to their environment" (12). The distinction by Spacks seems plausible, but in the literature I have been surveying, it does not hold up for long. Characters who struggle against boredom very often acquire a sense of their own superiority vis-à-vis their environment. While it takes years for Edna Pontellier to develop this sense in *The Awakening*, it comes to Emma Bovary suddenly at the start of her marriage, and it seems to have overwhelmed Hedda Gabler during her honeymoon tour with Jurgen Tesman.

32. Hedda Gabler refers several times to her need to find a way to "kill time." This idiomatic phrase, which construes time as a dreadful enemy, dates to the late eighteenth century, and by Ibsen's day, it had become commonplace. "Time like space has become a container, indifferent to what fills it" (Taylor, *A Secular Age*, 58).

33. Stephen Kern, *The Culture of Time and Space: 1880–1918* (Cambridge, MA: Harvard University Press, 1983), 10–15.

34. Charles Taylor, *Modern Social Imaginaries* (Durham, NC: Duke University Press, 2004), 96–99.

35. Michael North, *The Political Aesthetic of Yeats, Eliot, and Pound* (Cambridge: Cambridge University Press, 1991), 77.

36. Walter J. Ong, SJ, "Where Are We Now? Some Elemental Cosmological Considerations," *Christianity and Literature* 50, no. 1 (2000): 9.

37. Robert Jenson, *Systematic Theology*, vol. 2, *The Works of God* (New York: Oxford University Press, 1999), 34.

38. Ibid., 47.

Chapter 6 "I Will Restore It All"

1. Wallace Stevens, *Letters of Wallace Stevens*, ed. Holly Stevens (Berkeley: University of California Press, 1966), 378.

2. Not long before he died, Northrop Frye said that throughout his intellectual life, "Wallace Stevens remained something very central." He explained that when *The Great Code*, his study of the Bible and literature, came out in the early 1980s, interviewers asked him why he had "put so much Wallace Stevens in" the book, "and I couldn't tell them why, except that he just seemed to fit what I had to say." David Cayley, *Northrop Frye in Conversation* (Concord, ON: House of Anansi Press, 1992), 109.

In the epilogue to a reissued edition of his classic study of modern narratives, Frank Kermode admitted that when he reread his book, he was "struck by the ubiquity of Wallace Stevens. It is true that my head was full of Stevens at the time [1967], so much so that my friend the late John Wain, another admirer of Stevens, described the book as a love letter to the poet." *The Sense of an Ending: Studies in the Theory of Fiction, with a New Epilogue* (New York: Oxford University Press, 2000), 195.

3. Kermode, *Sense of an Ending*, 62–63. In the history of modern theology, the question of *chronos* and *kairos* has led to sharp disagreements among scholars. Frank Kermode follows the line of argument developed by Oscar Cullmann. For a strong critique of that argument, see James Barr, *Biblical Words for Time* (1962; repr., Eugene, OR: Wipf & Stock, 2009), 21–85.

4. Oscar Cullmann, *Christ and Time: The Primitive Christian Conception of Time and History*, rev. ed., trans. Floyd V. Filson (Philadelphia: Westminster, 1964), 39.

5. Ibid., 43.

6. Kermode, *Sense of an Ending*, 58, emphasis added.

7. For the full discussion of *chronos* vs. *kairos*, see Kermode, *Sense of an Ending*, 45–53; the quotation is from p. 52.

8. Cleanth Brooks, *William Faulkner: The Yoknapatawpha Country* (New Haven: Yale University Press, 1963), 348. Joel Williamson, in his study of the role of history in Faulkner's fiction, appears considerably less amenable to Christianity than does Brooks. Yet even Williamson acknowledges the strength of Dilsey and her faith: "It was almost as if the white aristocracy from the golden age of the antebellum South had somehow passed on the torch of truth to Dilsey and she carried it forward as they stumbled and fell. The light that Dilsey shone burned brightly." *William Faulkner and Southern History* (New York: Oxford University Press, 1993), 427.

9. Kermode, *Sense of an Ending*, 39.

10. Albert Raboteau, *Slave Religion: The "Invisible Institution" in the Antebellum South*, updated ed. (New York: Oxford University Press, 2004), 311.

11. Colin Gunton, *The Christian Faith: An Introduction to Christian Doctrine* (Malden, MA: Blackwell, 2002), 170.

12. Ibid., 170–72.

13. Paul Ricoeur, *Time and Narrative*, vol. 2, trans. Kathleen McLaughlin and David Pellauer (Chicago: University of Chicago Press, 1985), 26–27. For Buffon and the "dark abyss of time," see Paolo Rossi, *The Dark Abyss of Time: The History of the Earth and the History of Nations from Hooke to Vico*, trans. Lydia G. Cochrane (Chicago: University of Chicago Press, 1987).

14. Barbara Hardy, "Towards a Poetics of Fiction: 3) An Approach through Narrative," *Novel: A Forum on Fiction* 2, no. 1 (1968): 5.

15. Louis O. Mink, "History and Fiction as Modes of Comprehension," *New Literary History* 1, no. 3 (1970): 557–58.

16. Alasdair MacIntyre, *After Virtue*, 2nd ed. (Notre Dame, IN: University of Notre Dame Press, 1984), 212, 216.

17. Hans Urs von Balthasar, *A Theology of History* (1963; repr., San Francisco: Ignatius, 1994), 70–71.

18. Ibid., 76, 78. John Paul II makes a similar point: "Revelation renders this unity [of truth] certain, showing that the God of creation is also the God of salvation history." *On the Relationship Between Faith and Reason* (Washington, DC: United States Conference of Catholic Bishops, 1998), 51; and Karl Barth: "Does it need such a great imagination to realize, is it not the simplest thing in the world, that . . . in the history of Jesus, we have to do with the reality which underlies and precedes all other reality as the first and eternal Word of God, that in this history we have actually to do with the ground and sphere, the atmosphere of the being of every man, whether they lived thousands of years before or after Jesus?" (*CD* IV.1.53).

19. MacIntyre, *After Virtue*, 213.

20. Michael J. Sandel, *Democracy's Discontent: America in Search of a Public Philosophy* (Cambridge, MA: Belknap Press of Harvard University Press, 1996), 5. The argument I am making here does not deny the role of providence in our lives, nor does it downplay the powerful shaping agency of social, biological, and economic forces. What the argument is intended to do, however, is to recognize the vastly expanded role that the notion of self-determination has come to play in the way we think of everything, from the choice of our professions to the engineering of our bodies and reproductive lives.

21. Alexis de Tocqueville, *Democracy in America*, ed. Olivier Zunz, trans. Arthur Goldhammer (New York: Library of America, 2004), 514–15.

22. Robert Langbaum, *The Poetry of Experience: The Dramatic Monologue in Modern Literary Tradition* (1957; repr., Chicago: University of Chicago Press, 1985), 21.

23. Colin Gunton, *The One, the Three and the Many: God, Creation and the Culture of Modernity* (Cambridge: Cambridge University Press, 1993), 93–94.

24. Karl Barth, *Dogmatics in Outline*, trans. G. T. Thomson (New York: Harper, 1959), 58.

25. William C. Dowling, *Ricoeur on Time and Narrative: An Introduction to "Temps et Récit"* (Notre Dame, IN: University of Notre Dame Press, 2011), 49.

26. John Paul II, *Between Faith and Reason*, 19.

27. Ibid., 65–67.

28. Keith L. Johnson, *Karl Barth and the "Analogia Entis"* (London: T&T Clark, 2010), 202.

29. Dietrich Bonhoeffer, *Letters and Papers from Prison*, enlarged ed., ed. Eberhard Bethge (New York: Collier, 1972), 168.

30. Ibid., 169.

31. Ibid., 170.

32. Irenaeus of Lyons, *Against Heresies*, in Robert M. Grant, *Irenaeus of Lyons* (London: Routledge, 1997), 173.

33. W. H. Auden, *Forewords and Afterwords*, ed. Edward Mendelson (1973; repr., New York: Vintage, 1989), 18.

34. Hans Urs von Balthasar, *The Glory of the Lord: A Theological Aesthetics*, vol. 2, *Studies in Theological Style: Clerical Styles*, ed. John Riches, trans. Andrew Louth, Francis McDonagh, and Brian McNeil, CRV (San Francisco: Ignatius, 1984), 31–32.

35. Gunton, *The One, the Three, and the Many*, 158–59.

36. Gunton, *Christian Faith*, 64. Catherine Keller lodges a sharp complaint against Irenaeus and the theory of recapitulation. Her objection focuses on the second-century theologian's reliance on the doctrine of creation *ex nihilo* and its gendered narrative of power and domination: "I will argue that it is not a latent biblical logic but the polemic against 'heresy' that crystallized earlier narratives of beginning into the 'orthodox' doctrine of origin; that this absolute origin extrudes the Christian metanarrative as a single line stretching from the beginning to the end of history; and that this rhetorical extrusion draws its driving omnipotence from a drama of gender. . . . As it hardens, this narrative of omnipotent origin vaporizes any residual, female-tinged chaos." *The Face of the Deep: A Theology of Becoming* (London: Routledge, 2003), 43–44.

In a recent essay, Bruce Benson works out several narrative implications of Keller's assertions. When we think of God not as the *author of* history but as a supremely skillful *improviser within* the limits of history, our concept of art and storytelling changes. The idea that "even God works with material that is already there," argues Benson, means that "the very being of life is improvisatory—by which I mean that it is a mixture of both structure and contingency, of regularity and unpredictability, of constraint and possibility." "In the Beginning, There Was Improvisation," *Verge* 1, no. 1 (2011): 11.

37. Hans-Georg Gadamer, *Truth and Method*, 2nd rev. ed., trans. Joel Weinsheimer and Donald G. Marshall (New York: Crossroad, 1989), 356–57.

38. MacIntyre, *After Virtue*, 213.

Chapter 7 Defending a Great Hope

1. David Bromwich, *Skeptical Music: Essays on Modern Poetry* (Chicago: University of Chicago Press, 2001), 174.

2. Emily Dickinson, *The Letters of Emily Dickinson*, vol. 3, ed. Thomas H. Johnson and Theodora Ward (Cambridge, MA: Belknap Press of Harvard University Press, 1958), 728.

3. Dickinson, *Letters*, 2:514.

4. In the following pages, I will be discussing three works we have already encountered—Tracy Fessenden, *Culture and Redemption: Religion, the Secular, and American Literature* (Princeton: Princeton University Press, 2007); Amy Hungerford, *Postmodern Belief: American Literature and Religion Since 1960* (Princeton: Princeton University Press, 2010); and Pericles Lewis, *Religious Experience and the Modernist Novel* (Cambridge: Cambridge University Press, 2010)—along with a fourth: John A. McClure, *Partial Faiths: Postsecular Fiction in the Age of Pynchon and Morrison* (Athens: University of Georgia Press, 2007).

5. Lewis, *Religious Experience*, 23–24.

6. McClure in particular seems anxious about the "troubling" revival of fundamentalism, which he appears to conflate with evangelicalism in general. The "totalizing language" of that fundamentalism leads to repressive social order and "the fierce enclosure of consciousness" (16, 19).

7. Fessenden, *Culture and Redemption*, 217.

8. McClure, *Partial Faiths*, 7; Gianni Vattimo, *Belief*, trans. Luca D'Isanto and David Webb (Stanford, CA: Stanford University Press, 1999).

9. Edward T. Oakes, *Pattern of Redemption: The Theology of Hans Urs von Balthasar* (New York: Continuum, 1994), 243, 247.

10. Vattimo, *Belief*, 49–50.

11. McClure, *Partial Faiths*, 31, 12, 196, 16.

12. Ibid., 3.

13. Elton Trueblood, *The Predicament of Modern Man* (New York: Harper, 1944), 59.

14. Hungerford, *Postmodern Belief*, xiii, xv, xxi.

15. Ibid., 107–8.

16. Ibid., 108–9.

17. Ibid., 109–10. Hungerford is quoting here from Paul Tillich's *The Courage to Be*.

18. Dinesen borrowed the kernel of this story from Søren Kierkegaard, a writer of great importance to her work: "What the philosophers say about reality is often as deceptive as when you see a sign in a second-hand store that reads: Pressing Done Here. If you went in with your clothes to have them pressed you would be fooled; the sign is for sale." Søren Kierkegaard, *Either/Or: A Fragment of Life*, trans. Alastair Hannay (London: Penguin, 1992), 50. For an insightful discussion of Dinesen's "The Poet," see Robert Langbaum, *Isak Dinesen's Art: The Gayety of Vision* (Chicago: University of Chicago Press, 1975), 110–18.

19. The possibilities and limits of the conversational model were clearly delineated in an exchange between Nicholas Wolterstorff and Richard Rorty. The discussion had been prompted by a review essay published by Rorty in the 1990s. In it, the philosopher argued that religion had no legitimate role to play in public life and did not deserve a seat at the conversational table of the culture. Instead, it belonged to and ought to stay within the boundaries of the private life. "The main reason religion needs to be privatized is that, in political discusson with those outside the relevant religious community, it is a conversation-stopper," Rorty complained. Richard Rorty, *Philosophy and Social Hope* (London: Penguin, 1999), 171.

Wolterstorff responded to Rorty several years later and pressed him on key points of his argument. That challenge prompted Rorty to reconsider and revise his position. The change is significant in one sense but not substantial in a major way, as the final sentence of Rorty's reply indicates: "We should do our best to keep the conversation going without citing unarguable first principles, either philosophical or religious. If we are sometimes driven to such citation, we should see ourselves as having failed, not as having triumphed." It's meaningful to be at the table, but we ought to be levelheaded and clear to ourselves about what we might accomplish there. For Wolterstorff, see "An Engagement with Rorty," *The Journal of Religious Ethics* 31, no. 1 (2003): 129–39. Rorty's response can be found in the same issue, pp. 141–49; the cited passage appears on pp. 148–49.

20. John Updike, *Odd Jobs: Essays and Criticism* (New York: Knopf, 1991), 620, 622.

21. Friedrich Nietzsche, *Untimely Meditations*, trans. R. J. Hollingdale (Cambridge: Cambridge University Press, 1983), 60–61.

22. In rejecting God's creation, Ivan recognizes that he is also explicitly rejecting the moral order that undergirds it. He concludes that "everything is permitted," even egoism to the point of crime. Albert Camus sees Ivan, a fictional character, as a turning point in modern culture: "With this 'everything is permitted' the history of contemporary nihilism really begins. . . . The same man who so violently took the part of innocence, who trembled at the suffering of a child,

who wanted to see 'with his own eyes' the lamb lie down with the lion, the victim embrace his murderer, from the moment that he rejects divine coherence and tries to discover his own rule of life, recognizes the legitimacy of murder." *The Rebel: An Essay on Man in Revolt*, trans. Anthony Bower (1956; repr., New York: Vintage, 1991), 57–58.

23. Borrowing an image from Friedrich Schiller's poem "Resignation," Ivan says he hastens to return his "ticket" to the eternal harmony; accepting the suffering of innocent children is simply too high a price of admission. See the discussion of this in Joseph Frank, *Dostoevsky: The Mantle of the Prophet, 1871–1881* (Princeton: Princeton University Press, 2002), 394–97.

24. Diane Oenning Thompson, *"The Brothers Karamazov" and the Poetics of Memory* (Cambridge: Cambridge University Press, 1991), 247.

25. One of the fullest critical treatments of *The Assault* can be found in Jolanda Vanderwal Taylor, *A Family Occupation: Children of the War and the Memory of World War II in Dutch Literature of the 1980s* (Amsterdam: Amsterdam University Press, 1997), 23–59. Taylor quotes Dutch critic Jaap Goedegebuure as to the meaning embedded in the novel's ending: "Only when [Anton] can fathom *his* history and thus *history* (on a large scale) does he have a future and is he capable of maintaining the unity of his personality" (59).

26. Colin Gunton, *The Christian Faith: An Introduction to Christian Doctrine* (Malden, MA: Blackwell, 2002), 23–24.

27. Ibid., 24.

28. There are sharp disagreements within the scholarly community about whether or not it is legitimate to narrate the history of modernity as a return of gnosticism. For the primary argument, see Hans Jonas, *The Gnostic Religion: The Message of the Alien God and the Beginnings of Christianity*, 2nd ed., rev. (1958; repr., Boston: Beacon, 1963). Cyril O'Regan cautions against a loose and generalizing application of the term "gnosticism" to the modern world, while at the same time he acknowledges that "the battle for meaning between Gnostic and Christian discourses in modernity, what we might call the narrative agon, is a battle for truth, specifically the truth to which narrative gives one access." *Gnostic Return in Modernity* (Albany: State University of New York Press, 2001), 16.

29. Hans Urs von Balthasar, *The Scandal of the Incarnation: Irenaeus Against the Heresies*, trans. John Saward (San Francisco: Ignatius, 1990), 6.

30. Colin Gunton, *The One, the Three, and the Many: God, Creation and the Culture of Modernity* (Cambridge: Cambridge University Press, 1993), 97–98.

31. Ibid., 98.

32. Gunton, *Christian Faith*, 25.

33. Robert Jenson has several extended and constructive discussions of the tension between space and time in Christian theology. He speaks of the dominance of spatial metaphors in Western thought, and he seeks creatively to define space as "the form of consciousness that enables distinguishing other reality from oneself, [and] we must say that this distinction is first made by God. God opens otherness between himself and us, and so there is present room for us." *Systematic Theology*, vol. 2, *The Works of God* (New York: Oxford University Press, 1999), 47.

34. Dietrich Bonhoeffer, *Letters and Papers from Prison*, enlarged ed., ed. Eberhard Bethge (New York: Collier, 1972), 336–37.

35. Balthasar, *Scandal of the Incarnation*, 53.

36. Gunton, *Christian Faith*, 170–71.

Chapter 8 Dwelling in Possibility

1. Colin Gunton, *The Christian Faith: An Introduction to Christian Doctrine* (Malden, MA: Blackwell, 2002), 13.

2. Ibid., 19.

3. H. Richard Niebuhr, *Christ and Culture* (New York: Harper, 1951), 217–18.

4. Paul Ricoeur, *Hermeneutics and the Human Sciences*, ed. and trans. John B. Thompson (Cambridge: Cambridge University Press, 1981), 181.

5. Helmut Thielicke, *I Believe: The Christian's Creed*, trans. John W. Doberstein and H. George Anderson (Philadelphia: Fortress, 1968), 5.

6. John F. Kennedy, *The Burden and the Glory: President John F. Kennedy's Second and Third Years in Office as Revealed in His Public Statements and Addresses*, ed. Allan Nevins (New York: Harper, 1964), 133.

7. Richard Rorty, *Consequences of Pragmatism: Essays, 1972–1980* (Minneapolis: University of Minnesota Press, 1982), 150. In a series of elegant and provocative articles and books, Rorty labored to transform all intellectual inquiry into a form of literary enterprise. To be a modern person living at the dawn of the twenty-first century, he said again and again, is to realize that truth is not something we *find* but something we *make*. For a critique of the tradition that runs from Nietzsche (through Shaw) to Rorty, see my *From Nature to Experience: The American Search for Cultural Authority* (Lanham, MD: Rowman & Littlefield, 2005), esp. 17–40, 71–97.

8. Paul Ricoeur, "The Model of the Text: Meaningful Action as a Text," in *Hermeneutics and the Human Sciences*, trans. and ed. John B. Thompson (Cambridge: Cambridge University Press, 1981), 201–2.

9. Ricoeur, "The Metaphorical Process as Cognition, Imagination, and Feeling," in *On Metaphor*, ed. Sheldon Sacks (Chicago: University of Chicago Press, 1979), 150.

10. Ibid., 151–52.

11. Douglas Berggren, "The Use and Abuse of Metaphor," *The Review of Metaphysics* 16, no. 2 (1962): 243; Ricoeur, "Metaphorical Process," 151, 155.

12. Ricoeur, *Hermeneutics and the Human Sciences*, 180–81.

13. Jonathan Swift, *Major Works*, ed. Angus Ross and David Woolley (Oxford: Oxford University Press, 2003), 470–71.

14. Joel Weinsheimer's study of eighteenth-century hermeneutics contains an illuminating discussion of Swift. Highlighting the latter's *Tale of a Tub*, Weinsheimer says Swift understood the questions of language and interpretation to be marked by "the dichotomy of knaves and fools. Two inalienable though incommensurate interpretations of interpretation divide the field: . . . credulity and curiosity. Defined as the 'wisdom which converses about the surface of things,' the credulity of the hermeneutic fool consists in being passively open to the obvious, taking things to be what they seem and words to mean what they say. Correlatively, defined as the 'reason [which brings] tools for cutting and opening and mangling and piercing [things] and offering to demonstrate that they are not of the same consistency quite through,' interpretive curiosity consists in ferreting out the real beyond the apparent, the meaning behind the word." As proved to be the case with the word and the thing, so too is the relationship between the text and the interpretation a matter of considerable tension and complexity. Joel C. Weinsheimer, *Eighteenth-Century Hermeneutics: Philosophy and Interpretation in England from Locke to Burke* (New Haven: Yale University Press, 1993), 1.

15. What is remarkable is that during the primary campaign of 1968, Kennedy often balanced a powerful sense of idealism with a tragic awareness of life. On the night of the assassination of Martin Luther King Jr. (April 4, 1968), he gave an extemporaneous speech to a racially mixed crowd in Indianapolis. After telling them of King's death, Kennedy outlined the stark challenges before American society. Quoting Aeschylus, he said, "In our sleep, pain which cannot forget falls drop by drop upon the heart until, in our own despair . . . comes wisdom through the awful grace of God." And he concluded with a charge to his dazed and disconsolate audience: "Let us dedicate ourselves to what the Greeks wrote so many years ago: to tame the savageness of man and make gentle the life of this world." *American Speeches: Political Oratory from Abraham Lincoln to Bill Clinton*, ed. Ted Widmer (New York: Library of America, 2006), 693–94.

16. Allen Dwight Callahan, *The Talking Book: African Americans and the Bible* (New Haven: Yale University Press, 2006), 194–95.

17. John B. Cade, "Out of the Mouths of Ex-Slaves," *The Journal of Negro History* 20 (1935): 318. For the relationship between slave rebellions and reading restrictions, see Callahan, *Talking Book*, 4–18; and Daniel Walker Howe, *What Hath God Wrought: The Transformation of America, 1815–1848* (New York: Oxford University Press, 2007), 323–27. Howe notes that the restrictions extended even to many regions in the North because "literacy was associated with citizenship, a status that few states accorded their black residents" (644).

18. William S. McFeely, *Frederick Douglass* (New York: Norton, 1991), 29.

19. Perry Miller, *The New England Mind: The Seventeenth Century* (1939; repr., Boston: Beacon, 1961), 3–34.

20. Peter Brown, *Augustine of Hippo*, new ed. (Berkeley: University of California Press, 2000), 144–45, 150.

21. John Calvin, *Institutes of the Christian Religion*, vol. 1, trans. Ford Lewis Battles (Philadelphia: Westminster, 1960), II.1.8, 251.

22. George M. Marsden, *A Short Biography of Jonathan Edwards* (Grand Rapids: Eerdmans, 2008), 137.

23. Reinhold Niebuhr, *The Nature and Destiny of Man*, vol. 1, *Human Nature* (New York: Scribner, 1943), 96–97.

24. Henry Louis Gates Jr., *Loose Canons: Notes on the Culture Wars* (New York: Oxford University Press, 1992), 54.

25. Ibid., 57. The passage from Hegel to which Gates refers is this: "In Negro life the characteristic point is the fact that consciousness has not yet attained to the realization of any substantial objective existence—as for example, God, or Law—in which the interest of man's volition is involved and in which he realizes his own being. This distinction between himself as an individual and the universality of his essential being, the African in the uniform, undeveloped oneness of his existence has not yet attained; so that the Knowledge of an absolute Being, an Other and a Higher than his individual self, is entirely wanting. The Negro, as already observed, exhibits the natural man in his completely wild and untamed state." *The Philosophy of History*, trans. J. Sibree (New York: Dover, 1956), 93.

26. Robert W. Jenson, *Systematic Theology*, vol. 1, *The Triune God* (New York: Oxford University Press, 1997), 63–64.

27. Jenson, *Systematic Theology*, 1:64–65.

28. Ibid., 66.

29. Ibid., 66–67, 69.

Chapter 9 A Good Man Is Hard to Find

1. Paul Ricoeur, *Hermeneutics and the Human Sciences*, ed. and trans. John B. Thompson (Cambridge: Cambridge University Press, 1981), 142.

2. Hans-Georg Gadamer, *Truth and Method*, 2nd rev. ed., trans. Joel Weinsheimer and Donald G. Marshall (New York: Crossroad, 1989), 375.

3. Charles Norris Cochrane, *Christianity and Classical Culture: A Study of Thought and Action from Augustus to Augustine* (1940; repr., London: Oxford University Press, 1957), 410–11.

4. Jean Paul Friedrich Richter, *Flower, Fruit, and Thorn Pieces*, trans. Edward Henry Noel (Boston, 1863), 279.

5. Henry David Thoreau, *Thoreau on Land: Nature's Canvas*, ed. J. O. Valentine (New York: Mariner, 2001), 37.

6. Walter Harding, *The Days of Henry Thoreau: A Biography* (1962; repr., Princeton: Princeton University Press, 1992), 464.

7. H. Richard Niebuhr, *The Kingdom of God in America* (1937; repr., Middletown, CT: Wesleyan University Press, 1993), 193.

8. Jaroslav Pelikan, *Jesus Through the Centuries: His Place in the History of Culture* (New Haven: Yale University Press, 1985), 206.

9. Jay Fliegelman, *Prodigals and Pilgrims: The American Revolution against Patriarchal Authority, 1750–1800* (Cambridge: Cambridge University Press, 1982), 1.

10. Charles Taylor, *A Secular Age* (Cambridge, MA: Belknap Press of Harvard University Press, 2007), 300.

11. Richter, *Flower, Fruit*, 279.

12. Helmut Thielicke, *The Evangelical Faith*, vol. 1, *Prolegomena: The Relation of Theology to Modern Thought Forms*, trans. Geoffrey W. Bromiley (Grand Rapids: Eerdmans, 1974), 236–37. "Reality without God becomes incalculable. There are no barriers. Hence anxiety arises. If everything is possible, everything is to be feared" (237).

13. Emily Dickinson, *The Letters of Emily Dickinson*, vol. 3, ed. Thomas H. Johnson and Theodora Ward (Cambridge, MA: Belknap Press of Harvard University Press, 1958), 754–55.

Works Cited

There are many passages of fiction, poetry, and autobiography quoted in this book. To minimize interruptions within the text and to reserve the notes for the citations of scholarly articles and books, full bibliographical citations for the works of literature are given below. In addition, the page numbers are given within parentheses in the main body of the text. (In some instances, the passage is as brief as a sentence, while in other cases, the discussion of a particular work extends over a number of pages.)

Adams, Henry. *Novels, Mont Saint Michel, The Education.* Edited by Ernest Samuels and Jayne N. Samuels. New York: Library of America, 1983. *The Education of Henry Adams.*

Aeschylus. *The Oresteia.* Translated by Robert Fagles. New York: Penguin, 1977. *Agamemnon.*

Auden, W. H. *Selected Poems.* Edited by Edward Mendelson. New York: Vintage, 1989. *In Time of War.*

Barth, Karl. *Church Dogmatics.* 4 vols. 13 parts. Edited by G. W. Bromiley and T. F. Torrance. Edinburgh: T&T Clark, 1956–62. Citations will include the volume, part, and page numbers: e.g., (*CD*, I.2.203).

Borges, Jorge Luis. *Collected Fictions.* Translated by Andrew Hurley. New York: Penguin, 1999. "The Gospel According to Mark."

Buechner, Frederick. *Godric.* 1980. Reprint, New York: Harper, 1983.

Chopin, Kate. *Complete Novels and Stories.* Edited by Sandra M. Gilbert. New York: Library of America, 2002. *The Awakening.*

Crane, Stephen. *Prose and Poetry.* Edited by J. C. Levenson. New York: Library of America, 1984. "The Blue Hotel."

Dickinson, Emily. *The Poems of Emily Dickinson.* Edited by R. W. Franklin. Cambridge, MA: Belknap Press of Harvard University Press, 1999.

Dinesen, Isak. *Seven Gothic Tales.* 1934. Reprint, New York: Vintage, 1991. "The Poet."

Dostoevsky, Fyodor. *The Brothers Karamazov.* Translated by Richard Pevear and Larissa Volokhonsky. New York: Farrar, 2002.

Douglass, Frederick. *Autobiographies.* Edited by Henry Louis Gates Jr. New York: Library of America, 1994. *My Bondage and My Freedom; Narrative of the Life of Frederick Douglass, an American Slave.*

Dreiser, Theodore. *Sister Carrie.* Edited by Neda Westlake. New York: Penguin, 1981.

Eliot, T. S. *The Complete Poems and Plays, 1909–1950*. New York: Harcourt, 1971. *Four Quartets*; "The Love Song of J. Alfred Prufrock"; *The Waste Land*.

Emerson, Ralph Waldo. *Essays and Lectures*. Edited by Joel Porte. New York: Library of America, 1983. "The American Scholar"; "Divinity School Address"; "Experience"; "Self-Reliance."

Faulkner, William. *As I Lay Dying*. 1930. Reprint, New York: Vintage, 1990.

———. *The Sound and the Fury*. 1929. Reprint, New York: Vintage, 1990.

Frost, Robert. *Collected Poems, Prose, and Plays*. Edited by Richard Poirier and Mark Richardson. New York: Library of America, 1995. "Never Again Would Birds' Song Be the Same."

Hardy, Thomas. *Tess of the D'Urbervilles*. Edited by David Skilton. London: Penguin, 1978.

Hawthorne, Nathaniel. *Collected Novels*. Edited by Millicent Bell. New York: Library of America, 1983. *The Scarlet Letter*.

Hemingway, Ernest. *The Short Stories*. New York: Scribner, 1995. "A Clean, Well-Lighted Place."

Hopkins, Gerard Manley. *Poetry and Prose*. Edited by W. H. Gardiner. 1953. Reprint, London: Penguin, 1985. "As Kingfishers Catch Fire."

Keats, John. *Selected Poems and Letters*. Edited by Douglas Bush. Boston: Houghton, 1959. *Lamia*; "Ode to Melancholy."

Lewis, C. S. *The Weight of Glory: And Other Addresses*. New York: Harper, 2001. "The Weight of Glory."

Mann, Thomas. *Death in Venice and Seven Other Stories*. Translated by H. T. Lowe-Porter. New York: Vintage, 1989. *Death in Venice*.

Melville, Herman. *Melville's Short Novels: A Norton Critical Edition*. Edited by Dan McCall. New York: Norton, 2002. *Bartleby, the Scrivener*.

———. *Moby Dick: A Norton Critical Edition*. 2nd ed. Edited by Hershel Parker and Harrison Hayford. New York: Norton, 2002.

Miller, Arthur. *The Crucible*. 1953. Reprint, New York: Dramatists Play Service, 1998.

Milosz, Czeslaw. *New and Collected Poems 1931–2001*. New York: Ecco, 2001. "An Appeal"; "Either-Or."

———. *The Witness of Poetry*. Cambridge, MA: Harvard University Press, 1983.

Mulisch, Harry. *The Assault*. Translated by Claire Nicolas White. New York: Pantheon, 1985.

O'Connor, Flannery. *Collected Works*. Edited by Sally Fitzgerald. New York: Library of America, 1988. "A Good Man Is Hard to Find"; *Letters*.

Shakespeare, William. *The Complete Works*. Edited by Alfred Harbage. 1969. Reprint, New York: Viking, 1977. *Hamlet*; *King Lear*; *Macbeth*; *Romeo and Juliet*.

Shaw, George Bernard. *Back to Methuselah: A Metabiological Pentateuch*. New York: Brentano's, 1921.

Stevens, Wallace. *Collected Poetry and Prose*. Edited by Frank Kermode and Joan Richardson. New York: Library of America, 1997. *Adagia*; "The Pure Good of Theory."

Swift, Jonathan. *Gulliver's Travels*. Edited by Claude Rawson. Oxford: Oxford University Press, 2005.

Thomas, Dylan. *The Poems of Dylan Thomas*. Edited by Daniel Jones. New York: New Directions, 2003. "Do Not Go Gentle Into That Good Night"; "Fern Hill."

Thoreau, Henry David. *A Week, Walden, The Maine Woods, Cape Cod*. Edited by Robert F. Sayre. New York: Library of America, 1985. *Walden*.

Whitman, Walt. *Poetry and Prose*. Edited by Justin Kaplan. New York: Library of America, 1982. "Out of the Cradle Endlessly Rocking"; "Song of Myself."

Wilbur, Richard. *Collected Poems: 1943–2004*. Orlando, FL: Harcourt, 2004. "A Barred Owl"; "Lying."

Williams, William Carlos. *Selected Poems*. Edited by Robert Pinsky. New York: Library of America, 2004. "Asphodel"; "so much depends."

Wordsworth, William. *The Prelude: A Parallel Text*. Edited by J. C. Maxwell. London: Penguin 1971.

Yeats, William Butler. *Selected Poems and Four Plays*. 4th ed. Edited by M. L. Rosenthal. New York: Scribner, 1996. "Nineteen Hundred and Nineteen"; "A Prayer for My Daughter"; "Sailing to Byzantium."

Index

Abrams, M. H., 104, 238n1, 238n4
Adams, Henry (*The Education of Henry Adams*), 28
Adams, John, 28
Adams, John Quincy, 28
Aeschylus, 245n15
   Agamemnon, 34
Anderson, Benedict, 125
Anselm of Canterbury, 90
Aquinas, Thomas, 89–90, 116, 148
Aristotle, 38, 116, 144, 147, 204
Arthos, John, 96–97, 237n37
Athanasius, 13, 226n4
Auden, W. H., 151–52
   In Time of War, 43–44
Auerbach, Erich, 23, 123–25
Augustine, 7, 89–90, 116, 200–201
   on the doctrine of sin, 35–36, 201–2, 228n10
   on life as journey and pilgrimage, 198–99
   and the theory of language, 93–94, 236n36, 237n30
   and the trinitarian critique of classical antiquity, 211–12
   on the vestiges of the Trinity, 70, 72, 91
   view of sacraments, 67
Auld, Hugh, 195–97, 199–200, 202
Auld, Sophia, 195–97, 200, 202

Balthasar, Hans Urs von, 5, 162, 226n5
   and the challenge of gnosticism, 152, 178
   and the doctrine of recapitulation, 180
   and the dramatic nature of theology, 99

on the importance of the *Logos*, 13–14
on Jesus Christ and language, 59–61
on Jesus Christ and narrative form, 144, 146
on the theology of experience, 81–82
Barrow, John, 146
Barth, J. Robert, 68
Barth, Karl, 8–9, 225n5, 236n24, 237n32
   and the critique of natural theology, 80, 87–91, 94–95, 236n24
   on the distinction between sin and finitude, 228n6
   on the doctrine of creation and the narrative shape of human experience, 147–50, 233n32, 241n18
   on God's patience, 130–33
   on God's speech, 236n28
   on the Hegelian understanding of God, 107–8
   on the Incarnation, 77–78, 95–97, 218–20, 237n30
   on the joy of theology, 4–5
   on myth and the immanent cosmos of modernity, 71–74, 79, 84, 178
   and the secular parables of the gospel, 80–91
   on the theology of experience, 80–82, 87–88, 233n31
   and vestiges of the Trinity, 67–72, 74, 234n39, 234n40
   view of language and revelation, 91–95, 99–101, 233n32, 236n28

Barthes, Roland, 227n19
Bate, Walter Jackson, 46
Benson, Bruce, 242n36
Benveniste, Emile, 60–61
Berger, Peter, 54–55
Berggren, Douglas, 193
Berkeley, Bishop, 17
Bethge, Eberhard, 150
Blake, William, 22, 44, 46
Borges, Jorge Luis ("The Gospel according to Mark"), 112
Bromwich, David, 156
Brontë, Anne, 217
Brontë, Charlotte, 217
Brontë, Emily, 217
Brooks, Cleanth, 36–37, 118–19, 228n5, 241n8
Brooks, David, 3
Brown, Peter, 198
Buechner, Frederick (*Godric*), 162
Buffon, Comte de, 142

Calvin, John, 67, 89, 147, 201–2, 236n25, 237n32
Calvinism, 42, 124, 185
Camus, Albert, 244n22
Chopin, Kate (*The Awakening*), 126, 131, 240n31
Christian doctrine
  Christology
    Christ and the narrative arc of creation and human experience, 142–54, 184–90
    Christ in the literature of late modernity, 210–19
    Jesus Christ as the divine Word, 2–3, 13–14, 142
    and the kenotic self-emptying of God, 8, 28–29
    and modern debates about the nature of language, 61–62
    and the presence of Christ in the sacrament of communion, 45, 65–67
    prophetic office of Christ, 88–90
    twentieth-century renewal of, 9, 218–23
  divine patience
    and the challenge of ordinary time, 119–27

in contrast to human myth, 178
as a key to the interpretation of history, 147–48
space, time, and the patience of God, 127–33
Incarnation, 8–9
  and the challenge of modern materialism, 178–80, 219–23
  as a challenge to the secularism of life, 94–101
  and modern language theory, 12–14, 59–62, 93–96, 237n30
  and the redemption of time, 127–29
  and the romantic quest for "spots of time," 138–40
recapitulation, 135, 149–52, 179–80, 184, 242n36
revelation
  and the discovery of truth, 50, 58
  and the divine grasp upon language, 87–94, 100–101, 236n28
  as function of trinitarian self-disclosure, 68–71, 234n40
  as the opposite of myth, 178
  and the romantic theory of the self, 107–9, 181–82, 238n4
  in tension with natural theology, 88–89, 148–49, 241n18
sacraments, 39, 45–46, 61
  as clues to the nature of language, 65–68, 233n27
Trinity
  as challenge to the fatalism of late antiquity, 211–12
  and modern language theory, 99–101
  in the theology of Karl Barth, 68–74
  the *vestigia trinitatis*, 69–74, 87–87, 90–95
Cicero, 40
Cobain, Kurt, 114
Cochrane, Charles Norris, 211–12, 228n10
Coleridge, Samuel Taylor, 22, 107
  on the symbolic imagination, 44–46, 68, 230n41, 233n30
Covey, Edward, 200
Crane, Stephen, 78
  "The Blue Hotel," 114
Culler, Jonathan, 19–20, 227n32
Cullmann, Oscar, 137–38, 237n38, 240n3

Darwin, Charles, 3, 105, 108, 230n42, 73
  and the demise of the argument from
    design, 46–48, 73
  and the emergence of the structuralist
    paradigm, 48–49, 230n42, 230n44
  as a shaping influence upon modern natu-
    ralism, 22–23, 47–48, 157, 184, 191
Dawkins, Richard, 80
DeLillo, Don (*White Noise*), 8, 158–61,
  165–66, 168, 208
de Man, Paul, 230n41
Descartes, René, 167–68, 203
Diana, Princess of Wales, 121–22
Dickens, Charles, 217
Dickinson, Emily, 2, 5, 8, 12, 31, 57, 88, 105,
  183, 207, 239n11
  belief and unbelief as themes in her
    poetry, 88, 109–12, 136, 143, 157–58,
    216, 239n12
  on God's silence and absence, 9, 78, 109–10,
    130–31, 211–13
  and the modern sense of time, 119–21,
    125–26, 132–33
  on nature and its relationship to language,
    50
  on poetry and possibilities, 185, 188, 195,
    210
  view of Christ, 61–62, 217–23
Dickinson, Lavinia, 2
Dinesen, Isak, 9, 243n18
  "Poet, The," 166–67
Donoghue, Denis, 76
Dostoevsky, Fyodor, 8, 160
  belief and unbelief as themes in his
    fiction, 9, 78–79, 88, 157, 211
  Brothers Karamazov, The, 171–73, 176,
    216, 244n22, 244n23
Douglass, Frederick, 5, 9, 120, 217
  and African American views of narrative,
    202–5
  and the closed circle of slavery, 194–96
  experience with evangelical Christianity,
    199–201
  My Bondage and My Freedom, 199–200
  *Narrative of the Life of Frederick Douglass,
    an American Slave*, 194–98, 202–3
  on the nature of suffering, 198–99
  on reading as the path to freedom, 9,
    196–98, 210
  view of history and social order, 201

Dowling, William, 147–48, 237n42
Dreiser, Theodore (*Sister Carrie*), 27–28
During, Simon, 81–82
Durkheim, Émile, 4, 82

Eagleton, Terry, 231n50
Eaton, Mark, 226n10
Edwards, Jonathan, 89, 201–2
Eliade, Mircea, 162
Eliot, George, 114, 203, 217
Eliot, T. S., 103, 163–64
  and a Christian view of time, 128–29
  on ennui and the modern sense of time,
    122–23, 127–29, 133
  Four Quartets, 27, 75–76, 103, 127–29,
    133, 223
  "Love Song of J. Alfred Prufrock, The,"
    123, 127
  Waste Land, The, 122
Emerson, Ralph Waldo, 46, 92–93, 215
  "American Scholar, The," 107
  "Divinity School Address," 214
  and epistemological skepticism, 22, 138,
    144, 170–71
  "Experience," 22, 138, 170
  on language and reality, 60, 163–64
  "Self-Reliance," 105, 160
  and the theology of experience, 92–93,
    107, 160
  view of Christ, 214–16, 219
Evans, C. Stephen, 236n24

Faulkner, William, 8, 105, 163
  As I Lay Dying, 57, 73–75
  fiction and myth, 139–41
  on the limits of words, 73–75
  and the modern sense of time, 119–20,
    132–33
  Sound and the Fury, The, 31–37, 105,
    117–19, 139–41, 173, 176–78, 228n3,
    228nn5–6, 241n8
  and the theory of language, 36–37, 51
Fessenden, Tracy, 82–87, 92, 161, 166–67,
    235n14, 237n34
Feuerbach, Ludwig, 79
Fiddes, Paul, 229n26
Fitzgerald, F. Scott, 114, 124, 193
Flaubert, Gustave, 126, 240n31
Fliegelman, Jay, 215

Frei, Hans, 23, 104
Freud, Sigmund, 3, 23, 82
Frost, Robert, 1–2, 188
   "Never Again Would Birds' Song Be the
     Same," 163
Frye, Northrop, 136, 240n2
Funkenstein, Amos, 232n20

Gadamer, Hans-Georg, 5, 8, 228n6, 237n30
   and the ancient Greek understanding of
     the word, 37–39
   on the art of the question, 211, 218
   critique of structuralist model of lan-
     guage, 58–59
   on the demystification of language, 42
   on experience, word, and thing, 33–37,
     231n4
   language, incarnation, and Trinity, 94–97,
     99–101
   on suffering and wisdom, 153
   on the theological dimensions of language
     theory, 59–63, 69, 236n28
   on the word as picture, 62–67
Gates, Henry Louis, Jr., 203, 245n25
Geertz, Clifford, 81, 165
Gerhardt, Paul, 150
Goedegebuure, Jaap, 244n25
Green, Garrett, 86
Gregory, Brad, 226n10
Gunton, Colin, 141–42, 146, 152–53, 177–80,
   184

Hale, Emily, 127
Hallström, Lasse, 78
Hamner, Everett, 235n14
Hardy, Barbara, 143
Hardy, Thomas, 188–89, 217
   Tess of the D'Urbervilles, 27
Harris, Sam, 80
Hart, Darryl, 82
Hart, Trevor, 234n39
Hauerwas, Stanley, 80–81
Havelock, Eric, 229n14
Hawthorne, Nathaniel, 188
   on personal and moral identity, 63–65
   and the power of naming, 37
   Scarlet Letter, The, 37, 63–65, 217

Hayes, Roland, 9, 222–23
Hebblethwaite, Brian, 236n28
Hegel, G. W. F., 17, 79, 107–8, 203, 246n25
Heidegger, Martin, 10, 35, 192
Hemingway, Ernest, 114
   "Clean, Well-Lighted Place, A," 20–21
Hitchens, Christopher, 80
Hoen, Cornelius, 66
Hollingdale, R. J., 230n42
Homer, 23, 37, 47, 151–52, 169
Hopkins, Gerard Manley ("As Kingfishers
   Catch Fire"), 89–90
Hughes, Langston, 194
Hungerford, Amy, 82–87, 92, 161, 164–67,
   237n34
Hunsinger, George, 89

Ibsen, Henrik, 126, 240n31, 240n32
Irenaeus of Lyons, 135, 151–53, 178–80,
   242n36

Jacobs, Harriet, 203
James, Henry, 85, 160
James, William, 17, 80–81, 109, 192
Jameson, Frederic, 21, 51
Janz, Paul, 227n21
Jean Paul, 212, 216–17
Jeffrey, David, 93
Jenkins, Jerry, 165
Jenson, Robert
   on God, time, and space, 129–31, 133,
     244n33
   on the Lutheran view of communion,
     66–67, 233n27
   narrative and the life of God, 204–5
John (the Evangelist), 12
John of Damascus, 130
John Paul II, 5, 81, 241n18
   on the Eucharist and the unity of signifier
     and signified, 66
   on history and the revelation of God, 148
   on language and the power of divine
     revelation, 50
Johnson, Keith L., 148–49
Johnson, Lyndon, 190
John XXIII, 158
Jonas, Hans, 228n8, 232n14

Joyce, James, 85, 163
Jüngel, Eberhard
  on the cross and theological metaphor, 94
  on the incarnation and the secularity of
    the world, 100–101, 103
  on language and the revelation of God,
    236n26, 236n28
  on the *vestigia trinitatis*, 234n35
Justin Martyr, 226n5

Kafka, Franz, 72, 85, 217
Kant, Immanuel, 17, 80, 115–16
Kartiganer, Donald, 228n3
Kean, Edmund, 44
Keats, John, 188
  Lamia, 44
  "Ode to Melancholy," 131
Keller, Catherine, 242n36
Keller, Timothy, 5–6
Kennedy, Edward, 190–91
Kennedy, John F., 158, 190–91
Kennedy, Robert, 190, 192, 194, 245n15
Kermode, Frank, 5
  on the distinction between myths and
    fictions, 136–43, 149, 156, 168, 175,
    240n2, 240n3
Kierkegaard, Søren, 109, 186, 243n18
King, Martin Luther, Jr., 245n15
Kubsch, Ron, 239n24

LaHaye, Tim, 165
Langbaum, Robert, 146
Larkin, Philip, 86
Lawson, Charles, 199
Lewis, C. S., 105
  on medieval and modern models of the
    universe, 72–73
  and the storied order of human
    experience, 115–17
  "Weight of Glory, The," 115–17
Lewis, Pericles, 82–83, 85–87, 92, 161, 164,
    166–67, 237n34
London, Jack, 26
Luhrmann, T. M., 3–6
Luther, Martin, 90, 160, 201
  and the sacrament of communion, 45,
    66–67
Lyman, Joseph, 57
Lyotard, Jean-François, 5, 105

definition of postmodernity, 120–22,
    132–33, 239n24

MacIntyre, Alasdair, 7
  and the constraints of human identity, 153
  on the dominant characters of modern
    culture, 112–13
  view of narrative, 143–47, 156
  on the virtues, 116
Mann, Thomas (*Death in Venice*), 131–32
Marsden, George, 202
Marx, Karl, 3, 23
  history and freedom, 238n8
  and the search for expressive unity
    between nature and society, 108
McCarthy, Cormac, 164
McCarthy, Mary, 207–8
McClure, John, 161–68, 243n6
McCormack, Bruce, 67–68, 87, 233n31
Melville, Herman, 9, 74–75, 88, 160
  Bartleby, the Scrivener, 189
  belief and unbelief as themes in his
    fiction, 157, 215, 222
  Billy Budd, 217
  on God's silence and absence, 211–12,
    216–17
  Moby Dick, 74, 212, 217–18
Mencken, H. L., 82
Miller, Arthur (*The Crucible*), 63–65
Miller, Perry, 197–98
Milosz, Czeslaw
  "Appeal, An," 155, 181–82, 184
  belief and unbelief as themes in his poetry,
    186–88, 193
  "Either-Or," 186–88
  on the influence of Darwin, 47–48
  view of language and reality, 181–82
  Witness of Poetry, The, 47–48
Milton, John, 160, 185
Mink, Louis, 143–44
Morrison, Jim, 114
Morrison, Toni, 164
Mulisch, Harry, 8
  Assault, The, 169–78, 244n25
  on the meaning of symbol, 169–70
  on resistance to narrativity and the past,
    170–73
  on stories and their relationship to truth,
    173–75

narrative
and divine promise, 204–5
and the doctrine of creation, 129–30, 144–49
and the doctrine of the Incarnation, 94–95
the eclipse of biblical narrative, 23
and the imaginative creation of possible worlds, 192–93
naturalism and the master narrative of modernity, 19–20, 48, 157–58
and the postmodern critique of metanarratives, 119–23, 239n24
as reconstituted in romanticism, 105–7, 238n1
and secularization, 83–85, 160–61
and the storied order of creation, 105–6, 117, 122–23, 143, 149–50, 179, 184
in twentieth-century literature and theory, 136–44, 168–76
Niebuhr, H. Richard, 185, 214
Niebuhr, Reinhold, 202, 228n10
Nietzsche, Friedrich, 9, 23, 86, 216
influence on contemporary theories of fiction and truth, 17, 109, 142–43, 192, 245n7
influence of Darwin on, 46–48, 230n42
and the theme of the orphan, 78–79
view of history, 170–71, 230n43
Noll, Mark, 226n2

Oakes, Edward, 162
Oakley, Francis, 15–16
Ockham, William of, 15–16, 63–64
O'Connor, Flannery, 3, 5, 9
on the centrality of the sacraments, 207–8
"Good Man Is Hard to Find, A," 209–10, 216
Letters, 207–8
Oecolampadius, Johannes, 66
Ong, Walter, 40–41, 129
O'Regan, Cyril, 244n28
Orsi, Robert, 165
Ozment, Steven, 63–64

Paul (apostle), 3, 8, 28–29, 107
and the fullness of time, 138, 142
God, language, and story, 92, 180–81

on the gospel and the closed world system, 98, 185–86, 222
on the limits of human knowledge, 124
as source for the doctrine of recapitulation, 151
view of sin, 35–36, 97–98, 198, 202
Pelikan, Jaroslav, 214–15, 232n16
Pirandello, Luigi, 77, 79, 98–99, 132
Plantinga, Alvin, 19, 27, 48
Plato, 36–39, 47, 72, 179, 229n14, 237n30
Pope, Alexander, 193
Proust, Marcel, 85

Raboteau, Albert. 141, 183–84
Reformation, 63–68, 104, 157
Ricoeur, Paul, 10, 229n14
and the critique of structuralism, 97–99, 237n42
fiction and myth, 142–43
on the hermeneutics of suspicion, 23
literature and possible worlds, 185–86, 192–93, 195, 203, 210–11, 237n34
modernity and the search for a univocal language, 42–43
on narrative, 147–48
Robinson, Marilynne, 165
Rorty, Richard, 5, 143, 162, 243n19, 245n7
view of literature and truth, 16–18, 20–22, 24, 192–93
Ryle, Gilbert, 167

Salinger, J. D., 164
Sandel, Michael, 145
Saussure, Ferdinand de, 5, 19, 137, 237n42
on the arbitrariness of signs, 51–52, 58–59, 143, 227n32, 231n50
and the development of structuralism, 48–50
on the relationship of signifier and signified, 48–49
theological significance of his theories, 62, 97
Schiller, Friedrich, 161, 244n23
Schleiermacher, Friedrich, 79
Scholes, Robert, 20–21, 23–24, 42, 227n32
Shakespeare, William, 8, 26, 168, 188
Hamlet, 24, 188
King Lear, 34, 53, 77–79, 221

Index

Macbeth, 26, 32
Romeo and Juliet, 11–12, 14–16, 18, 24,
28, 37, 53
Shaw, George Bernard, 245n7
Back to Methuselah, 191–92
Shelley, Percy Bysshe, 160
Sheridan, Richard Brinsley, 197
Smith, James K.A., 239n24
Spacks, Patricia Meyer, 240n31
Spender, Stephen, 122
Sprat, Thomas, 44
Stanford, W. Bedell, 193
Steiner, George, 10, 40–41, 43, 229n32
Stevens, Wallace, 105
Adagia, 136
literature as religion, 136–37, 240n2
myth and fiction, 140–43, 156, 175
"Pure Good of Theory, The," 137
structuralism
on the arbitrariness of language, 20–23,
227n21, 227n32
as a central paradigm for modern
language theory, 8, 18–24
and the master narrative of late
modernity, 48–54, 167–68, 178
Ricoeur on the limits of, 97–98, 237n34,
237n42
in the strictly immanent cosmos of
modernity, 71, 79, 91–93
Swift, Jonathan, 245n14
Gulliver's Travels, 193–94

Taylor, Charles, 108, 226n4
on the buffered self, 215–16
on the dominance of structuralist models,
18–19, 227n19
on sacred and profane time, 123, 234n41
secularism and the subtraction story, 83
the shift from cosmos to universe, 72, 108,
226n4, 227n19, 234n41
Taylor, Yolanda Vanderwal, 244n25
Tennyson, Alfred, 108
Thielicke, Helmut, 188, 216–17
Thomas, Dylan
"Do Not Go Gentle Into That Good
Night," 25–26
"Fern Hill," 25–26, 35
Thomas, Keith, 229n29
Thompson, Diane Oenning, 172–73

Thoreau, Henry David, 60, 120, 163
Walden, 213–15
Tillich, Paul, 165, 243n17
time
as *chronos* and *kairos*, 137–39
as depicted in modern narratives, 119–26
and eschatological hope, 180–82
in the fiction of William Faulkner, 32, 73,
117–19, 139–41, 146
and figural interpretation, 123–25,
172–73
and the problem of finitude, 25–26
redemption of, 12–13, 75–76, 147–54
relationship to the patience of God,
127–33
sacred and profane time, 119–27
Wordsworth and "spots of time," 106–12,
122
Tocqueville, Alexis de, 145
Toulmin, Stephen, 42
Tristan, Flora, 240n31
Trueblood, Elton, 164
Turner, Nat, 196
Turner, Victor, 81
Twain, Mark, 60
Huckleberry Finn, 217

Updike, John, 169
"Pigeon Feathers," 6–8

Vattimo, Gianni, 161–62
Vendler, Helen, 239n11
Vesey, Denmark, 196
Virgil, 36

Wachterhauser, Brice, 231n4
Wain, John, 240n2
Ward, Graham, 235n12
Weber, Max, 82, 161, 235n12
Webster, John, 225n5
Weinberg, Steven, 115–17, 149, 179, 239n17
Weinsheimer, Joel, 58–59, 61–63, 228n12,
231n53, 236n28, 245n14
Wells, H. G., 6
Westcott, Brooke Foss, 12–13
Wharton, Edith (*Ethan Frome*), 26–27
Whitehead, Alfred North, 15
Whitman, Walt, 120, 213–14, 219